T0106120

I'm Stalking Jake!

BECKY HEINEKE

iUniverse, Inc.
New York   Bloomington

I'm Stalking Jake!

The story contained herein is true. Names and identifying characteristics of some individuals have been changed. Dialogue has been re-created from memory.

iUniverse books may be ordered through booksellers or by contacting:

iUniverse
1663 Liberty Drive
Bloomington, IN 47403
www.iuniverse.com
1-800-Authors (1-800-288-4677)

Because of the dynamic nature of the Internet, any Web addresses or links contained in this book may have changed since publication and may no longer be valid. The views expressed in this work are solely those of the author and do not necessarily reflect the views of the spublisher, and the publisher hereby disclaims any responsibility for them.

ISBN: 978-1-4502-5213-3 (pbk)
ISBN: 978-1-4502-5214-0 (ebk)

Printed in the United States of America

iUniverse rev. date: 8/27/2010

To Mom and Dad,
for always encouraging me,
even when the things I want to do are weird.

Contents

Q: Do you know Jake?

A: If by "Do you know Jake?" you mean, do we have a deep, personal knowledge and understanding of his every dream and desire that we may have projected onto him, then yes.

If by "Do you know Jake?" you mean, "Do we know Jake?" then no.

—"Unfrequently Asked Questions,"
Jake Watch, February 1, 2007

Hey, Remember When *Brokeback Mountain* Didn't Win the Oscar for Best Picture? Because I Do.

It was *Newsweek*. The November 21, 2005 issue.

In fact, I can narrow it down to two specific sentences within an article entitled "Forbidden Territory":

"Gyllenhaal and Ledger don't dodge it. The kissing and the sex scenes are fierce and full-blooded."[1]

No wonder I was excited. *Newsweek* made it sound like my two favorite actors had made a porno.

A year and a half earlier, in May 2004, I was spending the last weekend of my senior year of college at a music festival. As we walked from the parking lot, my friend Amy casually mentioned that she'd been chatting online with Anne Hathaway.

"You *know* Anne Hathaway?" I gasped, my tone indicative of how much this impressed me (greatly). "Like, *the actress* Anne Hathaway?"

In the four years that I'd known her, Amy had never once mentioned that she'd gone to high school with, and had been on the softball team with, and was still occasionally in contact with *the actress* Anne Hathaway. Nor did she act like it was any big deal to break the news to me as we walked across the parking lot.

Amy was a bit concerned that Anne was stuck doing princess flicks. "But I think she's starting a movie with Jake Gyllenhaal soon," she said. (At this I sighed dramatically to indicate my approval.)

"Yeah," she continued, "she's going to play his wife, but I think he's gay in the movie or something."

Anne Hathaway married to a gay Jake Gyllenhaal sounded like the absolute worst idea for a movie I'd ever heard of. So I promptly forgot about it.

Until that *Newsweek* showed up.

---

1   http://www.newsweek.com/id/51191.

The movie, of course, was *Brokeback Mountain*.

So that's where we'll start, with me at the kitchen table, devouring every word of the tantalizingly titled "Forbidden Territory" article, which was making this film I'd first heard about eighteen months earlier sound oh-so-much better than I'd originally thought. I had just gotten home from my first day at a new job, and the more I read, the more I couldn't believe my luck. Jake Gyllenhaal and Heath Ledger? In the same movie? And they were *in love with each other*? It was as if the universe had handcrafted a gift just for me and then stuck it in my mailbox, like some congratulatory gesture for landing steady employment.

Yes, I would say that was the catalyst. It was reading that article. Because after I read that article, I was excited about *Brokeback Mountain*. And being excited about *Brokeback Mountain* meant I was eager to see it as soon as it hit theaters.

Heath and Jake (and in that order) already occupied the top two spaces on my arbitrary list of things that made a movie worth seeing. The two of them together was enough to leave me faint with anticipation.

When opening day arrived, December 9, 2005, I called my friend Alex and insisted he see it with me. Alex and I saw movies together every Friday afternoon, and that Friday he had his heart set on *Aeon Flux*. I convinced him to switch his vote to *Brokeback,* a film he hadn't yet heard of, by talking it up as a "western."

But to my utter dismay, when I flipped open the paper that afternoon, I couldn't find a show time anywhere. The film's December 9 opening day turned out to be a limited release.[2] It would be another five weeks before it made it to my part of the country.

I wound up seeing *Aeon Flux* after all.

And by the time *Brokeback Mountain* did make it to us, in Memphis, Tennessee, Alex was more educated on the film's subject matter and politely declined my second invitation.

––––––––––

When I was eleven or twelve, my mother got out her Beatles Box. The Beatles Box was just that, an old cardboard box full of Beatles memorabilia; it had sat untouched in a closet in her parents' house for decades. It came

2   http://www.indiewire.com/article/big_numbers_for_brokeback_debut/. Its first week, the movie played in only five theaters in three cities across the United States.

home with us after a trip up north one summer, and when Mom started pulling things out of it in the living room, I helped her dig through it. There were newspaper clippings and concert ticket stubs, some trading cards, a coin purse, even a set of replicated birth certificates. And there, buried at the bottom of the box, was a magazine with the blazoning headline: "Paul McCartney Dead: The Great Hoax."

Even at eleven or twelve, I knew that Paul McCartney was not and never had been dead. Intrigued, I left Mom to her trading cards and sat down to read.

I didn't leave the couch until I had read the magazine cover to cover, by which point my head was swimming with the astonishing things I'd learned. Apparently, Paul McCartney was not only dead, but he'd been dead for *ages*, and the other Beatles had decided to replace him with a look-alike so that no one would find out. And wracked with guilt over deceiving the public, they planted clues in their albums to let us know what they had done. Like, did you know that Paul is barefoot on the cover of *Abbey Road*? And that means that he's *dead*? Who knew?!

One magazine, an hour or so's worth of reading in the living room, and suddenly I was a Beatles fan.

I saved up my allowance money so I could buy Beatles CDs and find the clues I'd read about. Mom and Dad didn't have a functioning record player, so I spent hours at our computer trying to get bits and pieces of songs to record and then play backward. My memories from middle school are full of ups and downs: The day I heard the words "turn me on, dead man" groan out of the speakers for the first time was a banner day. The day I was forced to admit that John Lennon was really saying "cranberry sauce" and not "I buried Paul" at the end of "Strawberry Fields Forever" was not.

In my head, John, mystical and untouchable for having died before I was born, was the mastermind. I envisioned him plotting this elaborate hoax decades earlier, and I, worldly as I was in the sixth grade, was connecting with him somehow by searching for the evidence he had so whimsically left behind. I never once thought Paul was actually dead, but for years I thought that the "clues" (many of which I made up myself) were far too plentiful to be explained as mere coincidence.

By the time I was thirteen, I considered myself enough of an expert on the Paul-is-Dead conspiracy to write a book about it. I called it *The British Encyclopedia of Paul McCartney Death Clues*, and those lucky enough to have received an original copy from me in the mid-1990s would have gotten forty pages: a hand-drawn cover of a *Sgt. Pepper*–era Paul with a question mark where his face should have been, fifteen pages of single-spaced death clues, and twenty-four pages of photocopied pictures and album covers. I finished the first edition in eighth grade. In ninth grade, I revised it and passed out copies in the cafeteria during lunch one day. I used the copying machine at my dad's office, and Dad put a stop to my excessive paper use after only four copies. Those four circulated, though, and word of mouth was such that I received a phone call shortly thereafter from a local DJ who wanted to interview me on the radio. The interview never materialized, but he did refer to me on air one Saturday morning as "local author and Beatles expert Becky Heineke." I was fourteen then, and I've lived as many years again in the interim, but I've never stopped aspiring to live up to the description of "local author and Beatles expert."

The funny thing about Beatles music, though, is that even the songs without death clues are kind of wonderful. I gave up on my Paul-is-Dead research about the time *The Beatles Anthology* aired on TV, and I spent the duration of my high school years filling in the gaps in my Fab Four knowledge. They were an indelible part of my daily existence. They still are. The Beatles influenced every part of my life, to the point that even now I associate them with my identity more than almost anything else.

I'm Becky. I'm sporadically creative. I'm a Beatles fan.

In elementary school, I was a *Little Mermaid* fan.

I walked into my classroom every morning with a *Little Mermaid* backpack and a *Little Mermaid* lunch box. I got *Little Mermaid* dolls for Christmas and used that same copying machine at Dad's office, along with scissors and masking tape, to create elaborate *Little Mermaid* posters to hang on my walls.

I *still* love *The Little Mermaid*. To this day I blame Disney for instilling in me an unnatural bias toward men who look like Prince Eric …

In college, it was *Buffy the Vampire Slayer*.
It was intense.
I'm not really sure how (or why) my roommate, Kathryn, put up with me.

And for a while there, back in late 2005/early 2006, I thought this time it would be *Brokeback Mountain*.

In the time that elapsed between the day I *thought* I was going to see *Brokeback Mountain* and the day I *did* see *Brokeback Mountain*, I went from being casually excited about it to completely preoccupied with what I was missing. I lost many long hours lurking on fansites and reading every review I could get my hands on. I downloaded (and repeatedly watched) a behind-the-scenes special and familiarized myself with the characters. The only thing I didn't do was read the original short story by Annie Proulx, upon which the film was based. I decided I didn't want the ending spoiled in advance.

I saw the movie for the first time with my friend Megan, a better choice than Alex for many reasons, not the least of which was that Megan had sat next to me at nearly every Heath Ledger movie of the past four and a half years, starting with the summer we saw *A Knight's Tale* more times than I'd care to admit.

On the Saturday that *Brokeback* opened in Memphis, we squeezed ourselves into a sold-out theater, stuck in the front row in a couple of the last available seats. The guy sitting next to me leaned over to warn, "I'm going to cry!" He pulled a handkerchief out of his pocket as if to prove his point.

"Oh, I'll probably cry too," I said. I'd heard it was a sad story. The lights dimmed, and the audience broke out into spontaneous applause. You could *feel* the anticipation in the room. It wasn't just me. Everyone there had been waiting for this.

When I think back to how Megan and I felt walking out of the theater that night, how the crying prediction came uncontrollably true and how we spent the remainder of our respective weekends under clouds of crushing depression, I sometimes wonder why I thought it was a good idea to go back the next weekend and see it again.

But I did. And again the weekend after that. And by the time I'd finished my fourth and final viewing, I'd dragged every half-willing person I knew to the theater with me.

There's no easier path to longevity than amassing a group of devoted fans, and that is exactly what *Brokeback Mountain* did.

It's just that I wasn't one of them.

With only four viewings, I was put to shame by those who clocked in *dozens* of trips to the theater.[3] Those people, the true *Brokeback*

---

3   However, for all the press it got, the film wasn't exactly a box-office juggernaut. It grossed just over $83 million domestically. By comparison,

aficionados, have their own stories. There are books about them, and by them, already.

I was a mediocre fan. A wannabe. The closest I came to truly getting involved was to write a blog entry about the movie, my first blogging experience ever. I saw the film with three good audiences and one bad one, and it was the bad one that I felt deserved a response. In the tradition of my generation, I pounded out something self-righteous and quasi emo and posted it on MySpace for all the world to read.

I got two comments; I knew neither person, and neither had seen the movie. And that was pretty much the beginning and the end of my attempt to make a name for myself as a *Brokeback Mountain* fan.

I was twenty-four at the time, or rather I'd turned twenty-four sometime between viewings two and three. The four leads of the film (Heath Ledger, Jake Gyllenhaal, Michelle Williams, and Anne Hathaway) were all within three years of my age.

I'd graduated from college two years earlier with a degree in biology and no idea what to do with it. On a whim, I thought it would be fun to design movie posters, and I spent a restless summer taking art classes and being turned away from every master's program in art that I could find. I wound up in art school as an undergrad all over again the following fall, stuck in intro-level courses next to eighteen-year-olds fresh out of high school. Miserable, I finished out the semester and then ran off to Cork, Ireland, for half a year, where I worked through a temp agency.

When my visa expired, I was forced to come home, no more sure about the direction I should take than when I left. I was twenty-three by then, living with my parents, with no career prospects and no interest in going back to school.

I signed up with a temp agency in Memphis, hoping I'd find the kind of friendly work environments I'd loved in Ireland, and the first job I was sent to was at an apartment complex where my boss was a girl I'd gone to high school with. She recognized me vaguely. "Weren't you, like, our valedictorian?" she asked.

Vin Diesel's family flick *The Pacifier*, released the same year, pushed past $113 million (http://www.boxofficemojo.com/yearly/chart/?yr=2005). The general *Brokeback Mountain* story line (the "gay cowboy movie") permeated pop culture in a way that was disproportionate to the number of people who saw the film.

"Salutatorian," I corrected her. When I finished filling her in on what I'd done since high school, she asked me what I was doing working for a temp agency.

"I honestly don't know," I told her.

I was supposed to be there three days. I was there three months, during which time I grew increasingly depressed, and then I quit, both the job and the temp agency.

Needing an income, I tried another agency. I worked one shitty job after another until one day I found myself working retail at an upscale clothing store. I watched as the store's owner got down on all fours to roll around on the floor with a customer's dog so the customer could browse in peace, and I decided that if that was where my life was headed, I didn't want any part of it. I finished out the day and then quit that temp agency too.

It was late 2005, and I was still without a job, without money, and without prospects.

But then, by a sheer stroke of luck, I got a job offer, out of the blue, to work at a financial services office. The work wasn't appealing, but it promised a steady paycheck, so I signed on. And when I came home after my first day on the job, there was a *Newsweek* waiting for me with a very interesting article inside …

Brokeback Mountain wasn't just an intriguing movie; it was the first thing I'd been enthusiastic about in *months.*

I wanted to be excited about it the same way I'd been excited about other things, when I was less depressed about life in general. I guess it makes sense that during this period, when I was trying to figure out where to go next, I latched on to the first thing that caught my attention.

And if we take into consideration just who, specifically, was involved in this movie, we can add yet another layer to the complexity of my psychological motivations. Though the details were different, my story was very similar to that of my friends. We were all in our early to midtwenties, and all had worked hard in school and followed the path that had been laid out in front of us. And we were all struggling as we tried to find our places in the world. Every one of us seemed to be floundering.

Our age and *not* floundering? Heath, Jake, Michelle, and Anne. *Brokeback Mountain* was earning them award nominations right and left.

Prior to the 2006 Academy Awards, I had never had much interest in Hollywood's awards season. But that year, those four actors were responsible for a universally acclaimed film that was winning just about everything in sight. I never thought of them as distantly glamorous movie stars. Heath and Jake made the movies I watched during midterm study breaks. Michelle was still best known as Jen Lindley from *Dawson's Creek.* Anne and I apparently shared mutual friends.

I would have seen any movie that the four of them made together, but the fact that they had made *this* movie, which was so widely celebrated and had affected me so deeply, and that they had done it at this stage in their lives, impressed me. I wanted these actors, and their movie, to win. Their achievement made it seem possible that there was hope for the rest of us. It was nice to see a group of twentysomethings get some recognition. It was especially nice that it happened to be that group.

I got sucked into awards season that year. If a movie was competing against *Brokeback* in one of the eight categories for which it had received an Academy Award nomination, I went out of my way to see it. I read every film analysis I could get my hands on. I followed online discussions of who would win, who should win, and who couldn't win. And then I watched the Golden Globes, and learned what the SAGs were, and the BAFTAs, and the Independent Spirit Awards.

All of the energy that I had poured into waiting for the film I redirected to the awards circuit, all in preparation for the big night. *The* night. Oscar night.

And when the night arrived, in March of 2006, I parked myself in front of my television and sat through the whole damned ceremony.

"I finally saw it and can see why it won Best Picture," an anonymous reviewer on Facebook wrote in 2008, regarding *Brokeback Mountain.* No one rushed to correct the guy. In fact, several other reviewers similarly expressed the opinion that the movie had been worthy of its Best Picture win.

Except at the end of the Academy Awards that night, when Jack Nicholson walked up to the mic to announce the winner in the category of Best Picture, he didn't say, *"Brokeback Mountain."*

He said, *"Crash."*

And I never really recovered.

It was a rough night. I went to bed numb and woke up crushed that I lived in a world where such a horrible miscarriage of justice could take place. While other people railed about intrinsic homophobia within the voting populace of the academy, I saw it as a judgment of another type. My *entire generation* had been snubbed. I took the loss personally.

But the interesting thing about *Crash*'s out-of-left-field win—aside from the fact that two years later no one remembered it—was that it solidified the devotion of the *Brokeback Mountain* fanbase in the way only large-scale, public insult could. A fascination that probably should have ended with the awards season, for me and for so many others, was prolonged by the perceived indignity of its loss. Instead of letting go, fans dug in for the long haul, and I was among them. Those who were truly devoted to the movie remained so. But aside from the film purists, there were those who had grown attached to Heath; for others, it was Jake. People grouped together based on their common interests.

I don't think there was ever any question; it was either going to be Heath or Jake for me. About a month after the Academy Awards, when the dust had settled and I looked around to see where I'd fallen, I found that I had instinctively gravitated toward the one who looked more like Prince Eric from *The Little Mermaid*.

Honestly, any celebrity could have been at the center of where the story goes from here. But for me, via that gay cowboy movie, it wound up being Jake Gyllenhaal.

of Jake Gyllenhaal. But it wasn't *Brokeback Mountain* that did her in. No, it was another of Jake's 2005 offerings, *Jarhead*, that caught her attention.[2]

Her idea to start a blog was largely rooted in a desire to keep her writing skills sharp as she approached graduation. She didn't start out with the idea of writing about Jake. She contemplated many options for her subject matter, and the one she finally settled on was tea. Then at the last minute, she radically changed course and decided to go with the guy from *Jarhead*.

Susie didn't know much about Jake, so before she started, she went online to do a little research. She became an active member of a couple of online communities centered around him, but like many new fans in that era, she wasn't satisfied with what the internet was offering her. In those days the options for a burgeoning Jake fan were fairly traditional. There were sites dedicated to his movies (*Brokeback Mountain* sites most prominent among them), there was his profile on the Internet Movie Database (IMDb), and there was the fansite I Heart Jake (www.iheartjake. com). There was no competing with I Heart Jake (IHJ). There's *still* no competing with IHJ. But for a guy whose movie roles tended toward the obscure, his audience was ripe for something slightly less conventional.

Despite this, when Susie first started shopping around her idea for a Jake blog, she was widely discouraged.

Blogs about celebrities were nothing new. There were lots of them already, many of them very successful. But blogs about celebrities were about *all* celebrities, and they focused on gossip. A blog about a single celebrity was not one for which there was much precedent. Susie's idea was opposed by those who thought it was unlikely one person—much less Jake Gyllenhaal—could provide her with enough material to blog about. Because sure, he may grace the cover of supermarket tabloids now, but back then he was just a single guy leading a low-profile life, best known for his Oscar-nominated role in a movie few people saw. He didn't sell magazines, and he certainly didn't generate celebrity "news" on a regular basis. People wondered how the hell anybody could write about him day after day, week after week.

Susie, however, was not one to fold to the expectations of others.

She called it Jake Watch, and it debuted on April 3, 2006, the first blog on the internet to focus solely on the life of Jake Gyllenhaal. Her first

---

2   Of Jake's three '05 theatrical releases, *Proof* was the only one that did nothing for the fan recruitment effort.

post, titled "Welcome Fellow Stalkers," was more about the readers Susie was hoping to attract than Jake himself.

> *It's okay to admit that you have a problem and don't worry, I understand. Think of this blog as group therapy; a place to express those feelings and thoughts about the wondrous Monsieur Gyllenhaal that you perhaps shouldn't share with friends or colleagues or children or pets or local political and religious leaders. They won't be able to comprehend your need to know his every movement: where is he walking his dog today? has he received a parking ticket? who is he talking to? who is that touching him? how high are his socks today? These are all valid questions that, frankly, need answering.*
> —"Welcome Fellow Stalkers,"
> Jake Watch, April 3, 2006

The blog's tagline? "Well somebody has to keep a damn eye on him."

That was all it took for Susie to know success: a one-paragraph post, a catchy title, and a picture of Jake Gyllenhaal. Jake fans showed up in droves and within hours. They left her encouraging comments like, "OK I've just discovered my new favourite blog!!" and she reacted by posting more, seven entries in all on her first day as a blogger. Her posts were all short, all slightly irreverent, and all offered Susie's own unique spin on who Jake was.

I cannot overstate the instantaneousness of her success. One day there was Jake Watch and the next day the internet was full of Jake blogs. And I do mean the *next day*, as in April 4, 2006, because Jake Watch may have been the first, but its reign of exclusivity lasted less than twenty-four hours. This idea that Susie had had, which was thought to be so crazy and radical and doomed to fail, was proven to be none of the above as soon as she put it into practice. People *loved* the idea of a blog about Jake. They loved it so much that, in mass numbers, they decided that they, too, should start blogs about him.

And they did. And if people were unsure of Susie's ability to maintain a blog of general Jake subject matter, they must have been floored by the narrow focuses of those who popped up in her wake.

There were Jake-is-gay blogs, focusing on those pesky rumors of homosexuality that every individual who is both male and famous must contend with. And there were personal blogs, in which the author talked about his or her day-to-day life, and how that revolved around Jake. There were blogs devoted to poetry about Jake, blogs filled with pictures of Jake, blogs that were about the entertainment industry in general but talked mostly about Jake. There were Jake blogs that spawned other Jake blogs, Jake blogs that came and went quickly, Jake blogs that outlasted even Jake Watch. A lone blog popped up focusing on Jake's career as an actor (improbably successful despite such ordinary subject matter). And when, a year or so later, Jake started dating the actress Reese Witherspoon, there were, naturally, blogs focusing on that relationship as well.

There was even a blog devoted exclusively to the facial hair Jake grew in the summer of 2006. It was called "Save Our Dill,"[3] and the girl who dubbed his beard "Dill" and started the blog experienced short-lived notoriety within the fan world. (Unfortunately, the beard was lost before summer's end, and the site had to be abandoned in light of a newly clean-shaven Jake. Such were the risks one took when starting a Jake specialty blog.)

But back on April 3, there was only the one. And that was Jake Watch, born into an atmosphere so crazed for Jake coverage that a fan could make a name for herself just for loving the guy's stubble. Susie's timing couldn't have been better. She was able to capitalize on the frenzy surrounding *Brokeback Mountain*, and she did so with a blog, right as blogs themselves were reaching new heights of popularity. She didn't even have to advertise much; everyone was talking about her. I found Jake Watch a couple of days after it sprang into existence as I skulked around on a *Brokeback Mountain* message board one afternoon. Someone had posted a link along with a sentence or two of praise, so I clicked to check it out and … I simply never left.

> *'When I was in* Jarhead, *I felt really good about my body, really confident.' (quote by Jake Gyllenhaal)*
>
> *I felt really good about your body in* Jarhead *too, Jake. Wait, let me rephrase that—I wish I could have felt your body in* Jarhead *or any other film for that matter.*
>
> —"Quote of the Week," Jake Watch, May 30, 2006

Jake Watch appealed to me (and so many others) because it was humor-driven rather than gossip-driven. In her first few days, Susie established her tone by introducing several regular features that she would fall back on

---

3   Sadly (or perhaps not), this blog has since been deleted.

in the months ahead when there was nothing new to report. She mocked suspicious behavior in paparazzi pictures in a segment she called "Blatant Stalking," entered a faux-jealous rage in her "Back Away From My Man!" entries, and lamented poorly executed photo shoots in "Whose Idea Was This Then?" But nothing matched the popularity of her most notorious creation, "Sock Watch."

> *Unfortunately there has been no sighting of Jacob Benjamin Gyllenhaal so far today, so for now we must go back to March 25th for the latest sock news (is that an oxymoron?). The height, colour and type of Jake's socks is indespensible information to us all so hopefully we'll have some up-to-date action soon.*
> ** COLOUR: White, perhaps greying slightly, black rims.*
> ** TYPE: Ribbed for sporting pleasure*
> ** HEIGHT: Dangerously High*
> ** OVERALL STATUS: Satisfactory*
> —"Sock Watch," Jake Watch, April 3, 2006

It was a gentle mockery of the obsession of fandom, but it was also exactly the type of detail-oriented reporting that people were desperate for. Of all else that came from Jake Watch, the blog was, through its final days, consistently associated with Jake Gyllenhaal's socks.

Susie posted several entries a day, which was monumental in helping readers develop the habit of routinely checking the site. As an early reader, I found a new headline waiting for me every time I checked: "Now You Can Drink Water, Just Like Jake!" "IMDb Thread of the Moment: Is Jake Black?" "Jake Has Fatal Effect On Women."

Doubters be damned, Susie was an unstoppable success, even amid the sudden onslaught of Jake blogs around her. By the end of her first month, she was pulling in a good five thousand readers a day.[4] People read Jake Watch from all corners of the earth. Many were not native English speakers; a few would later confess that they used the blog to help them learn the language. Within a matter of days, it became, and would remain, the second largest online Jake fan community, after IHJ.

---

4   Which was *a lot*. The *Brokeback* frenzy died down very quickly, and with it went many of those readers. For the vast majority of its lifetime, Jake Watch had between one thousand and twenty-five hundred visitors daily (traffic always increased when Jake was promoting a movie).

The blog embraced the nonserious fan and the fan who didn't necessarily know all that much about the man in question. As long as one was not averse to looking at Jake and wielded the ability to laugh, he or she was welcome.

Seeing as how I fulfilled both prerequisites, I landed quite conveniently within Jake Watch's target demographic. Though I read religiously, I wasn't an active member of the community, in that I didn't write comments at the end of Susie's posts as others did, nor did I e-mail with any of the other readers. But I was fascinated by what she had created.

Adding to the site's allure, Susie kept her identity strictly under wraps. Back then she was, to me and to everyone else, simply "britpopbaby." She called herself a "stalker," and she wasn't afraid to ridicule the absurdity of being a fan, though she simultaneously celebrated the fun of it. She hardly ever broke character.

I never had any aspirations to write for Jake Watch myself. On the contrary, the thought never crossed my mind. The blog was Susie's venture, and she was solely responsible for it. I didn't know her, she didn't know me, and we lived six times zones apart. But from my desk at home, I watched it all unfold before me—her staggering popularity, her unique way of expressing herself as a fan—and found in Susie the answer to a question I didn't know I'd been asking.

The thing was, I liked Jake. Quite a bit. I thought he was good-looking and talented, and I liked that he was never caught stumbling drunk out of a nightclub in the wee hours of the morning, but instead had a reputation for being thoughtful and intelligent and politically aware. *dreamy sigh* Okay, I'll admit it. I had a crush on him.

But he was barely a year older than I was[5], and every time I sat down to find out more about him, like to watch an interview he'd given or read up on his career (which are perfectly reasonable things to do, I might add), I found myself stopping midway through. My standards for learning about famous people had been set a decade earlier with The Beatles. As I grew older, I was finding that no one else could come close to grasping my attention with the urgency they had. There was so much to know there … and it seemed so *important*. I never felt that with Jake. It was like I was reading about some guy who had sat next to me in English class. I just didn't have the proper level of awe toward him as a celebrity to research him appropriately.

---

5   And he still is. Even now, Jake Gyllenhaal is a year older than I am.

What I learned from Susie's example was that it was possible to be a fan and make it more about "being a fan" than obsessing over the object of your affection. Susie's focus wasn't solely on Jake; it was also on britpopbaby's reaction to Jake. The character she created was as important to the blog as the subject himself. People didn't come to Jake Watch to learn what Jake was *actually* doing. They came to read how britpopbaby had *interpreted* what he was doing, her ideas being usually incorrect and always amusing.

I liked that idea. I liked it much more than sitting in front of a computer screen and watching old talk show interviews. I just wasn't sure what that meant for me yet.

If ever there was a time when MySpace was the be all and end all of social-networking sites, it was 2006. We can add that to the list of ways the internet has changed between now and then, and throw in with it the fact that in those days, the "status update" had yet to be integrated into our collective consciousness, and the wall of one's profile was (if you can imagine) for other people to write on. If you wanted to talk about yourself, you wrote a blog entry. MySpace trendily had a blogging feature built into every profile.

As already mentioned, I had made use of my MySpace blog for the first time with an entry about *Brokeback Mountain* a couple of months earlier. After that, I continued to write there. My blog had about three readers, and I had never progressed past writing about anything other than what was currently going on in my life. But in mid-April 2006, it just so happened that my life included discovering Jake Watch. So that's what I wrote about:

> *britpopbaby is pretty much the British, slightly-more-internet-savvy version of me. She also might have more time on her hands than I do, but the jury's still out on that one. Her blog is less than two weeks old, so I'm getting you in on the early end of this, before it starts becoming "cool" to read Jake Watch. Trust me, it's worth it for the Sock Watch entries alone ...*
>
> —MySpace blog entry,
> April 13, 2006

On a whim, I decided I should e-mail Susie to let her know that I'd written about her (as if I thought Susie, with her five thousand readers a day, could somehow benefit from my promotion of her on my poorly read

MySpace blog). And I'll be damned if she didn't write me back. She also read my blog and left me a comment, which was more than I'd done for her at that point.

Two days later, subscribing to the theory that imitation is the highest form of flattery, I followed her lead and created an online identity of my own. I became "Prophecy Girl," a title I nicked from an episode of *Buffy the Vampire Slayer* of the same name, and I created a new blog, separate from MySpace, to write about, of all things, human overpopulation.[6]

Susie and I continued to e-mail, and she unwaveringly supported me, even though she barely knew me and even as I struggled to find an audience, having to work for readers in ways she'd never experienced. She left me comments anywhere I wrote, and I began returning the favor on Jake Watch. Before I knew it, we were, in the truest internet-sense of the word, friends.

One of the first things I learned about Susie was that she was never satisfied with the status quo. She was always expanding, always changing the look of Jake Watch, always coming up with new projects on the side. A benefit to being in her inner circle was that sometimes I got to be a part of her ventures.

Like me, several other Jake Watch readers had blogs of their own. Late in April, Susie suggested that the writers among us form a blogging ring so we could support each others' efforts. The blogging ring, which was little more than a list of blogs we all tried to read each day, begat a blog review site we called Sparkle Motion.[7] Our little group of five, headed by Susie, took turns ranking and discussing blogs other than our own. And while that venture was short-lived, Sparkle Motion indirectly begat Susie's second-most-popular creation after Jake Watch: her (mostly) autobiographical blog, Memoirs of a Gin Harpy.[8]

---

6   The creatively titled "Overpopulation Blog" ("The OP" for short) was my first attempt at forming my own blogging niche. My readership was in the double digits. On a good day. (http://overpopulationblog.blogspot.com).

7   *Donnie Darko* reference. Because we were *nerds*. This site has also since been deleted. Too bad, as I recall that Susie assigned me to review a low-brow semi-pornographic blog for my first piece and, not wanting to be harsh my first time out, I concocted some sort of idiotic rationale for giving it seven out of ten stars.

8   http://ginharpy.blogspot.com/.

Between Jake Watch and Memoirs of a Gin Harpy, Susie amassed not just readers but a following, and all before Jake Watch was six weeks old. I did whatever I could to support her online empire, all the while continuing to write entries of my own that no one read.

The first time Susie asked me for help with Jake Watch, she was trying to design a T-shirt. She had a vague vision she was working toward but asked if I could take a look at it, maybe turn her idea into something polished and professional looking. I took my assignment unbearably seriously and would be lying if I said I didn't feel a twinge of disappointment when she wound up personally throwing together a design at the last minute, disregarding the eleven options I had optimistically submitted to her.

But because the logistics of selling T-shirts to a widely international audience proved overly complicated, Susie only sold one batch before temporarily getting out of the clothing business. There were other things, though, that she needed help with. Sometimes it was as little as e-mailing people for her. Sometimes it was as big as designing the layout for the Jake Watch message board she was planning and then acting as a moderator once it went live. She asked me to do these things though I'd never so much as posted on a message board before, much less moderated one, and my graphic design qualifications consisted of a single intro-level Photoshop class I had taken in college.

She never doubted me. She never doubted herself, either, and she didn't know much more than I did. Neither of us had any formal education in anything internet related. Everything we did was through trial and error. She'd come up with an idea, she'd ask me if I could help her, and most of the time, we managed to fumble our way through it. If we couldn't, we simply moved on to the next thing. Despite the fact that my contributions were not nearly on the same level as hers, it was around this time that she started to refer to her blog as "ours," a britpopbaby/Prophecy Girl production.

And that was Jake Watch: an online community of (mostly) girls with a crush, led by a writer with few inhibitions. There was no master plan. Susie was just a fan, and I was just lucky enough to share her interests and gain her trust. When I think back on that time, I remember the sense of solidarity above all else, not just between Susie and me, but among everyone. We were excited about Jake. We were excited to have found each other.

I commented once that I hadn't seen one of Jake's earlier movies, *Highway*, and a woman I'd only had fleeting contact with online mailed her copy of the movie to my house so I could watch it. That's what it was like in those days. Everyone was polite and gracious and willing to help out, even though we didn't know each other very well yet. And for a lot of people, the experience of being part of an online fandom was as new to them as it was to Susie and me.

And Jake Watch was still new too. The message board opened two months to the day after I e-mailed Susie for the first time. The possibilities back then seemed endless. It was a good time to be a Jake fan … but it was a great time to be a part of Jake Watch.

When I was a sophomore in college, I, like many fans of *Buffy the Vampire Slayer*, thought that Spike the vampire was the coolest thing on television.

The actor who played him, James Marsters, had a band, and sometimes he would play twenty-one-and-up gigs in Los Angeles. At twenty, and in Memphis, I thought it was wretchedly unfair that there were people who got to spend their Saturdays at James Marsters concerts while I was in my dorm room doing chemistry homework. I would read the accounts people posted online after the shows, look at the pictures they'd taken, and pout in jealousy as they talked about how nice James was to his fans.

That was my primary reference for fan encounters, and it spurred one of the defining realizations of my young adulthood: now that I was twenty-four, I could do that sort of thing. I was old enough. I had the money. I definitely no longer had any chemistry homework. If a comparable Jake-related opportunity arose, I could make the most of it. *I* could meet Jake. And I could get a picture. And he would be nice to me.

Jake was not, however, the reason I went to Los Angeles for the first time, in May of that year. I went because two of my best friends, Greta and Crystal, lived in the city. But when I told Susie that I was headed out for a long weekend, she threatened me with physical violence if I didn't track Jake down and nab some sort of Jake Watch exclusive for her.

Knowing me as they did, Greta and Crystal were aware of my interest in Jake and tolerated my hysteria with the patience of two people who had witnessed me moon over James Marsters in our dorm. But Jake, as if sensing my impending arrival, jetted off to the East Coast shortly before I left and remained there for the duration of my stay in L.A. Fortunately for me, Jake's participation was never really required when it came to a Jake Watch exclusive.

Just prior to my arrival on California soil, a certain Mr. Gyllenhaal had been photographed not once, but twice, in as many days, coming out of Sprinkles, a trendy little shop specializing exclusively in cupcakes, this particular branch being in Beverly Hills. Sprinkles slowly rose to legendary status in the online Jake world, regardless of the fact that he was never photographed there a third time. I made a point of telling Greta and Crystal that it was an absolute necessity for me to visit Sprinkles during my weekend in Los Angeles, as the experience of setting foot in a shop where an actor once bought some cupcakes was an experience no fan should be without.

It was Greta who greeted me upon my arrival in the city, and she one-upped me. "I know where Jake went to high school!" she said. She'd already mapped out the route, complete with a smiley-face sticker at the site of the school. She'd put a smiley face where Sprinkles was too. Greta did all of the research that weekend. In fact, as will soon become evident, all of my Jake-related travels from here on out were planned and researched by people other than myself. Though adept at many things (Photoshopping multiple—if unusable—T-shirt designs, for instance), when it came to stalking, I never quite mastered the skill.

We didn't head toward Sprinkles until the second day of my visit, by which time Crystal had joined us with her car. We cruised around Beverly Hills for a good ninety minutes before Greta, exasperated, exclaimed, "Is Jake just *smarter* than we are?"

Apparently he was because he'd been able to find Sprinkles twice, and the three of us, with a map, couldn't find it once.

It was another thirty minutes before we located it, identified only after one of us spotted a horrifically long (and, okay, glaringly obvious) line snaking down the sidewalk, and it was a further forty-five minutes before we exited the shop, cupcakes firmly in hand. Greta and Crystal became the first in a long line of my friends who continued to speak to me after vacations in which I demanded things of them that no sane person should tolerate.

But far from being annoyed, they both seemed pretty thrilled about the cupcakes.

"We should find a place to eat these!" I said, a little thrilled myself.

"I was thinking we should eat them at Jake's high school!" Greta said.

My squeals of delight are probably still echoing down Rodeo Drive.

Finding Jake's high school was infinitely easier than finding Sprinkles, although the welcoming committee was decidedly less friendly. Jake went to a private school, complete with gates and a guard shack. We weren't exactly waved into the grounds so much as Crystal just kept driving when the security guard didn't jump in front of the car to stop her.

She maneuvered us to a parking lot, and we cautiously climbed out, surprised to see a few students wandering the campus even though it was Saturday. (I'm sure we blended in well; maturity-wise, we looked about as old as we were acting.) We made our way over to an outside patio, and I snapped a few pictures of our uneaten cupcakes ("For Jake Watch!") before we all three finally sat down to eat them.

And we laughed and we laughed and we laughed.

And then we piled back into Crystal's car and drove down the road a ways to sneak into a high school where scenes from *The O.C.* were filmed.

When I got back to Memphis, I wrote a detailed travel account on MySpace, heavily featuring the Sprinkles run and the subsequent high school trespassing jaunt. Susie linked to my four-part vacation journal on Jake Watch under the title "First Official Jake Watch Stalking Mission: FAILED!" and thus the legend of Prophecy Girl was born.[9] Though I was already well known among the Jake Watch crowd, suddenly I was recognized across the spectrum of Jake fansites as That Girl Who Ate Sprinkles Cupcakes At Jake's High School.

Jake Tourism, as that which I just described would later be categorized, experienced a spike following my adventure. Fans hunted out locations where paparazzi pictures had been taken and then took photos of themselves in those same places. One particularly popular spot was the track where Jake once worked out with Ryan Phillippe (in an era when that interaction would have been significantly less awkward than it might be now … oh, the social incest of Hollywood![10]), although several places in Beverly Hills got attention, including Sprinkles. I remember one fan, who had published quite a few pictures of herself in various locations, actually managed to

---

9   http://jakegyllenhaalwatch.blogspot.com/2006/06/first-official-jake-watch-stalking.html.

10 Because at that time, Ryan was still married to Reese Witherspoon. By the end of our story, Ryan and Reese will have divorced, and Reese will have moved on to a young buck named Jake, with whom she fostered a relationship on the set of the political thriller featured heavily in Chapter 13.

track Jake down while he was filming scenes for *Zodiac*.[11] Seeing him in the flesh was somewhat traumatizing for her, and she quit posting photos after that. Something about realizing he was a mere mortal after all …

But yes. I think of that as my first real contribution to the fan world: helping to popularize this genuinely creepy trend of picture taking.

My travel account was the closest I came to writing for Jake Watch until a month or so after I got back from L.A. For it was then that Susie wrote to say that she would be going to Italy on vacation for two weeks. I could totally say no if I didn't want to do it, but she was worried about the blog sitting idle for that long and, "I was wondering, nay begging you, to keep an eye on it for me?"

Me? Write for Jake Watch?

"I won't let you down, I promise!!!" I wrote back immediately.

It was a major break for a small-time blogger like me, with my cursory knowledge of Jake and six months of intermittent, amateur blogging experience behind me. I was completely confident in my abilities though, if slightly intimidated by the specifics. Up until that point, I'd thrown myself behind every idea Susie had come up with, but never before had it been me coming up with the ideas. It wasn't the creative aspect that gave me pause so much as the basis for inspiring it. I had no idea where to find Jake news. I got all my Jake news from Jake Watch. Devoted as I was to the projects Susie gave me, I was at a loss as to how she ran her operation. I hadn't the first clue what she did on a day-to-day basis to sustain such a large blog. I imagined it to be a labor-intensive and systematic process, considering how many times a day she managed to update.

Or not.

"I've realised I fly by the seat of my pants in a most unorganised fashion so there is not a lot I can say," Susie wrote when I prompted her for tips.

She told me to check IHJ for new pictures and not to freak out when a bunch of people I didn't know inevitably started e-mailing me. "You have creative control so if anything pops into your head roll with it," she wrote. She ended by telling me that her favorite of Jake's two dogs, a little puggle named Boo, should probably have his own MySpace profile.

And off she went.

On July 15, 2006, three and a half months after the blog began, Prophecy Girl made her Jake Watch debut. Tackling the most serious

---

11   Jake's first post–*Brokeback Mountain* movie, *Zodiac*, was about the Zodiac killer who terrorized San Francisco in the late 1960s. He was filming it throughout the first months of Jake Watch.

issue first, my first post was a brazen plea to readers to send me Jake news to write about.

When Jake found out that I was going to be taking over for britpopbaby for a couple of weeks, he kindly came over to my house, donned an Uncle Sam outfit (complete with wig and beard) and sat still for several hours so I could hand-paint this exciting and completely original promotional poster begging you, the reader, for help. What a guy! Also, damn, I should have been in advertising. Maybe I'll sell this idea to the U.S. Army when I'm done with it.

—"Jake (Watch) Wants You!"
Jake Watch, July 15, 2006[12]

12   Graphics were a huge part of Jake Watch, nearly as important to the blog as the writing itself. Unfortunately, very few of those graphics have made it into this book. Though the majority of the pieces I planned to include were original creations, most incorporated (in various stages of modification) photos taken by others. Because the internet affords such free and unregulated distribution of material, it was often difficult if not impossible to find a photograph's

Within hours, my inbox was flooded, with everything from movie rumors to a story about a contact lens company ranking celebrities based on the desirability of their eye color.[13] In fact, if anything can be said about my first two weeks on the job, it's that I was overambitious and often dampened my own creative spin to work in as much material as possible. I look back on those days in much the same way I look back on that first trip to Los Angeles, with fond memories of the enthusiasm, but legitimate embarrassment over the outcome.

And nowhere was that embarrassment more apparent than my involvement with Boo on MySpace.

A Short Subchapter on Boo the Puggle and His Popularity on MySpace

By the time I started writing for Jake Watch, even I, unskilled as I was in Jake research, knew that Jake Gyllenhaal had two dogs. Their names were Atticus (a German shepherd) and Boo (a pug + beagle = puggle), and they had been named after characters in the book *To Kill a Mockingbird*.[14] Susie, along with much of the rest of the Jake Watch community, was fascinated by the smaller of the two dogs, as well as by Jake's tendency to cradle him in his arms as he walked. Susie had even found a shirt online that read "Obey the Puggle!" and she somehow connived the designer into custom making a variation of the graphic with Boo's name on it for Jake. It arrived at her house the day before she left for Italy, and she shipped it off to Hollywood not long after she returned home.

I chose not to broadcast to my fellow Jake Watchers that under no circumstances would I classify myself as a dog lover, and I didn't think it was "cute" so much as "exceedingly weird" that Jake hauled his puggle around like it was a newborn human. It's a testament to both how much I wanted Jake Watch to succeed and how much I wanted to prove my worth while Susie was away that I threw myself into her suggestion for a MySpace profile the way that I did.

---

original source. In other cases, my request to publish a work in this book was denied by the photographer in question. Anything of importance that I could not include is still on Jake Watch, and can be found at the URLs that are footnoted throughout the book.

13 http://www.prnewswire.co.uk/cgi/news/release?id=176022. Jake ranked a disastrous 4 out of 5.

14 Hence Jake's beard being christened "Dill" by his highly literate fanbase.

Jake Watch already had a generic MySpace profile to advertise the blog, but that was Susie's project.[15] From here until the end of Jake Watch, Boo would be my responsibility. I started on his page the day that Susie left, and I attacked it with the grim determination of someone who's been weighted with an unpleasant task but wants to succeed for the common good. When I was finished, I was so mortified that I had fabricated a profile for a canine that I only admitted to my closest friends that it was my handiwork. To the internet as a whole, Boo's page was merely "created in affiliation with Jake Watch."[16]

I unveiled Boo's MySpace profile my second day on the job.[17] Because I believed in the blog, and because I wanted even its side ventures to prosper, my dedication did not end after the profile was set up. I made an early and fateful decision that everyone who wrote to Boo would get a response.

Boo got messages from exactly two types of individuals: those who thought they were writing to Jake himself (example quote: "OK, so this is just too damn cute for words!!!! You made MySpace pages for your dogs!!!! AWESOME!!") and those who wrote in the voices of their own pets (example quote: "I'm a beagle and only 3 years old, do you like older women? I hope we can be friends"). Boo's tendency to engage people in their delusions resulted in many of those who were writing as their dogs and cats to create new and separate profiles for their pets, notching up the weirdness level to heights I cannot say I was entirely comfortable with.

And it is this that I can claim as my second contribution to the fan world: helping to popularize this genuinely creepy trend of creating profiles for animals on social-networking sites.

Boo's popularity was such that after my initial Jake Watch post introducing his page, I didn't have to solicit friends for him. To this day, I have never logged into his profile without a friend request waiting for me. I don't know how people found him. I don't know why they wrote him. But they did. Starting the first day he was live on MySpace.

The messages were slow to trickle in at first, and it was easy when there weren't many of them. But as the days, weeks, months flew by, the messages kept coming … and coming … and coming …

Boo got unsolicited lifestyle advice:

---

15 www.myspace.com/jakewatch.

16 Atticus eventually got a profile of his own too, though it was created and maintained by one of our readers and was not formally associated with the blog (www.myspace.com/atticusfinchgyllenhaal).

17 www.myspace.com/booradleygyllenhaal.

"I think the next time Jake is at work he should take you & your brother [Atticus] along, imagine all that stuff to chew up, get tangled in & pee against!"

Unsolicited sexual advances:

"I just might have the girl for you?!!! …. my little baby girl named 'Gracie' would love to meet you. She's a black and tan little puggle and she's 4 mo. old. She's my baby and she's the most amazing thing that ever happened to me …. She will be in New York with me this week … would love to hang out!"

Unsolicited fitness information about other puggles:

"I weigh thirty-two pounds, which I guess is kinda big for a Puggle, but I am not fat. What do you weigh? I know Mom & Dad can't carry me around too long, but they are old anyway, so that is probably the reason."

Unsolicited attempts at humor:

"Is this a joke? Why does a dog have a myspace account??? Has there been a new discovery that dogs can now work a computer????? WOW!!!!"

Unsolicited glowing praise of Jake, punctuated by poor capitalization:

"IF HES HALF as nice as hes got talent for acting THEN HE WOULD BE one hell of a person to know! BUT OF COURSE you already know that!!!!!!"

Unsolicited greetings and queries meant to be passed on to Jake:

"Tell Jake I said Merry Christmas for me, and I wish him the best in Zodiac."

And:

"heya thur … so yea, can i date ur dad? lol…?"

Unsolicited personal questions:

"Boo, I love your belly! Do you like it when pretty women do the motorboat on your tummy? Or are you the kinda fella who prefers a good Ole fashion belly rub?"

Unsolicited therapy sessions:

"I think he's a great actor but it's really hard to get through to a famous actor. I'm more like a family guy and i know this may sound boring but i work for a software company and my dream to become a rockstar is stuck somehow, well my band is not unknown in germany but i realized that this is not what i really want to do …"

Unsolicited poorly translated creepiness:

"Hola Boo! I would like to reincarnate in your body like that Jake takes me as his pet and it would kiss it very much."

And, of course, unsolicited requests to promote people's bands …

"If you fancy taking a listen to a bunch of humans making noise—described as rock, heavyish but not the screamy shouting stuff! go to [website removed]"

Susie and I once contemplated compiling a book called *Letters to Boo*, which would feature all of the above quotes and hundreds more that currently lie in wait in Boo's inbox. But then we both reasoned that would be a horrible thing to inflict on the unsuspecting public.

So we'll just leave it at that and move on for the time being.
End of Subchapter.

Actually, I kind of like that subchapter idea. I'm going to keep doing that.

Other Adventures in Being In Charge

In addition to impersonating a dog, I also used my time in charge to write my first Sock Watch and Blatant Stalking posts. And there was news to be covered too. Those of you who were paying attention to celebrity news in the summer of 2006 probably remember that Lance Armstrong and Matthew McConaughey struck up a rather sudden and very public friendship fraught with bike riding and spandex. What you may not remember is that this power duo had a third amigo, and his name was Jake Gyllenhaal.

The first big news story of my budding Jake Watch career was Jake's trip to Europe with Lance to watch the Tour de France. I also had the task of live blogging[18] ESPN's ESPY Awards.[19] The entire trio showed up. Jake and Matt presented awards, and Lance hosted the event, although most memorable to Jake fans was the moment when Lance cracked a *Brokeback Mountain* joke at Jake's expense. I remember people being critical of that. I also remember people being critical of my (apparently) inaccurate transcription of what was said and my (apparently) unfair judgments about Jake's feelings regarding sporting events. The ESPYs were somewhat enlightening, as they gave me my first experience of seeing my words criticized by people outside of the Jake Watch community. My name showed up on fansites I'd never been to, and I wavered between being hurt and flattered by the scrutiny from people I didn't know.

---

18 Live blogging is the process of writing and publishing about an event as it happens—such as blogging about a television show as it is being aired.

19 I have no fucking clue what ESPY stands for.

And speaking of people I didn't know, throughout those two weeks I interacted with more fans than I ever had as a Jake Watch reader, mostly via e-mail. I made fast friends with a few who saved my neck by sending me tips. Many e-mails came from people who simply wanted to talk about Jake with me. One girl wrote me repeatedly with the suspected IP address of a reader she thought to be a stalker of Heath Ledger, though she never offered any reason as to why she suspected this person or explained what she wanted me to do about it. The most frequent e-mailer, though, was a woman by the name of Doris, who was older and didn't seem to require any input from me to carry on lengthy conversations about Jake ("Now 'Bubble Boy' ….. for the folks who say 'Jake did a good job' .. no … it wasn't just good … it was Brilliant!" [ellipses in the original]). Doris would later become disillusioned with me, and her introduction here serves only as foreshadowing to her one other appearance in this book, in Chapter 15. You'll probably have forgotten her by then, so I'll save the details of our correspondence for later.

The two weeks went by quickly.

When Susie came back, I was initially relegated to the occasional guest spot. Though I had been working full time since the inception of the blog, it had taken Susie—as a newly graduated university student—some time to find employment. Part of the reason that she had been able to put so much into the site was because she hadn't had a job, but once she found one, we began splitting the duties more evenly. It would be a few weeks before that happened, but when it did, generally I took the weekday shift and she took weekends, though there were many exceptions. As time wore on, we gradually slowed to posting five to seven times a week instead of several times a day, simply because we didn't have time to do more, and she abandoned Memoirs of a Gin Harpy and I my Overpopulation Blog. Later our roles would reverse completely, and I would be the primary writer, while she only intermittently posted.

But that's later. And this is now. And now that I've painted an idyllic portrait of our first few months, I must admit that things were slightly more complicated than I've let on. Thus far, our tale has been one of tranquility, but that's mainly because I have hitherto avoided mention of Jake's dad.

Seeing as how he plays a rather large role in the events that transpire next, I think it's time that I introduce you to Stephen.

The Saga of Stephen, Father of Jake

Sometimes I feel like a bit of an imposter being so high up in the ranking system, since I've only recently become a fan of Jake's and then, almost by default, the entire Gyllenhaal family. I tend to see Jake Watch as more of a creative outlet than anything else. It definitely has its own unique tone of admiration, but I think both Susie and I approach the blog as being just as much about creative expression as drooling over Jake.

—e-mail from me to Cantara Christopher,
July 27, 2006

Meet Stephen

Stephen Gyllenhaal, father of Jake and his actress sister Maggie, and (then) husband of writer Naomi Foner, was a Hollywood fixture in a family of Hollywood fixtures.

Best known for his directorial work in both movies and television, Stephen joins our story at a time when he was experimenting with a new medium: poetry. Now under normal circumstances perhaps the poetry of the father of a celebrity would not yield hysterical anticipation. But this was the summer of 2006. People were reverently referring to Jake's facial hair as a proper noun. Poetry of the father of *this* celebrity was *major* news, and rumor had it that Stephen had (wait for it ...) *written a poem about Jake.*

Best of all, this poem would soon be available to us (the public!) along with Stephen's other works in a book intriguingly called *Claptrap: Notes from Hollywood*. Now in order to fully appreciate the buildup to all that follows here, I must ask that we pause for a moment so we can reflect on what it was to be a Jake fan in the early days of Jake Watch.

The thing was, back then, it really wasn't the name "Jake" that had everyone excited. It was the name "Gyllenhaal." Any Gyllenhaal would do.

The myth of the Gyllenhaal family was heroic, and we, the fans, perpetuated it among ourselves as earnestly as we bought into it. In my Gyllen-crazed youth, I argued quite forcefully that the Jake Watch community was, in part, the product of the wholesomeness of the Gyllenhaal family. It was because of their innate goodness and intelligence that they attracted such good and intelligent fans. I truly believed that someone as talented as Susie must have been drawn in by an instinctual recognition of the talent she saw in them. Furthermore, I believed the readers at Jake Watch to be of a higher caliber than that usually associated with internet fan groups, and I connected that back to our common interest.

I didn't know of any other celebrity who had as many blogs devoted to him as Jake did, and I saw meaning in that. I saw creative output fomenting creative output. I don't know that I was necessarily wrong in that assessment either, but the truth of it isn't really the point here. The point is that we were delirious over the thought of Stephen writing a poem about Jake, as such an action rather audaciously reinforced our preconceived notions of a family with extensive artistic range.

Also, Maggie was pregnant at the time, the baby's father being none other than Jake's *Jarhead* (and later *Rendition*) costar Peter Sarsgaard. That dynamic, in turn, bolstered our idea of their familial closeness. This was a family who worked together and lived together and downright *functioned* in the dysfunctional world of Hollywood.

See? Just writing about them inspires me to use words like "audaciously" and "familial," as if these are words I might use in everyday conversation (which they are not). But at the time, that's the way we talked about them, because that's the way we thought of them. As intellectual … refined … possessing a sizable vocabulary …

Picturegate and Its Aftermath

Susie was merely keeping up with her audience, then, as she regularly checked Stephen's official website for information on his impending literary release. In May her diligence was rewarded when she ran across one of his poems. The piece was called "Land of the Free," and after she obediently published it on Jake Watch, we readers hurriedly converged in the comments section to talk about it.

"The colour pink, to me, has a lot of connotations to the superficiality of the modern American lifestyle," read one of our deadly serious comments. It's true; we voluntarily spent our time painstakingly deciphering poetry and arguing among ourselves about the American cultural and political landscape. On a Jake Gyllenhaal fansite. Had Stephen actively been looking for a base to buy his book, he would not have had to look further than his own son's fans.

It was on Stephen's official website that Susie found a previously unseen picture of Jake and his father around mid-May. Not having any immediate plans for it, she saved it, waited until news was slow, and then posted the photo on the blog one night before going out for the evening.

Over in central standard time, where it was only midafternoon, I turned on my computer and was as thrilled as the next poetry geek to see a new picture of Stephen and Jake under the latest Jake Watch headline. The photo was unremarkable; it simply showed the two of them looking at something on a computer screen (though it was obviously a recent picture, since Jake was sporting Dill). After reading what Susie had written on the main page, I clicked over to the comments to see what my fellow readers were saying.

Stephen, Jake, and Dill.[1]

At first it was just the usual chitchat—how hot Jake was, how sexy Dill was (or not, depending on one's persuasion), how Stephen's book would be available soon.

---

1   Photo by Robert Elswit. Used by permission of owner Cantara Christopher.

But then, about ten comments down or so …

She was not a commenter we had seen on Jake Watch before, but hers was a name we were familiar with. Cantara Christopher—*Stephen Gyllenhaal's publisher*—had left Susie a comment. And judging by what she had written, she was not happy that Susie had posted the photograph.

We would later learn that in addition to her publishing duties, Cantara was the sole administrator of Stephen's official website and the picture in question was owned by her. But all we knew at the time was that she was demanding the photo be taken down immediately and reprimanding the lot of us for prying entirely too far into the family's affairs.

For my part, I was *horrified*. *We*, the fine people at Jake Watch, invade the privacy of the *Gyllenhaal family*!? It was unthinkable. It was mortifying. It had to be corrected immediately.

I left a comment after Cantara's apologizing on behalf of all of Jake Watch and expressing just how highly we regarded not only Jake, but his entire family. Cantara didn't respond, but several other readers did, fortifying my response with apologies of their own.

A few hours later, Susie came home, by which point the drama had died down somewhat. She sent me an e-mail thanking me for mitigating the situation, and I felt then that I had earned her trust in being able to act responsibly on behalf of the blog in her absence. It would be another two months before I started writing for Jake Watch, but "Picturegate," as the controversy would later be dubbed, marked a turning point in the britpopbaby/Prophecy Girl dynamic.

So that brings us to Cantara's integration into Jake Watch, because while the obvious end here might be that we never heard from her again, the reality was quite the opposite. Considering how quickly she found the offending picture, I would imagine that she had been keeping an eye on the blog. That being the case, she likely had a good understanding of the level of hero worship going on with us. Fawning adoration is generally helpful when it comes to book sales, so we have to assume that she recognized our potential as an enthusiastic pool of buyers. And using this line of logic, we just might find some sense in what happened next.

For when Susie took down not just the picture but the entire post and then e-mailed Cantara personally to apologize, Cantara, despite her harshly worded rebuke of our interest in the family, offered Susie an interview in return.

With Stephen.

could discourage our collective desire to present ourselves as learned and studious.

At the reading, Stephen purportedly referred to us as "the girls," solidifying the image Cantara was feeding us of Stephen as the doting fatherly type, humbled by our interest in his work and thinking of us often.[4] Though it may not have been obvious to an outsider reading our anxious (but respectful!) poetry talk, it was implicitly understood within the community that all of us were being watched. We knew Cantara was watching us; she openly admitted it. And Cantara had taken every opportunity to hint that Stephen was also watching us. And if Stephen was watching us, it wasn't much of a leap to speculate that Jake might be too …

The perceived favorability that Stephen and Cantara directed toward Jake Watch vaulted the blog into the stratosphere. We went from being the chic new kids to a force to be reckoned with. Not everyone liked the attention; a negligible number of readers left us over fears we were getting "too close" to the Gyllenhaals, thinking the blog was suffering creatively under the pressure of trying to impress the family. But to most people, Jake Watch was a relentless success story. We had, in the course of a couple of months, achieved what no other fansite before us had: we had the Gyllenhaals reaching out to *us*.

Time passed.

June morphed into July, and Susie gallivanted off to Italy, leaving me to my aforementioned maiden voyage as a Jake Watch writer. I contacted Cantara personally for the first time while Susie was away, asking if I could publish another of Stephen's poems. Cantara and Susie e-mailed regularly, and Susie usually recapped the details, but it wasn't clear whether I, or my involvement with the blog, had ever come up between them. I didn't want to get in trouble for posting the poem without permission, so I used the opportunity to introduce myself and ask for her consent.

My request being short and to the point, I was floored to receive a nine-paragraph response in which I was granted permission to post the poem and (and!) asked to contribute to a scholarly blog about Stephen's film work, along with Susie. Cantara addressed me like she was speaking to an old friend:

---

4   http://jakegyllenhaalwatch.blogspot.com/2006/06/last-nights-poetry-affair.
    html.

"You have to understand, Becky," she wrote, "when I started out a year ago it was just to publish a little book of poems. Had no idea it was going to open up to this incredible new world with people like you in it. After the reading last month I was sitting next to Peter Sarsgaard on my left and I had just said to Stephen on my right that I thought the reading would be the end of it, but Stephen said something like Not on your life, kid, this is just the beginning, and when he went off to call Jake on his Blackberry I turned to Peter and asked him, Once you enter the Gyllenhaal circle, do you ever get your life back? And without a moment's hesitation, he grinned at me and said, 'No.'"

First e-mail. She shared a personal conversation she had with Peter Sarsgaard whilst Stephen was off calling the son who was at the center of my creative universe *in the first e-mail*. Not only that, but she expressed her sincere gratitude that I had sought permission to publish Stephen's poem (despite the many places his works had shown up online, I was the first person to have ever asked in advance), and, let us not forget, she'd offered me a writing gig. I fell all over myself writing her an enthusiastic thank-you in return.

It would be years before the nuances of the relationship between Cantara and the Gyllenhaal family fully revealed themselves, so we have to look at what she wrote as I saw it the first time I read it.[5] When she said to me, "You have to understand, Becky," I *did* understand. I understood perfectly because like her, I was getting in deeper every day. All I'd done was see a movie, and six months later I had an audience of thousands at my fingertips.

And now I ask that *you* understand just how humbling and flattering I found it, on my eleventh day of writing for Jake Watch, to have this woman confide in me. Cantara, who had sat between Peter Sarsgaard and Stephen Gyllenhaal (like she was one of the family!), had written to me and trusted me with a private story. She was a publisher, and she had deemed me worthy of contributing to a blog about Stephen's films. She was a professional, and she had treated me as an equal. I could envision the scene she had laid out before me, with Stephen jovially telling her it was "just the beginning." I wanted it to be "just the beginning" for me too. I wanted in, on anything Cantara could get me in on.

And I wanted her to know that she could rely on me not to overstep my bounds when it came to her client's work:

---

5   For Cantara's take on this story, check out her memoir, *A Poet from Hollywood: Love, Literature, and Stephen Gyllenhaal*.

"I'll always ask first!" I assured her.

Stephen Speaks

I posted the poem as scheduled, and despite the fact that Jake appeared publicly in spandex that same day, thus veering our intellectual discussion decidedly off course, Cantara linked to our comments about the poem on Stephen's official site anyway. The film blog went to the top of my list of things to talk to Susie about once she was back in England, but as soon as she was home, we were distracted by a much larger issue. Stephen, at long last, had finished answering our questions.

It was the second-to-last day in July, the day after Susie came back from Italy. It had been two and a half months since we'd sent the questions on their way, and Jake Watch had more than doubled in age in the interim. The interview sat overnight in Susie's inbox and then, to the aching joy of every one of us, she posted what he had to say.[6]

The finished interview ran sixteen questions long, the topics ranging from poetry to politics to the paparazzi. And while his answers were thoughtful and well constructed, they did not completely mesh with what Cantara had told us about him. Specifically, there was little indication that he was as interested in us as Cantara insisted he was.

Not once did Stephen mention Jake Watch by name. Nor did he explicitly acknowledge or thank us for our interest in his book. Nor did he give us any personal anecdotes, make more than a passing reference to his kids, or answer his questions with anything other than deadly seriousness. The closest he came to recognizing who he was talking to came when he wrote, "some [of you] I know contribute to the online forums and fanblogs."

Blogs? As in plural?

Susie commented to me in an e-mail that she got the impression he didn't have "a clue about what Jake Watch actually is all about." But Cantara had, frequently and emphatically, told us quite the opposite. In her e-mails to us, the same ones in which we were told of Stephen calling us his "daughters" and where hints were dropped that he was keeping up with every word we wrote, Cantara often referred to him, among other things, as "the big knucklehead." So Susie and I rationalized that perhaps he was just eccentric.

---

6   http://jakegyllenhaalwatch.blogspot.com/2006/07/ok-so-some-bloke-named-stephen.html.

It was Stephen's stance on the paparazzi, though, that dominated our discussion over the next couple of days. He brought up the issue of celebrity privacy early, first mentioning it in the short introduction he'd penned: "I have to admit, as I watch all this interest unfold around me, though, particularly around my kids, I'm often driven to ask, what about each of you? Everyone [*sic*] of us deserves attention. Lots of attention."

But he didn't get into specifics until he responded to a direct question about photographers:

"It affects us. It's sad. People will discover much more interesting things when they turn their cameras (and thoughts) on the people in their own lives, the people they know. The people they personally love. The people they personally hate. The people in-between. The rest of this is just an excuse for avoiding that far more interesting world. The world of their own lives."

Hindsight. It's wonderful, isn't it? You can see things clear as day that you missed the first time around. All of the things I'm emphasizing here are connected: the way he didn't address us directly, the way Susie noticed something was off but the two of us chose not to analyze it, the way Stephen took a question about the paparazzi and subtly twisted it so that his response was aimed at us and not the photographers. Together, these things coalesce into such a clear warning of the events in the following chapter that it's difficult for me to explain how it was that we all missed it.

But we did. We were just too excited. He was a Gyllenhaal, for God's sake. And he was talking to us! We didn't treat what he said or did with any cynicism; we were starstruck. Jake Watch still had that glossy feeling of newness that only a young internet community has, when its members are hopelessly optimistic and see nothing but good in the world.

"The thoughts and observations of the father make me want to be a better person," one commenter gushed.

"It just reminds me even more why I respect and admire people such as the Gyllenhaals so much," swooned another.

"I mean, really, who are we to get that level of intimacy out of him? I'm honored that I got to be a part of this," wrote yet another adoring fan. (Okay, confession, that last one was me, bravely overlooking the fact that my question had been attributed to Prophecy Girl and not Becky after all.)

That he'd taken so long to get back to us surely meant that he had thought at length about his answers. That he'd grimly shot back, "What do you do?" when asked what he did to relax certainly indicated that he was genuinely interested in hearing our answers to that. That Stephen, for whom the livelihood of every member of his family depended on public interest, had chastised us for our public interest ... well ... dammit, okay. That was a tough one. That one we didn't have a great explanation for.

"He comments about Hollywood and fame and people falling for that illusion, and what he says is all true, but still; it's a life he and his children chose for themselves," wrote one reader, before continuing, "I AM interested in Jake Gyllenhaal. I know I don't know him and I don't need to, but there is no crime in having fantasies, living in fantasies sometimes."

"I'm sure Stephen meant well by his comments, but it seemed a little disingenuous to me for him to discourage others from buying into the dream when his whole family is such a part of it," someone else wrote.

Those two comments were as close as anyone came to criticizing him outright. And since most of us felt that questioning him was disrespectful, we instead chose to take his advice. We looked inward. We talked among ourselves about our motivations for coming to Jake Watch and what it was about the community that kept us there. It was then that Susie said something that she and I would go back to over and over in the months to come: "This blog stopped being about Jake Gyllenhaal a long time ago. It was never truly about Jake Gyllenhaal to begin with," she declared in the comments. By that, she was acknowledging that while we had converged around a central subject matter, there was little connection to Jake beyond that. She never operated under the delusion that she knew who he was as a person, or that she was somehow doing this blog *for* him.

Another commenter agreed, "It's not about Jake, it's about the people I have come to know, and the thoughts and laughter they share with me ..."

Jake Watch made me feel like I was back in college, and in the best possible way. I'd been out of school less than two years; Susie had only been out a few months. We hadn't yet defined ourselves outside of the role of students.

But until Jake Watch, I hadn't had any real-life experiences that reinforced what school had conditioned in me. Cantara's interest in us and Stephen's engagement with us closely resembled the only model for success that I was familiar with: that hard work was always recognized, and that I, personally, was perceived as intelligent and talented by anyone who met me. It had been devastating to graduate and find myself in dead-end jobs where no one saw me as any different from the person sitting next to me. I was in one of those dead-end jobs at the time, and it was a relief beyond measure to find this other world where the rules I knew still seemed to apply.

We treated Stephen like he was a favorite professor, with our faux intellectualism and our deferral to his authority. But he was even better than a professor because this *wasn't* college. This was real life. We respected him, and we respected Cantara, and it's precisely because of that respect that when Cantara asked Susie to do something for her about a week after the interview went up, Susie didn't hesitate.

The Moral High Ground

On August 9, 2006, Jake Watch, already light on the tabloid rumors, became a no-gossip zone.[7]

From that day until the end of the blog, the posts on Jake Watch would contain no girlfriend rumors, no boyfriend rumors, no open speculation on what Jake's life was like when the cameras weren't rolling, and never again would we mention any of his non-famous friends by name.

Though Stephen's interview and a couple of private conversations with Cantara already had Susie contemplating this decision, she was swayed when Cantara confided that Jake, personally, didn't like people talking about his private business. Cantara was usually mum about our favorite family member, so when she did mention him, we paid especially close attention. If she had warranted his comments about privacy important enough to tell us about them, then that meant something.

We still posted paparazzi pictures (alas, even the two of us would have a hard time running a blog without those), and confirmable news stories, such as Maggie's pregnancy, were fair game … but when it came to gossip about Jake's private life, our policy was zero tolerance. We couldn't control what people wrote in the comments, but the standard for britpopbaby and Prophecy Girl was simple: if it was personal, we didn't write about it.

To the confusion of those who rightfully noted that we didn't publish much gossip anyway, Susie broadcast the new standards with as much fanfare as she could muster.

"I emailed Stephen about your pledge and your posting," Cantara wrote to Susie after she'd broken the news publicly. "I know it looks like

---

7   http://jakegyllenhaalwatch.blogspot.com/2006/08/goodnight-and-good-luck.html.

dreams had already come true, Cantara dropped another responsibility in our laps: Stephen's official website.

Official. Not "unofficial," not "run by fans," but *official.* In the world of online celebrity-fan interaction, the official website is the holy grail of responsibilities. It is the gateway through which information flows from the inner circle to the world as a whole. There are no filters, no third parties; there is only the source (and his representation) on one side and the unwashed masses on the other. For Susie and I to be named as gatekeepers? To be trusted as guardians of this most sacred of online thoroughfares? To be given the keys to the kingdom of Gyllenhaal? Of all the responsibilities Cantara had given us, this one was in a category all its own. For if we were in charge of his official website, that meant that Stephen, patriarch, poet, and privacy advocate, would be shown to the world through the lens that Susie and I shaped.

All right, so Stephen's site wasn't going to pay anything. And truthfully, I doubt Cantara was thinking much beyond lessening her own workload when she made the offer. But an ocean apart, Susie and I came to the same conclusion. If we got Stephen's official site, we were only one step away from Jake's official site. And if we could get control of Jake's official site, maybe someone would actually *pay us* for our services. Maybe we could make a living doing something we actually *liked.* Suddenly our afternoons of snickering over spandex were giving way to thoughts of creative fulfillment and legitimate careers.

These were pretty heady notions for a couple of recent college graduates who were working administrative jobs and were none too optimistic about their current career prospects.

With the tantalizing scent of money on the horizon, Susie went to work coming up with a basic design for Stephen's site, aiming for a complete overhaul of the simplistic layout Cantara had been using. Adding to the pressure to succeed was the theory that Stephen would be personally approving anything we came up with before we used it. We knew he was on board with our involvement because Cantara had told us as much: "Stephen's exact words re this website: 'Of course they have my blessing.' Let us therefore feel blessed."

Once she came up with an outline she liked, Susie passed it along to me, asking that I clean it up and add my own touches. *Days* were lost behind our computer screens. Jake Watch was still our top priority, and we made sure to post at least once a day, but behind the scenes, Stephen's site was a constant source of conversation and anxiety. We nervously e-mailed back and forth over every …

single …

detail.

And when we had a product that we thought was worthy of being unleashed to all of humanity, we updated Cantara on our progress. She requested some time to look things over. There was a brief period of pause.

So back to the film blog we went.

I volunteered to take the first essay, which Cantara decided should be on the 1993 Stephen-directed drama, *A Dangerous Woman*. I scoured the city of Memphis and loyally acted affronted when I couldn't find it.[9] I scoffed at the plebeian mind that would fail to stock the local shelves with a complete collection of Gyllenhaal films. In desperation, I turned to the internet and bought a used VHS copy on Amazon. It cost me $1.80 plus shipping, and again I sneered in disbelief. The going price for art these days!

And then I watched the film.

In the interest of full disclosure, I had never seen one of Stephen's films before. Neither had Susie. Then again, neither of us had previously whiled away our evenings discussing poetry like a couple of beatniks, but Jake Watch proved to be a gateway to all sorts of new experiences.

I watched *A Dangerous Woman* for the first and only time on a sunny weekend afternoon in late August. The quality of my tape was about level for what I'd paid for it. Jake and Maggie had small cameos at the start of the film and after that … I don't really remember. Something about masturbation and Gabriel Byrne.

For the very first time, it occurred to me that perhaps I wasn't meant to delve into the inner reaches of Stephen Gyllenhaal's mind.

There was a lot of pressure on me, going first and all. I anguished over it. Cantara wasn't helping either, what with her constant assurances that she was keeping Stephen informed of our progress and that we were doing a wonderful thing to help bring attention to his work.

Whatever enlightening commentary (a.k.a. "bullshit") I finally managed to wring out of my viewing has, along with the blog itself, long since been deleted. But I do remember Cantara saying it was good … good enough that she told Stephen about it.

---

9   Here's a fun exercise in humility: next time you're at a video store, walk up to the counter and say, "I'm looking for *A Dangerous Woman*."

Speaking (incessantly) of Stephen, he was still holding poetry readings. The first, mentioned earlier, was held in New York and attended by not only Jake Watch people but also the entire Gyllenhaal family, sans Jake. The second reading, in August in Martha's Vineyard, was attended by Jake Watch people, the entire family, *and* Jake. By the time the third reading was announced, also to be held in New York City, in mid-October, neither hell nor high water could have kept me away.

Let's Talk Internal Politics

Cantara, Susie, and I may have been a triumvirate of sorts, but I was unquestionably the least of three powers. As such, it didn't surprise me that when I e-mailed Cantara to let her know that I was planning to make the trip, she already knew I was coming.

I didn't always know what was discussed between Susie and Cantara. I would get bits and pieces of information about their conversations, sometimes full quotes, sometimes just summaries, and was often left with the nagging feeling that I was being left out. After her first e-mail, Cantara had written nothing to me personally, aside from her brief second invite to write for the film blog, which was addressed to Susie and me both. While we evenly shared the workload Cantara bestowed upon us, it was always Susie who got the information, Susie who was passing along instructions, and Susie who was relaying what Cantara had said in relation to something I'd done. I would never have known she read my *Dangerous Woman* essay, or that she'd liked the banner I made for the blog, had she not written Susie to tell her.

When I e-mailed Cantara then, to let her know that I was coming to New York, I wasn't sure she would respond. But she did and, slightly bewilderingly, she did so within a matter of minutes and began her e-mail: "Not only do I know you're coming, I told Stephen about it a couple of weeks ago." That prompted me to jump up from my desk at work and run down the hall to the bathroom so I could squeal in peace without arising the suspicions of my coworkers.

When I'd calmed down enough to return to my cubicle, I finished reading the e-mail. Cantara ended by inviting me to brunch before the reading, suggesting we talk about Stephen's official website then.

What she didn't mention was the plan that she and Susie had deviously devised between themselves long before I sent my e-mail. It involved me presenting Stephen with a card for his birthday (apparently the reading was in the vicinity of it) and another congratulating Maggie and Peter on the birth of their child (apparently the baby was due around this time as well, and while there was always the hope that Maggie and/or Peter would be at the reading, Cantara couldn't know for sure, and the plan conservatively assumed they would not be). And lastly, to prevent any damage that might occur to the cards during my flight, Susie would e-mail the finished products to Cantara, who would print them off and hand them over to me at brunch, before the reading.

And thus was I successfully circumvented from any and all stages of the planning process, with my participation required only at the execution stage. I didn't find out about any of this until a few days before I was due to leave, because Susie and Cantara were so wrapped up in the vision of me charming Stephen as I played the role of fan ambassador that they simply forgot to tell me. I wasn't upset with them, though. I was still stuck on the fact that Cantara had *told Stephen I was coming.* I mean, my God. How amazing was that?

As Baby Gyllenhaal-Sargaard's arrival drew closer, Susie began toying with the idea of coupling the card with a gift of some sort. She came up with the idea of adopting an animal at the Chester Zoo in the baby's name. I thought that was a great idea and lobbied for a monkey. Susie argued that the red pandas didn't cost as much.

We went with a red panda.

> *Just in case you forgot to mark this momentous occasion down in your diaries/laptop/sidekicks/fence post in back yard I thought I should remind you it's Jake Watch's sixth month anniversary. Aaah, the memories, the dramas, the socks, the achievements, the lawsuits—who would have thought?*
>
> *In all seriousness though, I'd like to say AHA mutherfuckas! to those naysayers who reckoned it wouldn't last, my Dad who told me to stop wasting my time on Jake Gyllenhaal and get a frickin job, all the jackasses who tried to correct my spelling and grammar and lastly, Blogger, for working 76% of the time.*
>
> —"I'd Like to Thank the Academy, My Agent,
> My Grandpa Buster ..."
> Jake Watch, October 3, 2006

Regarding the Birth of the Gyllengaard Child

The baby was born the day Jake Watch turned six months old.

Cantara broke the news in the comments section of our anniversary post: "STEPHEN JUST EMAILED ME. HER NAME IS RAMONA, SHE WAS BORN ABOUT 8PM NEW YORK TIME." Ramona had been around for all of an hour and sixteen minutes.

Susie was asleep (it was the middle of the night in England), and I was in the middle of watching *The Little Mermaid* (I can't believe I just admitted that), so the news sat in the comments for over an hour with only a few other commenters taking notice of it.

Perhaps sensing that her announcement was not achieving maximum impact, Cantara followed up by e-mailing three people: me, Susie, and Ally, the owner of IHJ. Of the three of us, I was the first to check my inbox. Under the exclamatory subject line "Maggie's Baby!" Cantara had written: "Becky. Stephen just emailed me. Baby came around 8 this evening. Her name is Ramona!"

I was very excited by this.

"AH!!!! That's so exciting!!!!!! Can I post this?!?!?!?" I wrote back (not yet realizing that she had already posted the news herself in the comments).

"God, I wish you would!!!" responded Cantara.

So I did. "It's a Girl!" I wrote, giving Ramona her very first internet headline.[10] Ally put up a similar announcement on her own site a few minutes later.

Then I went to bed.

The next morning, I began my day by hitting every major gossip website I could think of; I wanted to share in the joy of those who had heard the news overnight. But strangely, there was nothing. Ramona was nowhere to be found on any of the gossip sites ... aside from one. On a blog called Just Jared, she had grabbed the headline: "EXCLUSIVE: Maggie Gyllenhaal Gives Birth to Baby Girl."

Of course, it wasn't *really* an exclusive because the story, which was time-stamped, had gone up well after Jake Watch published the news. But I was willing to let it slide. Just Jared had been very good to Jake Watch.

The blog's administrator (whom I presume to be named Jared) was a reader. He didn't comment, but he did occasionally link to our stories and give us traffic boosts. The last time he'd paid us that favor was less than a

10 http://jakegyllenhaalwatch.blogspot.com/2006/10/its-girl.html. This post was edited the following morning to credit Cantara as the source, but this was done long after Just Jared had posted his story.

week earlier when he referenced a post I had written about the Gyllenhaal family visiting a very pregnant Maggie in New York.[11]

Neither Susie nor I had ever spoken to Jared personally, but knowing he read our blog, and knowing from his recent reference to us that he was watching us as we waited for the baby to arrive, we surmised that he might have gotten the Ramona story from us, even though he didn't mention us in his post.[12] Which was fine. Information is shared on the internet all the time. Two Hollywood stars had a kid. It's not like the news wasn't going to get out.

Just Jared had credited the details of his story to "a source close to the Gyllenhaal family," who "confirmed [the story] exclusively to JJ [Just Jared]." Jared would later adamantly declare that he did not take his story from Jake Watch or any other Jake site, but he did retract his "source close to the family" claim and give credit to an "anonymous e-mailer."

And again, none of this should have mattered. Maybe the anonymous e-mailer saw the story on Jake Watch and sent it to Jared, or maybe there really was a legitimate third party who sent in the details. But the reason it *did* matter is because much as Just Jared was watching Jake Watch, *US Weekly* was watching Just Jared.

Later that day, Cantara got a voice mail message. It was *US Weekly* asking her to confirm that Stephen had issued a statement about the birth of his granddaughter. When she didn't call the magazine back, *US Weekly* followed up with an e-mail. "I understand that Mr. Gyllenhaal has released a statement about his new granddaughter Ramona through Cantara Books [*sic*]. Can u pls forward me the statement?" wrote a senior editor. Again, Cantara ignored the query, but she did forward the e-mail on to Susie as a curiosity.

And Susie, as confused as I was and seeing a journalistic opportunity in the works, decided to e-mail the *US Weekly* editor herself.

She explained from the beginning … that the story had appeared first on Jake Watch … that it in no way qualified as a "statement" … that the baby's name was Ramona, but he wouldn't be able to verify that through any of us … Then, trying to understand how he had known to come to Cantara and why he thought her publishing company was involved, she asked where he saw the story.[13]

---

11   http://justjared.buzznet.com/2006/09/28/gyllenhaal-family-walk/.

12   http://justjared.buzznet.com/2006/10/04/ramona-sarsgaard/.

13   http://jakegyllenhaalwatch.blogspot.com/2006/10/actual-behind-scenes-action.html.

"we saw it on just jared," the senior editor snipped.

Which did not explain how he came to track down Cantara. At no point in his post had Jared used the words "statement," "Cantara," "Stephen," or "Cantarabooks." And I don't say that in order to foreshadow any revelations about this later in the book. I say it because it's a mystery; even now none of us knows how *US Weekly* came to write that e-mail. It doesn't make much sense if all they did was see the story on Just Jared, with Just Jared claiming a separate source that had nothing to do with any of Jake's fansites (all of which had credited Cantara).

The senior editor finished his e-mail by saying, "i think it's weird that a publisher [Cantara] forwarded a request from an editor to a fanblog. but thanks for expalining."

I could see his point. Although, to be fair, *I* think it's weird that a senior editor at *US Weekly* can't spell and doesn't use capital letters.

The magazine eventually got its confirmation of Ramona's name and birth date from Maggie and Peter's publicist. I dealt with the situation by changing my Facebook status to "Becky is celebrating the fact that she SCOOPED US WEEKLY!!"[14] Because I had. And because I was still a bit in awe of how a second-rate Jake fan such as myself had climbed the ladder so quickly as to be in the position to announce major celebrity news well before a noted American gossip magazine.

By the time Ramona was two days old, everyone had moved on to the next thing. I didn't hear anything more about *US Weekly*. That was early October.

A week later, it was time to leave for New York.

So that was where I stood as I got ready to leave for my trip. I was fresh off publishing a celebrity baby story ahead of the mainstream gossip machine. I had a head (and hard drive) full of ideas for Stephen's new official website, which I would be co-running, and my graphics were already showcased on the existing one. I had written the first academic piece for the revised Stephen Gyllenhaal film blog. I had read Stephen's book cover to cover. I had my plans in place for brunch with Cantara. And I continued to cowrite the most popular Jake Gyllenhaal blog on the internet, a blog that had exhibited unprecedented interest in Stephen's work and which had taken a bold stance in respecting his son's privacy.

I was ready.

---

14   Remember when everyone wrote status updates in the third person? Oh, 2006! .

Susie and I discussed whether I should mention our ambitions for Jake's official site to Stephen while I was in New York or wait until later. We decided I should assess that situation once I met him. Would he be at brunch? Would he expect a formal presentation of my business ideas? How long would it be before we made the leap from fans to official representatives? (Weren't we nearly there already?)

It was Megan, my good friend and fellow Heath Ledger aficionado, whom I saw last before my trip. I filled her in on my accomplishments and ambitions, and she remarked, "By the time this trip is over, your whole life may have changed."

I didn't disagree.

Never Sit Too Close to the
Stage at an Opera ...

(Sob ... sob ...) Where Is Jake? Not one single new sighting
since October 8! Not even a mention much less a picture!
—comment left on Jake Watch,
October 12, 2006

O Jake, Where Art Thou?

Jake's name was on the VIP list. Allegedly. That was the rumor on Jake Watch anyway, started by an anonymous commenter whose friend was supposedly working the New York Film Festival. Kirsten Dunst's new film, *Marie Antoinette*, would be premiering at the festival the night of my arrival in New York, and her ex-boyfriend (Jake) had worked his way onto the guest list.

Allegedly.

The premiere was two days before the poetry reading. Furthermore, it appeared that the day after Stephen's reading, Jake would be receiving an Americans for the Arts Award, also in New York City.

If Jake was due to be in the city both before the reading and after the reading, it seemed a logical assumption that he might also be *at* the reading. Even if he wasn't, I had options now for trying to track him down. And so it was that my business trip to work out how Susie and I might best represent Stephen was unexpectedly coupled with my Second Official Jake Watch Stalking Mission.

I connived my friend Kara into taking the trip with me. Kara and I had gone to college together and were good travel partners, having survived numerous trips together. She was living in Indiana, going to graduate school, and we hadn't seen each other in over a year. Like me, she'd never been to a poetry reading before, but she wasn't averse to the idea. She did, however, have a few questions about the cards I was supposed to be handing over to Stephen at some point. "Is this, like, going to be a formal presentation? Where you give a speech and then hand over the cards in front of everyone at the poetry reading?" she asked when I described my diplomatic duties.

"I have *no idea*. I don't really want to think about it too much or I might vomit," was my honest answer.

We arrived in New York City on Friday, October 13, 2006. Nothing could dampen our enthusiasm—not the date, not the fact that the airline lost Kara's bags, and not the discovery after we checked into our minuscule hotel room that we had only half as many beds as we'd paid for. It was as if my excitement was a communicable disease, and the longer Kara was exposed to me, the more infected she became. She kept asking me about the poetry reading and Gyllenhaal family history and, "When are you going to call Cantara?"

I had told Cantara that I would let her know when we arrived, but I wanted to get my bearings first. I needed to be mentally prepared for my first non-e-mail contact with her. I wanted to be calm. Collected. Full.

"I need to eat first," I answered, after we dumped our bags and admired the striking view of the brick wall just outside our window.

"Okay, where do you want to go?" Kara asked.

"I don't care. Someplace close," I said.

"Do you think there are restaurants by Central Park?"

"Definitely! It's New York! There are restaurants everywhere!"

"Then let's go to Central Park!" Kara said. Because of our hotel's close proximity to the park, a mere five blocks south, this plan seemed infallible. But ninety minutes later, when the two of us were staring out at the East River, it occurred to us that perhaps we should have brought along a map. We had both been to the city before and had apparently thought we would find our way to Central Park on instinct. Like carrier pigeons.

Another thirty minutes passed before we reached our destination. And once there, we found the area mercilessly devoid of restaurants. It was a full three hours after we left our hotel that we arrived back, feet sore and me slowly becoming tragically sick from the sandwich I'd eaten when we'd finally stumbled across food.

"I'm just going to go lie down," I whimpered, leaving Kara in the lobby with her laptop. She had some homework to do but promised to research the New York Film Festival as I shuffled off to writhe in pain in our room.

We had only a couple of hours before *Marie Antoinette* premiered. It was a highly inopportune time to fall ill over a sandwich.

I was in bed for an hour before mind won over matter. Forcibly willing myself to wellness, I stumbled back into the lobby.

"How are you feeling?" Kara asked.

"We're going to that damned premiere if it kills me," I said, slowly sinking into the chair next to her. She gave me an appraising look.

"All right. But we can't get tickets."

I had lain in bed just a few minutes too long; tickets went off sale a half hour earlier. Not that that was necessarily a deal killer. Kara and I had been carefully avoiding the subject of celebrity arrivals at the film festival all afternoon, as if in fear of jinxing ourselves. While it would have been fun to watch the film's debut screening, there were also positives to being *outside* the theater …

"I'm still up for going down there to *people watch*," I said carefully. Meaningfully.

Kara nodded in solemn agreement, understanding what I was implying. "Yes, we could *people watch*," she agreed. "But," she added pointedly, "let's take a cab."

Fifteen minutes later, the taxi dropped us near the theater. Though we were plenty early, we could see the red carpet was already in place. Next to the carpet was a semi-short line of people stretched down the sidewalk, waiting to enter the building. Otherwise, the area was pretty quiet. Having never been to a red-carpet affair of any sort, neither of us was sure about protocol.

"Um, where should we stand?" I asked Kara.

"I think all of those people have tickets," she said, taking in the line on the sidewalk.

"Do you think we'd be allowed to stand there? Since we don't have tickets?" I asked.

"I don't know. Should we ask?" Kara looked as indecisive as I felt.

"Well, we couldn't see the red carpet from where they're standing …," I said.

We opted to stand across the street.

"I think we'll be able to see better from here anyway," Kara assured me.

"Yeah, and this way we won't be in anyone's way," I agreed. It was very important to both of us that we not be in the way. We were distressingly aware of our lack of both tickets and knowledge of what was appropriate.

"So, we've got what? About an hour?" I said as I looked around for a distraction to pass the time. It didn't look as though anyone would be fighting us for our spots on the opposite side of the street.

Kara gave me a sideways glance. "You really think Jake will be here?" she asked. Truth be told, it had occurred to me earlier, while lying in agony over my sandwich, that logically, it just didn't make a lot of sense for Jake to show up to the premiere of his ex-girlfriend's movie, VIP list or not. After I admitted this to Kara, she nodded. "Yeah, I didn't want to burst your bubble, but I thought that too."

She thought maybe now was a good time to call Cantara. Maybe Cantara would know something about Jake's whereabouts, now that it had been decided that his whereabouts were not here. I weighed my promise to alert her to my arrival against the possibility that I would come off as stalkerish. A phone call seemed to leave too much room for error, so I opted for a text message, tapping out and deleting words for an embarrassingly long period of time until I came up with something inquisitive but not pushy. Appreciative but not overbearing.

Cantara texted back almost immediately. She welcomed me to New York, and that was about it.

"If she knows where Jake is, she's not telling me," I said.

We found some steps and sat down, spending several long minutes watching people mill about across the street. Kara directed my attention to a developing situation: a group standing across from the ticket line, adjacent to the red carpet.

"They don't look like they have tickets," she said hopefully.

"Yeah, but I'll bet they won't be able to stand there once famous people start showing up," I said. "I don't think you can just, like, *stand* right next to the red carpet at something like this if you don't have a ticket."

Kara conceded I was probably right.

And we still had some time to kill.

"I think we should check for a back entrance," I announced. I stood up. Kara followed suit.

As we crossed the street, we noticed a man in a uniform, radiating importance, frantically moving the barricades set up in front of the carpet. He shouted instructions at a few workers who were moving the carpet itself. We overheard him explain that "she" was going to show up soon, and "she" wanted to enter at a slightly different angle than the setup originally allowed for.

"I'll bet they're talking about Kiki!" I whispered, for Kara and I had rather suddenly taken to referring to Kirsten Dunst as "Kiki," as if she were our close personal friend.

"Maybe we should go back across the street!" Kara hissed back.

After a few seconds of paralyzing indecision in the middle of the road, we simultaneously came to the conclusion that we surely had time to scope out the back of the building before she showed up. So around the block we went. The men were still working when we arrived back where we started, so we walked around the block again. And then a third time. I'm not sure why we thought it was less suspicious to repeatedly circle the back entrance than to stand with the crowds by the front, but alas, that was our tactic. After the third loop, we headed back to our station across the street.

We had only been standing a few minutes when a black SUV pulled up, and out of the passenger side popped Kirsten Dunst in a black dress, clearly visible from where we stood. She was hidden from the crowds by the SUV, so no one standing on her side of the street realized she had arrived. We watched as she adjusted her dress and prepared to make her entrance.

"That's *her*!" I exclaimed.

"No, it's not!" Kara said.

"No, no, it's her!" I insisted.

"Are you *sure* that's her?"

Spring break our senior year of college, Kara and I had gone to London and spent a day at Windsor Castle. It was just the two of us and a couple of bobbies when Queen Elizabeth II drove up in her car (yes, she was behind the wheel) and then walked into St. George's Cathedral not ten feet from where we stood. We had the exact same conversation then. Except in my case it was capped at the end with a panicked "Can I take a picture?!" because I felt weirdly intrusive doing so with so few people about. A kindly bobby told me it was fine, and then Kara, dazed, asked, "So that *really* was her?"

It *really* was her this time too, and I wasn't about to make the picture-snapping mistake twice (my pictures of the queen didn't turn out so well unless you're well-acquainted with her backside). Kirsten was walking around the front of her car, and the noise of the crowd grew as she came into view. I noticed that no one was being shooed off the sidewalk by security on the other side of the street, and as Kirsten walked to the red carpet, she was no longer visible from where we stood. Grabbing Kara, I broke into a run and dragged her with me toward the red carpet.

"That's *definitely* her, and I want a better picture, dammit!"

Suddenly, there were people everywhere. The small crowd that had gathered prior to Kirsten's arrival had doubled in size. And the press … there were camera crews and paparazzi and reporters everywhere. In the time we'd spent making our lazy laps around the building, everyone else had been positioning themselves for the main event.

We squeezed our way through the crowd to get as close as we could to the red carpet, coming up just short of the rope line as Kiki started giving interviews, though we were too far away to hear what she was saying. I took as many pictures as I could through the heads in front of me. "A person up there got Kirsten's autograph!" a woman beside me said, clearly impressed, possibly hoping. Kiki never came back over to the spectators, though. She slowly made her way from one camera crew to the next.

More of the movie's stars arrived (some we knew, some we didn't), and each gave interviews and posed for photographers. Friends and family members of the cast wandered the short red carpet, but many seemed at a loss as to where to go and what to do. Even from my sphere of inexperience, I could tell that this was pretty low-key for a premiere. For the most part, the stars hovered near the news media and away from us gawkers. Kara and I took advantage of a break in arrivals to dart around the block one more time, just in case anyone important was sneaking in while all the excitement was up front. But no. We were back in time to watch as Kirsten paused one last time for photographers before entering the building. Her back was to us; we were standing directly across from the flashbulbs, and it was deafening and blinding all at once—everyone shouting her name, everyone snapping picture after picture after picture.

We made one final sweep.

And when we came back to where we started, all the stars had gone inside. The black SUVs were no longer on the street, we were tired, and as expected, there had been no sign of Jake.

Back at our hotel, I parked myself in the lobby on Kara's computer with the intention of checking out what exciting Jake Watch activity I had missed while I was busy staking out movie premieres. Instead, I became distracted looking at the pictures I'd taken and chose e-mailing Susie over reading the blog. Susie dutifully posted my celebrity photos on Jake Watch the next morning.[1] As it turned out, her previous post had been about her

---

1   http://jakegyllenhaalwatch.blogspot.com/2006/10/guess-who-went-to-premiere-of-that.html.

crush on another celebrity and had had nothing to do with Jake. That didn't go over too well.

Also not going over well were my pictures of Kirsten. The next morning, as Kara and I took turns quickly checking our e-mail before we headed out sightseeing, I finally made it over to Jake Watch. I skimmed through the comments, which included the likes of "Why is precious JW cyber space spent on KD?" and "An event without Jake in it isn't worth our attention in my book," and also some harsher ones that Susie later deleted.

I kept scrolling.

One reader had written a two-stanza poem for me in honor of my travels to New York, but further down the line was something even more startling: Jake had turned up in the Lone Star State with Lance Armstrong.

"He's in Texas!" I said.

"Texas?" asked Kara, looking up from whatever it was I was distracting her from. There was no question which "he" I was referring to.

"Texas. With Livestrong." No question who "Livestrong" was either.

"Why is he in Texas?"

"How did these people even *find out* he's in Texas?" I asked, not able to answer her question. "I have no idea how any of this works. I'm so out of the loop."[2]

"That takes some of the pressure off tomorrow then."

I looked up from the computer screen. She had a point. His geographical location did lower the probability that he would be attending the poetry reading. And with the fate of my professional career on the line, perhaps the fewer distractions, the better.

"True. This might actually be a good thing," I admitted.

That day, Saturday, was our day to be tourists. It was still early as we sat in the lobby. Susie had e-mailed me something about … something … but I was having difficulty concentrating because I was too busy being bewildered about Texas. And the concierge was staring at me.

"Maybe we should get a map," Kara said.

"Huh?" I asked.

"Of Manhattan. And then we can see which places we can walk to and which ones we'll need to take a cab to," she said.

Yes, a map. A map would have been helpful the day before, but now we had quite a long list of sights to see, so it was a necessity. Kara and I

---

2   I still don't know how people used to do it. Nowadays, a celebrity's every move can be tracked by following the sightings of him people report on Twitter.

were of the same mindset when it came to transportation while traveling, in that we didn't pay for it if at all possible. Over the course of that day, we would walk over seventy-two Manhattan blocks. It took my feet days to recover, but at least we didn't get lost. Or spend any money.

"Okay," I said, hoping she would ask the concierge herself so I wouldn't have to go over there. She stood up and looked at me expectantly. So I stood. We walked over together.

"Do you have a map of New York?" I asked him.

"You mean of Manhattan?" the concierge said.

"Um, yes. That's what I meant to say." I'm such an informed traveler.

"Right here," he said, pulling out a map. He showed us some places to eat, the fastest way to get to Central Park (not via the East River, crazily enough), and a few places on our sightseeing list, sending perplexed glances at me as he talked.

"Well, thanks," I said, trying to duck out before things got any weirder.

"Wait!" he said. And then he hesitated. And then he asked, "Haven't I seen you on TV before?"

It took me a moment to realize he was serious.

This would happen on other Jake Watch–related trips as well, me inexplicably being mistaken for some vague celebrity of unspecific origin. It's never happened during any other times in my life.

"I wish!" I told him, which was a lie, because I've never had any interest in being on television (except when I was nine and thought it would be cool to be on *Full House*, but that doesn't count).

"But no. I'm sorry," I finished.

Kara laughed. I laughed. The concierge didn't laugh, but he did look a little sad. He was smiling, though, when we waltzed (okay, hobbled) back through the doors of the hotel at the end of the day. So I guess he wasn't too disappointed.

Which Brings Us to Sunday

I woke up Sunday morning with a knot in my gut. Kara didn't help matters by referring to Stephen as my "future father-in-law" at every possible opportunity.

We walked around the city that morning and then ate an early lunch before heading back to the hotel so Kara could study and I could get ready

her to initiate a discussion, and again she let the opportunity slide. I was starting to get the sense that I had misinterpreted things and then, still trying to fit the cards in my purse, I heard Cantara announce to the group, "I'd love to meet Jake."

And I froze.

She was saying something about how she hadn't gone to the reading in Martha's Vineyard, the only one he'd attended, but my mind was racing. She hadn't met Jake. Holy fuck, *she hadn't met Jake.* Which meant my preconceived notion of her place in family affairs was all wrong …

"I don't know if he'll show up tonight or not. I'm sure *you'd* love it if he did," she ended, looking at me once again. My purse and the cards lay forgotten on the floor. Yet again, all eyes at the table turned to me.

"No, he's in Texas," I answered automatically. Jesus Christ, *she hadn't met Jake!* "With Lance Armstrong."

I snapped out of it when I realized what I'd said. Shit, these women were going to think I was unbalanced, following his every move like that. I clarified, "Well, at least that's what someone wrote on Jake Watch." Cantara nodded, and the flow of conversation picked up again. Some other topic.

"Are you intimidated by us?" the woman across from me asked after several minutes went by and I hadn't spoken. "If I were you, I'd be really intimidated."

I had hoped that the incident with me and the Bloody Mary at the bar would be the low point of the afternoon. Unfortunately, it wasn't. But rock bottom didn't come in the form of a stranger insinuating I should be scared of her, either. I answered her diplomatically ("I really appreciate the opportunity to be here; I'm just sort of taking it all in."), and then our food came. And *that's* when it really went downhill. Because by that point, some at our table were on their second Bloody Mary, and that appeared to be the signal that it was all right to start talking about the Gyllenhaals.

Some of the women had been to Stephen's first reading in New York, the one the Jake Watch reader had gone to. And as they started talking, both about that reading and the family as a whole, they started sharing things that I couldn't quite wrap my head around. Because I had read accounts of that reading. I had championed that family. And the people at the table with me … they were saying things that sounded foreign to my ears. They were talking about the Gyllenhaals like they were gossiping about their neighbors.

"They raided the refreshment table before the volunteers even got a chance to eat!"

gasp

"No!"

They were talking about their flaws. And their financial situation. And about Google-Earthing the family home. And zooming in on Naomi's car.

"You know, [poem x] isn't really about his mother; it's about Naomi*!"*

And Cantara didn't get along with Naomi (what?!). And Cantara thought she was in love with Stephen (no, seriously, *what*?!).

"I don't think any of them are really *that supportive of Stephen's poetry."*

And:

"You wouldn't believe the tension behind the scenes on that movie!*"*

And:

"Everyone in Hollywood has a story about what a piece of work she is!*"*

"Intimidated" was not the right word for what I was at that table. The word was "paralyzed." I didn't want to know *any of these things*. I had shown up to talk about design options and gimmicks to pull in higher traffic volume, and goddamn, that Tabasco sauce was out of control. How was anyone else drinking this stuff?!

I bowed out of the conversation for the duration of the meal, lost in trying to mentally decipher how I had read the situation so incorrectly coming into it. Maybe Cantara was just waiting until people left, and then we would talk about the website? Maybe? Maybe Stephen would want to talk to me about things? Maybe we'd meet up with him before the reading?

After what seemed like an eternity, Cantara paid for our meals, and the group began to dissipate. One of the other women at our table was also attending Stephen's reading that night (she had not been at the previous one), so she and Cantara offered to take me on a walking tour of the surrounding area to kill the hour or so left before we headed over to the poetry bar. We said good-bye to the others and then headed out ourselves.

As we ambled along, Cantara glanced at me and asked in a deceptively polite tone, "Do people dress fashionably in Memphis?"

Mortified, I self-consciously looked down at my striped pink sweater and then quickly surveyed the people in our vicinity. I was definitely overly colorful. "Well, we don't go around wearing all black, if that's what you mean." I looked over at Cantara and … sure enough. She was wearing all black. Before I even had time to open my mouth to apologize, she had moved on, ostensibly unaffected by my unintended insult.

A short while later, we walked by a store with a window dressed for Halloween, and Cantara broke the silence again. "Is Halloween big where you live?"

I turned to look at her. Was she fucking kidding me?

"Um, well, we celebrate it. Is that what you're asking? Adults go to parties, little kids go trick-or-treating ..." I trailed off.

"Yeah, that's the way it is here too," she said thoughtfully, as if I'd just described some surprising aspect of foreign culture to her. As if the state in which I lived was not part of the same country as the state in which she lived.

On we walked.

We wound our way around until we ended up at a park a few blocks behind the poetry bar. There were blockades up and notices stating that a Will Smith movie (*I Am Legend*) was going to be filming there after dark. I made a mental note to ask Kara if she wanted to scope it out after the reading. And speak of the devil, she called, just as Cantara finished explaining that sometimes they had to block off whole streets for movie crews.

"Yeah, I know. Movies have been filmed in Memphis before," I assured her slightly impatiently as I flipped open my phone.

"I'm so sorry! I just never got a chance to call you," I said in lieu of a hello.

"It's all right," Kara said. "So?"

"Um," I stalled.

"Are you still with them?"

"Yes," I said slowly.

Kara's excitement level went up a notch. "Is Stephen there?"

"Decidedly no."

"Huh. Was he at lunch?"

"Not so much."

"Interesting," she said. I could almost hear her thinking through the hints I was giving her.

"Are you headed over?" I asked, trying to keep the desperation out of my voice.

"Yeah. I'm headed out to catch a cab right now."

"Oh, thank God," I breathed.

I had no sooner hung up with Kara than my phone rang again. This time it was a Jake Watch reader who had driven in from North Carolina. I'd exchanged phone numbers with her earlier in the week, along with a promise to meet up with her at the reading. Cantara's husband arrived while I was still on the phone, meeting us as we strolled down the sidewalk. After I hung up, he and I headed over to the bar, while the other two walked off to run a quick errand.

A small crowd had already gathered outside the bar when we arrived. I recognized one of the middle-aged women in line, though she wasn't the Jake Watch reader I'd just been talking to. She was a Jake Watch reader who repeatedly wrote to Boo on MySpace. As her dog. I'd never posted a picture of myself on Jake Watch, and even if I had, I'd never claimed responsibility for Boo's profile. She couldn't have possibly known who I was, but I still found myself watching her carefully for any sign of recognition. The other Jake Watch reader was nowhere to be found, so Cantara's husband and I made awkward small talk while we waited to go inside.

Eventually someone unlocked the door, and our group filtered down a set of stairs, leaving the sidewalk above us. We walked past a small bar and into a room that I can only describe as cave-like, as it was both dimly lit and underground. I stood for a moment to let my eyes adjust to the reduced light, the only source being tiny candles flickering on the few tables in the room. It looked like Stephen would be standing, reading to us as we sat across from him at the tables. Once we were all inside, there were about ten of us in the room, which brought us roughly a third of the way to capacity.

I sat down on a bench near the door to wait for Kara. There hadn't been a lot of intermingling between the groups outside, but after a short, pregnant silence in the dark, someone asked, "So where is everyone from?"

No one spoke, so I piped up, "I'm Becky and I'm from Memphis." I thought about the reader I was supposed to be meeting and wondered if I'd somehow missed her outside. I added, "Actually, I'm Prophecy Girl. From Jake Watch."

A chorus of "oooohs" followed my introduction, and everyone started talking at once.

"I *love* your blog," one woman gushed.

"You guys are so funny," someone added.

"Do you know who does the profile for Boo?" the woman I'd been watching outside asked.

"Um, yes," I answered, tackling the Boo question first. "That is done through Jake Watch, and I designed it." I carefully avoided admitting outright that I was behind any messages Boo may have sent her. But she saw right through me. "That's *you*?" she asked, dumbfounded.

"I had no idea who you were when we were standing out there," I heard from across the dark.

"Yeah, sorry, I wasn't really sure how to introduce myself. I honestly didn't know if you'd know who I was."

"You should have said something! I read your blog every day," another voice responded.

If there was any question as to whether the audience that night would be composed of a bunch of Jake fans, it was settled as soon as it became obvious every person in the room knew who I was. And there could not have been a bigger contrast between the reception I got in that darkened room and the one I'd gotten at brunch. For the first time all day, I started to relax.

A few minutes later, I saw Kara walk through the doorway. Squinting in the candlelight, she made a beeline for me and pulled me over to a table in a corner.

"Becky, there are people outside who know who you are! They were talking about you when I walked up!"

I looked at her in amazement. "Dude, everyone in this room knows who I am! It's so weird! Who was talking about me?"

"I don't know …" She paused and then pointed to the doorway. "That lady!"

I looked over, and standing in the doorway was the reader who had called me earlier. I waved.

"Becky?" she squealed.

I ran over to hug her and exchange formal introductions before again claiming my seat next to Kara.

"Have you met her before?" Kara asked.

"No. But we're friends on MySpace. She gets bonus points for knowing me by my real name 'cause most people here just know me as Prophecy Girl …"

Kara interrupted me to ask about brunch. We were alone at our table, so I plunged into a quick recap, which rapidly turned into a long recap, and then Cantara walked by, waving to me and whispering, "He'll be here soon!"

I hadn't seen her walk in, but I did notice moments later when the man of the hour, Stephen Gyllenhaal, walked unassumingly into the darkness.

Cantara was there in an instant to greet him. I half stood, expecting her to call me over to introduce myself, but she didn't. She bustled away to aid a man who had come in with a spotlight for the reading. I looked to Kara in a panic, wondering if my opportunity had passed.

"Should I just go up to him? I don't know how to do this!"

Kara looked as helpless as I felt, and several more minutes passed before I heard Cantara's voice calling from some blackened corner, "Becky! Have you met Stephen yet?"

When I replied to the negative, she enthusiastically told me to go talk to him. She then walked off in the opposite direction, and I realized that I wasn't going to have her help with this.

At least she'd told him repeatedly that I was coming tonight.

"Wish me luck!" I whispered to Kara.

By the time I had made my way over to him, Stephen was deep in discussion with someone else. I sat down on a bench nearby and waited my turn, shooting smiles at him at every opportunity. He gave me a very strange look in return. At the time I took it that he was nonverbally apologizing for not being able to get rid of the other person to talk to me. In hindsight, I'm fairly positive that look was meant to convey disapproval that I was so blatantly eavesdropping on his conversation.

Except I wasn't eavesdropping. I had completely tuned out their exchange (blah, blah, poetry, blah, blah), but then my ears perked up when Stephen said, "My daughter just had a baby, so she's not here, and my son is in [someplace that's not Texas]."

Not in Texas? Hmmm. I filed that away for later use and continued to people watch until the conversation ended.

The man Stephen had been talking to walked off. With one final perplexed look at me, Stephen did too. My mouth opened in protest, but no sound came out.

I went back to where Kara was sitting. "Well, that didn't go too well."

"You'll get to talk to him after the reading," she said.

Stephen Reads Some Poetry

The lights were in no condition to be dimmed, so instead, the start of the reading was preceded by the appearance of a spotlight. And then someone who was not Stephen got up to read poetry. In fact, it was the man whom I'd just been not-eavesdropping on.

Kara leaned over, "I didn't know there was going to be more than one poet."

"Me neither!" I whispered back, before noting, "I don't think I came into this very well-informed." A half hour later, Stephen stepped up to the plate. And he read some poems.

I suppose it was fairly typical, as far as poetry readings go, but from an observer's standpoint, two things of significance happened about halfway through:

1. Ally, creator of IHJ, came in and parked herself near the door; and
2. Naomi Foner, wife of Stephen and mother of Maggie and Jake, came in and parked herself at the bar outside the room we were sitting in.

Stephen noticed Naomi's arrival and cautiously called out to his wife. Her voice drifted in from the other room to confirm she was there.

"It makes me more nervous when she's at these things," he said, directing his attention back to us.

When the reading, which included renditions of Stephen's poems about both of his children and contained an anecdote about his recently born granddaughter, ended at last, he was swarmed by autograph-hungry fans. Seeing my opening in another arena, I left Kara at our table and bolted over to where Ally was standing.

Ally was a true celebrity in the online world of Jake. That day happened to be her sixteenth birthday, and she already had three long years of Jake-related hard labor behind her. She had gotten her picture taken with Jake at the New York premiere of *Jarhead* and had attended Stephen's first reading in New York. She was as well-known to fans as Jake himself.

By the time I had fought my way over to her, she was talking to another girl, whom I recognized as Danielle. Danielle was a Jake Watch reader and she, along with a co-blogger, ran The Sarsgaard Soiree, a blog devoted to Peter Sarsgaard. Both of them lived in New York City. With Danielle a freshman in college, it was one of the only times in my Jake Watch experience where, at twenty-four, I was the oldest person in the group.

I reached them right as Ally was saying, "I wasn't going to come, but then I found out that Jake was mad and …"

"Whoa, whoa, whoa," I said, disregarding the fact that these people had no idea who I was. "Jake is *mad*? About what? Oh, I'm Becky, by the way. A.k.a. Prophecy Girl."

Ally smiled. "It's great to meet you!" I then swapped introductions and hugs with her and Danielle.

"Okay, so seriously," I said. "Why is Jake mad?"

"You know, about the whole baby thing," Ally said, nodding at me, though I most certainly did not know. "I'm just here to apologize to Stephen personally because I feel so bad about what happened. I would *never* do anything to offend Jake, and it just makes me sick to think that we've upset him."

I turned to Danielle, still not comprehending.

"Yeah," she said, "I'm pretty much just here to apologize too."

"What are you talking about?" I asked. "What baby thing?"

There was a pause.

"You know, with Ramona's name?" Danielle said.

I gave her a blank look.

"You mean no one's talked to you about this?" Ally said.

"No," I said carefully. "What is *this*?"

"This" boiled down to the following, all of which was hastily explained to me in hushed tones as the three of us moved closer and closer to Stephen:

Stephen had shared the news of Ramona's birth with Cantara as one shares news with a close friend. As in, he never intended for her to pass Ramona's birthday or name on to anyone else, though this was obviously not clear to Cantara at the time. The rest of the Gyllenhaal family, upon learning that *US Weekly* had gotten hold of the information, became very upset, and then even more very upset when they found out that *US Weekly* had gotten it from Jake's fansites. (Which … did they? Because I think we're all still unclear on that matter …) And furthermore, Jake turned out to be the most angry out of any of them because, for whatever reason, he had taken strong personal offense to the fact that his niece, who was born to two celebrity parents, was of interest to a magazine that focused on celebrities.

What. The. Hell.

"I wasn't even going to come tonight, but I wanted to tell Stephen personally how sorry ..." Ally said.

"Jake's *mad*?!" I was pretty much shrieking by that point. "Because of Ramona's *name*?! *I* published Ramona's name! Me! *My* name is on that post! It went up first on Jake Watch, and the post says, 'It's a Girl!' blah, blah, blah, signed Prophecy Girl! That Just Jared dude reads our blog, so we're pretty sure he stole the story from us, and Susie heard directly from *US Weekly* that Just Jared is where they got the story.[3] So this all boils down to being *my fault*?!"

Ally and Danielle looked at me with vaguely concealed horror.

"And Jake's *mad*?!" I repeated for emphasis.

"You seriously didn't know about this?" Danielle asked at last.

"No!" I said. "Nobody tells me anything! This is the first anyone has said *anything* about *anyone* being mad that Ramona's name was on our sites. Or that there was any problem *at all* with us publishing it."

Ally and Danielle both continued to look horrified.

"I am so sorry," Ally said. "Someone should have told you. I guess Jake wanted us to ask for permission before we posted the name."

"Ask for *permission*?!" I really was shrieking now. "I *did* ask for permission! I have the e-mails ... where I asked Cantara ..." I was sputtering. "I ... I *always* ask for permission."

"Well, I didn't," Ally said.

"Yeah, I just posted the information after I saw it on your sites," Danielle said. "I didn't ask anybody ..."

"If you asked for permission, then you don't have anything to apologize for," Ally said. "I didn't ask. I just posted what Cantara said in her e-mail. But I just feel so bad that Jake was hurt by the whole thing, so I need to say *something*."

This was wrong. Wrong, wrong, wrong. I felt queasy. My outrage was gone, and dread was creeping in.

"I'm not going to apologize," I finished weakly, trying to think through this. I had to think, because I didn't understand what was happening. But there wasn't any time. Because we were up.

Stephen stood complacently before us, looking neutral, if not possibly a little tired. But he knew who I was, right? Surely once I introduced myself, this would all blow over. Cantara had told him on multiple occasions that I was coming. All the way from Memphis. And that I'd been writing for

3   Jared later apologized personally in an e-mail and again insisted he hadn't stolen the story from us. No hard feelings, Jared!

the Stephen Gyllenhaal film blog. And that I had done some design work for his official website. Which I would soon be running. And that I had submitted one of the questions that he had so painstakingly carried around in his pocket for weeks. I was Becky. From Jake Watch. And I was here on business. I would *never* knowingly compromise his family's privacy. Surely he must know ...

"I'm Ally, from I Heart Jake," Ally was saying. "We met before. I came to your first reading."

"Oh, right, right," Stephen said, not showing any sign of recognition.

I put on my brightest smile.

"I'm *Becky*, from *Jake Watch*." I watched his face. Absolutely nothing. In fact, he had already turned to Danielle.

"And I'm Danielle from The Sarsgaard Soiree."

"Ah," he noted wryly. "Another one."

It was about that point when all vestiges of hope disappeared and my mouth dropped to a half-open position before it effectively stopped working.

"We just wanted to apologize ..." I heard Ally say.

"Look, girls," he interrupted, "it's all about learning."

I was immobile, only taking in every other sentence or so. It was a completely one-sided conversation. He talked about "responsibility" and the media, and when he got to "asking for permission," Ally jumped in. I looked over at her dumbly and nodded my head in encouragement as she protested, "Cantara gave us the information, and we thought it was okay ..."

"This isn't about pointing fingers," Stephen said, cutting her off. And then my stupefied face was directed away from Ally and back to Stephen. He was still talking about "responsibility" and "learning" and ... the paparazzi?

"Maggie and Peter *haven't even been able to leave their house* since the baby was born," he stated flatly. "You have no idea how hard it is on my kids. Jake can't do *anything!* You just need to be more careful."

I looked over at Ally and Danielle. Was I hearing this right? Us? *Me?* On the same level as the paparazzi? But ... but ... but I didn't even take a picture of the Queen of England without asking a policeman first! I ... I had nothing to say. Of all of the thousands of scenarios I had envisioned in preparation for this weekend, not one of them, *not one*, involved me being lectured for being on par with the paparazzi.

No words came. Nothing to defend myself, nothing to defend the two teenagers standing next to me … nothing. Just open-mouthed staring. Everything crashed down around me. He didn't know who I was. And if he didn't know who I was, he didn't know about the film blog. Or the website. And maybe he'd acted like he didn't know about Jake Watch when he answered our questions because he *didn't know about Jake Watch.*

All of those e-mails to Stephen that Cantara had forwarded on to Susie and me … about our rules for respecting Jake's private life … about our relentless promotion of his book … How could he not know? Or had he not read them? Or had she even sent them? I had no idea anymore what was real and what wasn't.

I didn't understand what he was saying. It didn't make sense on the surface, because I stubbornly couldn't grasp that he didn't know me. And it didn't make sense on a deeper level, because he was assigning way too much importance to the three of us, not understanding that we had no influence or power beyond our small niche audiences. I understood that he was concerned about his kids' problems with the paparazzi, but we weren't the right people to talk to. We were fans. We didn't make any money. We didn't pay for any of the pictures we posted. We were nothing more than volunteers peddling free publicity. The closest Jake Watch had come to participating in the business side of the entertainment industry was that very thing he was lecturing us for: *US Weekly.* Who got nothing from us. Whose time Susie wasted spectacularly through repeated e-mails. The fans, the only people who didn't have a way to profit from the story of Ramona's birth, had gotten it before anyone else and then done nothing to help the press circulate it. I thought it was a victory. And not just that, but specifically a victory against everything he was railing about.

I was so blindsided and devastated all at once that I couldn't process it all. And he was still talking. And then he was dismissing us, and the other girls were leaving, and he was turning away, and I had to *do* something … oh God, I still had the cards. I had to give him those …

I fumbled around, finally digging them out of my purse and presenting Stephen with his birthday card, my mouth clumsily saying something about it being "from all our readers at Jake Watch" (still no sign of recognition). And then I muttered some explanation as I handed over our congratulatory card for Maggie and Peter (I was sensing some impatience now). And whereas before I was unable to speak, I was now producing words, except I wasn't saying the things I should have been saying but was instead robotically asking, "Could you sign my book?"

Stephen took it from my outstretched hand. "What's your name again?" he asked.

"*Becky*," I said, again placing special emphasis on the word in hopes that he still might make some connection. Nothing. He scribbled something across the title page before turning again to leave. "Oh, can I have a picture too?" I asked, really pressing my luck now. Why was I still talking? I felt like I was going to be sick. "Sure," he said, and Kara, who had appeared behind me at some point, grabbed my camera and snapped our photo.

Once he finally managed to release himself from my clutches, Kara grabbed me and asked if I got my book signed.

"What did he write?" she asked anxiously. She'd been in the line ahead of me and had hers signed minutes earlier. I didn't think she'd been able to hear what Stephen said to us, but she was scowling and casting suspicious looks in Stephen's direction, obviously having picked up that something was wrong.

"He just gave us a lecture," I said, my voice a little teary, before opening my book and reading, "Becky, It's all about learning. Stephen." I looked at Kara. "'It's all about *learning*?' What did he write in yours?"

She opened her book. "To Kara, May poetry teach us all."

I paused for dramatic effect. "It's all about *learning*? I am going to fucking *cry*, Kara. Jake is *mad* or some shit, and it's all my fault, and *nobody tells me anything*! And it's all ..."

"Why is Jake mad?" Kara interjected.

"Because of the stupid baby name thing, which I had no idea there was any problem with, and Stephen thought I was here to apologize, and *it's all about learning*?! Cantara mailed Susie a hand-signed copy of this book to fucking England and it said, 'To my britpopbaby, thanks for everything you've done, love Stephen' or some shit. And I thought I was here to ...," I stopped.

Kara looked at me sympathetically. "Do you want to go back to the hotel? I still need to hear the rest about brunch," she said.

"Yeah," I said. "I guess we're not going to talk about the website. He didn't know who I was. I feel like a complete moron. I can't even believe what a fucking idiot I am."

"Should you tell Cantara you're leaving?" she asked.

"Yeah," I said, taking a deep breath. "And I need to thank her for brunch."

Trying to salvage what was left of my dignity, I worked my way through the crowd over to where Cantara and Stephen were sitting and talking. Cantara looked up and asked if I was leaving. Stephen looked highly annoyed that I had interrupted their chat.

I told her we were headed out because we had a long day the next day; we were going to a taping of *The Daily Show*. She asked that I e-mail her when I got home, and then Stephen interrupted, "Look, I really don't have a lot of time here." She turned back to him and, not having accomplished all I had gone over to do, I leaned in and said, "I just want to thank you for everything." Engrossed in whatever they were talking about, neither even looked at me.

Kara and I made our way outside, where we found Ally and Danielle on the sidewalk, still discussing the night's events. Neither was happy. Ally apologized to me again. "I feel so sorry for you, Becky. I can't believe you didn't know what was going on."

"I don't know what just happened," I said, fighting tears. "But it's not your fault. I'll be okay. Oh, but you'll never guess." My tone hardened. "He signed my book 'It's all about *learning*!'"

It was at that moment that I turned around and saw—not ten feet away and clearly within earshot—Naomi.

Oops.

… It Spoils the Illusion.

Stephen Gyllenhaal is a muppet. He can blame us for whatever he wants to blame us for but to go around lecturing other people over issues they are well aware about like he's the grand master of the internet and then not even let them speak out for themselves is class A muppet behaviour.
And that is me being painfully polite.
—comment left on Jake Watch,
October 18, 2006

So the Poetry Reading Didn't Really Turn Out the Way I Thought It Might

Kara and I hopped in a cab. I mentioned the Will Smith movie that was filming in the neighborhood, but neither of us found that prospect appealing just then.

"Seventy-five percent of the family hates me," I moaned on the ride back to the hotel.

"They don't hate you!" Kara protested. A noble friend, she did not point out that it's difficult to hate someone whose existence you are unaware of. She instead indulged me in a several-hour rehashing of everything that had happened that day and didn't say a word when I hogged her computer for an hour to write Susie a novel-length recap. Susie responded the next morning, "Er … crap. I think the bottom just fell out of my internet world."

Needless to say, there were no more "future father-in-law" jokes that weekend.

The only thing that kept me from falling hopelessly into despair was the fact that Jake was still scheduled to receive his Americans for the Arts Award. And after sort-of-but-not-really eavesdropping on Stephen, I knew that he was not in Texas but fairly close to New York. If he picked up his award in person, there was a chance—a slim chance, but a chance—that

I could speak to him. Apologize even. Explain that no harm was meant. Let him know that I would never have published Ramona's name if I'd thought there would be a problem.

For a brief time after we arrived back at the hotel from the reading, I considered quitting Jake Watch. I had donated time, energy, vacation days … and what had I gotten in return? No one had talked to me about any of the internet projects; Cantara had treated me like I was too unworldly to know what Halloween was; and Stephen, either completely clueless or willfully ignorant of the fact that my website had played a large and very direct role in the number of copies of *Claptrap* he'd sold, had given me a (misdirected) lecture about the paparazzi.

All in all, it was not the best time I'd ever had in New York.

When Susie had offered to let me take over the blog for two weeks while she was in Italy, I had told my parents, "You never know where this could take me!" I thought Jake Watch could be a platform to bigger and better things. I thought all of this was *going* somewhere.

But there I was, three months into my Jake Watch career, no further than a crappy hotel room in New York City with a bruised ego and a desperate wish to apologize to someone I'd never met for something that wasn't my fault.

I didn't quit. (Obviously; it'd be a much shorter book.) But I didn't sleep either. By morning, I'd decided I was being stupid.

I didn't do Jake Watch for Stephen or Cantara. I didn't do it for Jake. I did it for those people sitting at the poetry reading with me, who told me they loved what I did. I did it for the thousands more who were sitting in their homes, all over the world, waiting to hear what I had to say about my weekend.

But mostly, I did it for me. I did it because I had fun doing it.

And I realized that I couldn't act like this was a substitute for college. No one was waiting for me at the other end with a gold star and an A+ for all my hard work. I couldn't pitch a fit and storm off because I'd done a bunch of stuff and no one noticed. I'd made a choice to put the effort in, it hadn't paid off, and now I could make the choice to stick with it or to expend my energy doing something else.

Removing all other variables, and thinking of it in those simplest possible terms, I decided the rest shouldn't matter. I shouldn't act like I wasn't in control of my own actions. And I certainly shouldn't forfeit all future experiences with the blog just because Jake's dad didn't give me the welcome I'd been hoping for. It wasn't like he was going to care if I quit. The only person who lost if I walked away was me.

I liked writing for Jake Watch. Therefore, I should keep doing it.

But it didn't escape my notice that I had a daunting task ahead of me in explaining the weekend to our readers. How the hell was I going to do that? My disappointment didn't belong to just me; it belonged to all of us.

All the more reason to snag a good Jake story for everyone, I reckoned. If only I knew where his awards ceremony thingy was going to be held. I honestly hadn't been paying that much attention when I'd read about it.

When the sun came up, I got on Kara's computer and spent about two minutes trying to find the answer myself, but it was hard and I didn't know where to look. And wasn't this why I had readers? I posted a comment on Jake Watch asking if someone could look it up for me. Sure enough, eighteen minutes later, I had my reply: "PG, Americans for the Arts National Arts Awards happens at Cipriani 42 St. on Oct. 16." October 16 being today. I pulled out our city map. We didn't know when the ceremony started, and we'd have to take a cab, but if we left *The Daily Show* and went directly to the awards ceremony, we just might be able to catch Jake … Well, we'd give it a try.

A month earlier, I had requested two tickets for *The Daily Show*. But because seating was not guaranteed, even for ticket holders, Kara and I got there early to secure a place in line. We stood outside the studio in the crisp New York chill for two and a half hours that day, during which time we took turns walking around the area to warm up and stretch our legs. At one point Kara came back with a couple of newspapers. She handed one of them to me, and we wordlessly started paging through them.

"Uh oh," she said, a few minutes into our reading. For there, on page 13 of the *New York Post*, was a paparazzi picture of Stephen and Maggie out for a stroll. By sheer coincidence, on the same page was Kirsten Dunst and the unrelated headline, "Just plane [*sic*] hypocrisy."

"Pictured here for the first time since giving birth to her first child, Maggie Gyllenhaal takes a walk through the Village with a friend," Kara read to me. I'd repeated Stephen's words to her enough times in the preceding twelve hours that I knew she knew what I was thinking. But I disbelievingly said it out loud anyway, "He said Maggie hadn't left her house."

"Well, she left yesterday, and he was with her," Kara said.

We let that sink in for a moment.

"Maybe he didn't mean she *literally* hadn't left her house," Kara said.

"Well then he shouldn't have said, 'Maggie and Peter *haven't been able to leave their house.*' I remember his words very specifically, and they don't leave a lot of room for interpretation," I retorted.

"Well, maybe yesterday was the first day she had," she said.

"So again, if she'd left the house, why did he say that she couldn't? Dammit! It seemed so plausible! I was envisioning their house surrounded on all sides by paparazzi. They don't even look annoyed in that picture." I paused. "Does it really say Maggie *'and friend'*?"

Kara snickered. "Yeah."

"Ha! That's hilarious," I said laughing.

Recognizing Jake

When *The Daily Show* ended, we hightailed it over to Cipriani Forty-Second Street.

The paparazzi were still hanging out when we got there, so we hadn't missed the arrivals by much. There were also a few civilians loitering on the sidewalk. Scarcely daring to hope, I walked over to a guy flipping through the pictures on his digital camera and asked him who was inside. He excitedly told me that Robert Downey Jr. had just gone in, and he'd gotten a shot of him. He rattled off a few other names, including Lance Armstrong, before I, tired of waiting, blurted out, "What about Jake Gyllenhaal?"

And then the words that sealed my fate for the evening were uttered with complete disinterest. "Oh, yeah. He's in there too."

"Are you sure?!" I asked.

Kara showed her first sign of fatigue, shooting a withering look in my direction. She, like I, had been hoping we'd catch Jake as he went into the building. But now that we'd missed that opportunity, we were looking at a potentially long wait. More standing in the cold. And we hadn't eaten in hours.

But the guy with the camera not only assured us that Jake was inside, but that he had taken a picture with a couple of girls on his way into the building.[1]

"Oh, sweet Jesus," I breathed. I turned to Kara, frantically searching my mind for some compelling reason for wanting to stay. How could I

---

1   One of the girls posted her account of meeting Jake online. It was, predictably, found quickly by Jake fans and brought to my attention after I arrived back home (http://greedybitch.livejournal.com/16575.html).

explain that it didn't matter what the wait was? This was my chance! It might be my only chance! I should have said something about my quest for redemption or my need to uphold the dignity of Jake Watch. But I was stuck on the two girls getting their picture with him.

So I went with MySpace.

"I gotta get my picture taken with him!" I cried out. Kara looked at me as if I'd lost my mind.

"For my MySpace profile!" I elaborated. "It'll be an awesome profile picture!"

"Becky," Kara said patiently, "We're not really going to stay, are we? We don't even know how long he'll be in there."

"Kara!" I whined, my mind still whirring. "This may be my only chance ever to say something to him about Jake Watch. Ally met him, and he said he'd heard of I Heart Jake! I'm sure he's heard of us too. I can't leave *now!*"

Kara was not convinced.

"You can take a cab back to the hotel," I said. "I don't mind at all if you leave me here, but I have to at least try." I actually did mind, but I owed it to Kara to act like I didn't. I searched her face as she hesitated.

"Well, can we at least eat?" she asked.

Food did seem like a good idea. And even the paparazzi were starting to wander off. In fact, by the time I conceded that it would be okay for us to leave long enough to run down the street to McDonald's, we were the only two people on the sidewalk, aside from a girl around our age who wandered over to introduce herself.

"Who are you guys waiting for?" she asked.

"Jake Gyllenhaal," I said without hesitation.

"Oh, me too!" she swooned. "He's so *gorgeous*! I *love* him. He took a picture with two girls earlier when he was going in, and I'm so jealous. I'll stay out here all night if I have to."

Ah. A kindred spirit. She shall hereafter be known as "Sex and the City Girl" for reasons that will become evident a few paragraphs from now. She hadn't been able to garner access to Jake when he arrived because the paparazzi were being a bit too pushy. She had a copy of the director's cut of *Donnie Darko* and a Sharpie with her. What she didn't have (and I did) was a camera. We exchanged e-mail addresses and MySpace information so that I could e-mail her the pictures of ourselves with Jake that we were going to be taking. I explained to her that I was THE Prophecy Girl from

THE Jake Watch. But she hadn't heard of Jake Watch so that didn't get the wowed response I'd been aiming for.

"I'm registered at I Heart Jake," she said.

"You need to check out Jake Watch!" I said. "We're huge now! I met his dad last night."

"Oh, really? His dad went in with him. And his mom."

"*What!?*"

"Becky!" Kara yelled, all patience gone.

"Right." I turned to our new friend. "We're going to get food. We'll be back!"

I turned after a minute and shouted back to her, "You don't think we'll miss him?"

"No!" she said. "And if you do, I'll make him wait for you!"

Sex and the City Girl and I laughed. Kara rolled her eyes.

I was practically skipping by the time we spotted the golden arches. *This* was what I had wanted this vacation to be. Sitting in the studio audience of *The Daily Show*, seeing my favorite movie star in the flesh … Everything was going to be okay. I'd see Jake, I'd explain, I'd get a picture, and we'd be back at the hotel in time to see the show we'd just watched being filmed. Yesterday didn't matter. Stephen and Cantara were peripheral. *This* was what it was all about.

I don't know if it was the bounce in my step or her Chicken McNuggets, but Kara got her second wind and agreed to hang around.

"Great! I can already tell this is going to be *so* much better than last night," I said.

"Yeah, I can't believe his parents are here," she said grinning.

"God, I'm so screwed," I said. "Maybe they've forgotten me since last night."

She sobered at that. "Actually, based on the way Stephen was looking at you last night, I really doubt he remembers you."

Back outside Cipriani, Kara, Sex and the City Girl, and I stationed ourselves on the sidewalk. It was implicitly understood that the steps between the sidewalk and the front door were strictly off-limits, although we soon found friends in the two doormen blocking our way. Both were similarly unimpressed that I was THE Prophecy Girl from THE Jake Watch, but they were incredibly impressed at the dedication we were showing by committing ourselves to standing in the cold for an undetermined amount of time to catch a glimpse of some actor. One guard was an aspiring actor himself and so, as it turned out, was Sex and the City Girl. They shared the experience of being extras on *Sex and the City*. Being an extra on *Sex and the City* seemed very exotic to me, and it occurred to me that Jake might be more interested in talking to a *Sex and the City* extra than the girl who blabbed his newborn niece's name to the internet two hours after she was born. I frowned as I listened to them swap stories of being on set. Kara looked on with detached fascination.

Apparently feeling sorry for us, or more likely hoping to score points with his *Sex and the City* comrade, the Actor Doorman (referred to hereafter as "Sex and the City Doorman;" the other doorman will just be "Other Doorman" as his role in this story is quite undeveloped[2]) proposed a deal.

"Go back to your hotel or wherever you're staying," he said, "put on a nice dress, fix up your hair, put on some earrings, and come back here. I'll be here, I'll open the door, and what happens from there is out of my hands."

Unbelievable. A doorman at a private function explicitly telling us he would aid in our endeavor to sneak inside the building. Yet it was a gesture rendered completely moot by the fact that I lacked a dress of a caliber that would make my appearance inside the building unsuspicious. (I didn't have anything like that at home, much less in my suitcase.) Sex and the City Girl probably could have pulled it off, but she lived in Brooklyn and was concerned that she would miss Jake if she went all the way back home and changed.

"I'll do it!" Sex and the City Doorman said again. "I'm telling you, just get dressed up, and I will open that door and ask no questions. It will be out of my hands!" He continued to tell us this throughout the night.

We knew when Jake received his award because the screen that was being used to broadcast the action to the back of the theater was visible from the sidewalk. The three of us excitedly huddled together across from the window to watch the soundless picture as Jake walked on stage and gave his acceptance speech. Sex and the City Doorman, continually amazed by the depth of our loyalty, pulled the ropes back and let me run to the window to take a picture of the screen.

Kara and Sex and the City Girl greeted me back on the sidewalk. They seemed impressed that I had actually run up to the window, although all I had gotten for my effort was an indecipherable image of my flash reflected across the glass. We were like three little orphans pressed together in the

---

2   Kind of like an extra. HA HA.

cold, bonding over the fact that we were social rejects, banished to the outside as long as we were dressed as we were, and desperately hoping for our moment of glory when the patrons inside left their shiny world and entered the cold New York night. But it was *fun*. We were having a good time, and there was genuine joy in our anticipation. Even Kara had gotten excited once she'd seen Jake's face on the screen. "He really *is* here!" she said, finally believing.

Two hours later, there was a little less good in the time we were having. After Jake got his award, we entered an interminable holding pattern. There was a moment of high alert when the SUV that Sex and the City Girl identified as Jake's ride pulled out from its parking spot in front of the building. We all tensed in anticipation while the SUV slowly crept forward along the curb. Then it abruptly swerved into oncoming traffic and, oddly enough, crashed into the car in front of it. Which happened to be a police car.

A man Sex and the City Doorman thought was Robert Downey Jr.'s bodyguard came rushing out of the building moments after the accident and made several frantic announcements into his sleeve. Not long after, a replacement SUV arrived, and we were back to waiting and pacing. At least the crash had given us something to talk about. Sex and the City Girl seemed intent on spending every moment speculating on what might happen once Jake left the building. Kara and I jumped on the opportunity for a subject change.

But as soon as the replacement vehicle arrived, we were back to Jake.

"I think I'm going to tell Jake it's my birthday," Sex and the City Girl said. Her theory was that if she did, he might be especially nice to us. "You never know," she said earnestly. "Wouldn't it be amazing if he invited us to go out with him?"

For what seemed like the hundredth time, I explained that my plan was to try to get a picture without either of Jake's parents seeing me, all the while silently keeping my fingers crossed for a chance for an apology. Kara chimed in at that point to voice her skepticism about our plans for photos.

"But those girls got a picture when he was going in!" I protested.

"I just don't want you to get your hopes up," she said. But I didn't feel like listening to such pessimism.

Sex and the City Girl also admitted that she'd staked out Jake's New York haunts several times before. She offered to meet up with me the next day so we could check out some of the restaurants she knew he frequented.

To her credit, despite the total of five hours of standing in the cold that I subjected her to that day, Kara never went back to the hotel. But I knew she was waning. Even I was waning. Just as I lost the final bit of feeling in my fingers and toes, and as Kara sank to the sidewalk in exhaustion, and as even Sex and the City Girl finally seemed to have run out of Jake-related topics to talk about, the doors opened.

"This is it!" I shouted. We all three jumped to our feet and turned to the doormen. Other Doorman was, well, doing his job, but Sex and the City Doorman was moving the rope line.

"I'm going to make sure he walks right by you!" he stage-whispered to us.

And sure enough, he roped off the steps so that everyone leaving the building was forced to walk right by us. Unfortunately, throngs of paparazzi had appeared out of thin air about the same time the doors opened, and suddenly our section of the sidewalk, which we had guarded so carefully throughout the night, was teeming with people. As the patrons began exiting the building, most ignored the crowd outside, but a few winked at the three of us among the photographers and said things like, "He's in there, girls!" or "I just saw him. He'll be out any minute!" No one had to ask who we were waiting for.

And then, almost too soon, Lance Armstrong walked out. He strolled down the steps, taking the path laid out for him, and stopped. Directly in front of me. I stared at his profile no more than a foot away and realized he was waiting for someone to open the door to his SUV. He then climbed in and was lost behind a tinted window.

I debated whether I should have said something to him, but the appearance of Lance most likely indicated the impending appearance of Jake, and I couldn't lose my focus. Despite the cold, I threw Kara my jacket. "I don't want to wear my jacket in the picture," I said.

"Uh, Becky, I'm not so sure ...," she started. But I wasn't listening. Because there was Jake at the top of the steps, talking to his mother. Sex and the City Girl was ready with her Sharpie and DVD. I was ready with my camera. Kara was standing back several feet behind us, watching Jake as raptly as we were.

I caught Sex and the City Doorman's eye, and he nodded. In an act of boldness that remained forever unmatched during my days at Jake Watch, he walked over to Jake, gently touched him on the back, and led him away from his mother and over to the steps. And Jake went with it. He looked down and made his way toward us.

All hell broke loose. With the paparazzi screaming and swarming, Sex and the City Girl made her move, quite literally jumping right in front of him, forcing him to stop. "It's my birthday!" I heard her shout above the noise of the photographers. He grabbed her DVD, signed it, looked up briefly to say, "Happy birthday," and then bolted to the car Lance had just climbed into.

In an act that defies both logic and physics, Jake managed to keep his back to me the *entire* time he was making his getaway. From the moment he left the steps to the moment he got in the car, no matter which way I was turned, he maneuvered himself so that the only view I had was of his back. I snapped a single picture of the back of his neck as he signed Sex and the City Girl's DVD and then screeched his name a couple of times as he charged to his SUV. But he didn't turn around. The door slammed shut in front of me, and all I could see was my own reflection in the tinted window.

I blinked at the image of myself a few times and then looked over at Kara, who stared back with a look of disbelief. I turned ninety degrees to see how Sex and the City Girl was holding up, and she was … my God, she was mouthing words of love at the car window. Clutching her signed DVD, she alternately kissed it and mouthed, "thank you" and "I love you" to the SUV with a sultry look on her face. Not to be outdone, I shot an incredulous look toward the window and mouthed a defiant, "But I didn't get anything!" though I honestly don't know if I meant an autograph, a picture, or if that was just a general statement about my weekend. The car started to pull away, and Sex and the City Girl followed along the sidewalk a ways, still licking her DVD cover.

"Uh, Becky," Kara said, motioning me over to her. "You might want to get over here."

"What? Why?" I asked, near tears.

"Jake's mom has been watching you the entire time, and she does *not* look happy. We're talking death glares. Just lay low, okay?"

"Fuck!" I yelled, not laying low. I stomped over to Sex and the City Doorman for some sympathy.

"You did it! You got your picture!" he congratulated me. "I saw you, you were right in there. I could see the light from your camera on his face!"

For one desperate moment I thought maybe I had imagined my version of events and my camera held the truth. Maybe I had actually been in front of Jake and gotten a picture that didn't suck. I whipped out my camera. No. My picture sucked.

Probably the best known picture ever taken of the back of Jake's head.

"All I saw was the back of his head," I sniffed.

"Hey," he whispered, "right there! Right there!" He pointed to our right, and about five feet away was Robert Downey Jr. talking to, of all people, Stephen.

"No, I can't go over there! That's Jake's dad, and I got a lecture from him yesterday!" I said.

"Who cares? Now is your chance! Go over there!" he urged me. "He's the one you wanted anyway, right?"

Sex and the City Doorman had spent a good part of the evening confusing Jake Gyllenhaal and Robert Downey Jr. I had initially found this to be mildly humorous, but now that the horror of reality was setting in, it wasn't funny anymore. I'd missed my opportunity. There were no other chances. I had *failed*. I could say something to Stephen, but what? And how? Interrupt another of his conversations?

Lost in thought, I halfheartedly snapped a few pictures of Robert until, abruptly realizing what I was doing, I was overwhelmed with guilt. Suddenly there weren't many people around, and yet here I was, creepily taking pictures of a private conversation. Like a paparazzo. Oh God! I really *was* as bad as Stephen thought I was!

The tears started welling up. I turned around to see Sex and the City Girl crying in earnest, but her tears were not of the same nature as mine.

"He looked in my eyes!" she gasped. "He has the most beautiful eyes! Oh, I will cherish this memory *always!*"

"Can I see your autograph?" I choked out. She had smeared Jake's signature before it had dried. Just his name. Nothing personal. He'd barely even looked at her.

I handed her DVD back to her and turned to where Kara was standing off to the side, looking appropriately freaked by the emotional display in front of her. Robert Downey Jr. then left, and Stephen looked over as he walked off, locking eyes with me for a second. Nothing. No sign of recognition. Naomi was already waiting for him down the sidewalk, and seconds later, they were around the corner and gone.

Sex and the City Girl dreamily drifted into the night, shouting back at me to let her know if I was up for stalking Jake the next day. I nodded, still a little stunned.

"Nice to meet you," I yelled eventually. "Check out Jake Watch!"

I turned to Kara. She handed me my coat.

"So, ready to go back to the hotel?" she asked. "We're really not that far. We can walk if you want."

And that's when I started crying.

I shrieked out his name several times, although I'm guessing my voice was lost in the midst of everyone else calling out to him. That's what I like to think anyway, seeing as I got nothing but a good look at his dandruff-free shoulders as he got into his car. The windows were so tinted that I couldn't tell if he was looking out the window or wisely facing forward and ignoring the hysteria. I say "wisely" because if he had been looking out the window, he would have seen me looking like my cat just died, Autograph Girl making out with her DVD cover, and poor Kara standing back a ways looking like she'd just learned something about me she'd rather not know ...

—"Prophecy Girl Gets Really Close to Jake and Then He Completely Ignores Her,"
Jake Watch, October 17, 2006

Babygate

I'm still waiting for PG's report. Damn, I remember when all this Jake stuff was fun. *pouts* The problem of course is fandom has a life of its own. I have friends because of this weird little hobby of lusting after Jake so I still want to talk to all the folks I've met and laugh over the silliness but this whole situation has been draining and unfun. I can get draining and unfun at work. I don't want to feel like my attention/ adoration is a burden.

—comment left on Jake Watch,
October 16, 2006

Now What?

I didn't stop crying for quite some time.

"I don't understand," Kara said, not unkindly, as we walked back to the hotel that night. "I thought you *wanted* to see him. And you did."

"I know. I did. I don't know," I said. Was it worse that I didn't react like Sex and the City Girl? Or better? Even if it had been my DVD Jake signed, I wouldn't have been as excited as she was. I hadn't apologized; I hadn't gotten any insight. I hadn't even gotten my stupid MySpace picture. I might as well have not even bothered. Did that make me weird for not being thrilled at the mere sight of him? Or would it be more weird if I was euphoric?

Whatever the "correct reaction" was, I was fairly certain I wasn't experiencing it. For all my calm rationalizing in the middle of the night, I had failed to anticipate the emotional impact of striking out with Cantara, Stephen, and Jake, all in less than thirty-six hours.

I didn't call Sex and the City Girl. In fact, we never talked again. I don't know if she visited Jake Watch, or if she ever ran into Jake as she casually made the rounds to his favorite New York restaurants.

"Are you sure you don't want to call her? I don't mind," Kara asked the next morning, our last in the city, as we packed up. But the guilt I felt over what I'd done to her vacation dominated all decision making for the rest of the day. Though she repeatedly assured me she hadn't minded the day in the cold, or my prolonged crying spell, or the way all our other plans had to be retrofitted around my agenda for the weekend, I still felt I owed her the opportunity to direct at least this, our final day.

"Honestly, what if we did run into him?" I hypothesized. "After staking out a bunch of restaurants? I'd feel weird." That was the other side of it. While in the midst of conversation, talking with another fan, it hadn't seemed all that bizarre that Sex and the City Girl knew where Jake liked to eat. But in the harsh light of day, I wasn't entirely comfortable with tracking him down while he was going about his daily life. Showing up to a public event, like the night before, was one thing, but …

"She was kind of, um, shall we say 'intense'?" Kara hazarded.

"I don't know. No more than most of the fans I talk to," I said. I noticed when Kara didn't answer me right away. I looked up from my suitcase; she was looking a bit worried.

"Becky, she wasn't like you," she said. "I'm not entirely sure that was healthy, the way she was acting."

I instinctively jumped to Sex and the City Girl's defense.

"What? She was *a lot* like me! I *understood* her. She's pretty much exactly like all the people on Jake Watch I talk to every day. I totally get where she was coming from."

But Kara wasn't buying it. "No, I'm sorry, you would never act like that," she said, and then she went back to packing.

To this day, I don't know if Kara really saw a difference in our behavior or if she just saw in me what she wanted to see. And likewise, I can't say if my defense of Sex and the City Girl was due to a genuine feeling of affinity or an unwillingness to admit that there was no affinity.

I do know, however, that a week later, I privately wrote of Sex and the City Girl's Jake encounter to several Jake Watch readers, telling them how "insignificant" the experience had appeared to me. "He looked up for a sec, told her what she wanted to hear, and she thought they'd made a connection of some sort!" I scoffed.

Every single person I wrote carefully avoided that portion of my story when e-mailing me back. The rest was fair game—the poetry reading, the *Marie Antoinette* premiere—but no one was willing to question Sex and the City Girl's reaction. (Susie might have, but she was too busy being angry at Stephen and Cantara on my behalf.) The unspoken defense was clear: Sex and the City Girl responded the way most Jake Watch readers would have.

Up until that point, I had thought everyone at Jake Watch was like me. And with everything else I'd lost that weekend, I wasn't ready to confront the notion, any notion, that I couldn't relate to other fans. Especially now, when I needed those fans to support me as I grappled with my downgraded sense of self-importance. Kara couldn't be faulted for being too emotionally stable to empathize with my meltdown.

But Jake Watch would understand.

And they did.

The night of the awards-ceremony near miss, I came back to the hotel and wrote a post about seeing (the back of) Jake, promising a full report on the poetry reading at my earliest opportunity. The stress of the weekend weighing on me, I lapsed out of character and wrote more as Becky than Prophecy Girl.

"I was pretty emotional last night when I posted and that won't be happening again," I apologized to Susie the next day. "I don't like to use that tone of writing on Jake Watch, but I was just so weirded out I couldn't help myself." (Months later, completely embarrassed by it, I rewrote the entry.[1])

My post only heightened the anticipation surrounding what I would say about the poetry reading. I didn't publish anything on that subject until the day after I arrived home, by which time rumors were flying.

Something had gone wrong; that much was common knowledge. Danielle and Ally had both published short and respectful (though detail-less) accounts of the evening on their respective websites. Despite their best efforts, though, they hadn't been able to stop the growing agitation across the fan community. "I got [a] 'weird' vibe from reading their posts …," a Jake Watch reader wrote, amid speculation of what had happened. Susie didn't say anything other than to comment, "Bear with us on PG's report because she's at the Jon Stewart show. Bit of a weird night."

Over the next couple of days, a vague sense of anger and anticipation sunk in. The post on The Sarsgaard Soiree, which was both an apology for

---

1   The replacement version is what is now online and what was quoted in the previous chapter:
     http://jakegyllenhaalwatch.blogspot.com/2006/10/prophecy-girl-gets-really-close-to.html.

publishing Ramona's name and a declaration of strict privacy guidelines for the future, received exactly one comment:

"I've never seen anything out of line on any of the websites including this one. I understand privacy, but when you become a recognized actor, you give some of that up. Congratulations on the new baby, and I hope the Gyllenhals [*sic*] can get over themselves."[2]

In March of 2007, months after the events described here, Patrick Enright wrote an article for MSNBC entitled "Jake Gyllenhaal Does Everything Right." As an example of Jake's flawlessness, Patrick pointed out that if you Googled the phrase "I hate Jake Gyllenhaal," you would only get three results.[3] In the atmosphere described in that MSNBC article, telling the Gyllenhaals to "get over themselves" was a fairly radical thing to say. And that comment was written before I offered my side of the story.

As the last of the eyewitnesses to come forward, whatever I said on the subject would dictate how the drama played out. If I followed Ally and Danielle, the whole thing would be buried with a few keystrokes. Discussion over.

But I didn't have to follow them. I could do whatever I wanted; I could make this whatever I wanted. That was the difference between the real world and the internet. In New York, I'd felt powerless. Online, I was in complete control. I didn't even have to defer to Susie on this one. My word would be law. And everyone waiting for me knew it.

It was a hero's welcome in my inbox when I got back to Memphis. E-mails poured in from all over the world ... from people I'd never spoken to, people who were full of praise, people who just wanted to say "hi," offer their support, send me a "hug," or simply introduce themselves because they'd been meaning to for a while but just hadn't gotten around to doing it until now (when I was suddenly so interesting!).

But there were also people warning me, telling me to watch what I wrote, suggesting I take one for the team. "The fact remains Cantara is our conduit to Mr. Gyllenhaal," one guy cautioned. "Venting the anger which is justified may only make a bad situation worse."

---

2 The Sarsgaard Soiree has since been deleted.

3 http://www.msnbc.msn.com/id/17300067/. You get more than three results now, though I always thought Mr. Enright's experiment more likely quantified Jake's fame level than (as he was suggesting) the success of any long-term career strategies.

Ally, over on IHJ, also e-mailed, explaining, "My post about the reading was VERY vague and modest because I did not want to make a big deal out of it. Yeah, I went home feeling like crap but I didn't want anyone else to."

Wading through the demands to tell the whole story and the pleas not to, I put off posting anything for twenty-four hours after I arrived home. Susie got impatient and offered to write my recap for me, but I turned her down and let everyone wait while I e-mailed Cantara, finally organized enough in my thoughts to know what I wanted to say to her. I was long-winded and included lots of details about my expectations for the weekend, my disappointment at Stephen's misunderstanding, and a declaration at the end that I felt she had wasted my time and, as such, I would no longer be offering her my services. (I thought that last one was a particularly well-placed blow). I even warned her about how I was going to address this publicly. "I'm an adult," I wrote (perhaps to reassure myself more so than her), "with a college education and a few years of life experience behind me ... I'm not so sycophantic that I'm going to roll over and pretend I didn't get my feelings hurt for the sake of appeasing a family that obviously has no consideration for the effort I'm putting in for them."

And then I waited nervously for her reply, compulsively checking my inbox, ready to defend my complaints and regain my footing.

Except that was all for naught because it was two months before she wrote me back. And by that time, we were deep into Chapter 8, and no one really cared.[4] But while we're still in Chapter 7, *everyone* really cared, and I couldn't put off writing my post any longer. Without word from Cantara (which I had generously hoped might soften the blow I was about to deliver), I dove in head first with what I perceived to be a damning indictment of poetry readings everywhere.

---

4   At which point Cantara suggested that the lecture had been given at Naomi's request. In 2009, however, Cantara backtracked and admitted that she had lied to us about the Gyllenhaals' interest in the internet in general (see final chapter). The complete story I still don't know, nor do I think I'll ever know, and I have since grown skeptical that Jake was ever even involved. While I patiently waited for her response, Cantara continued to correspond with Susie and even mailed gifts and books to her in England. When she did finally respond to my e-mail, Cantara sent her reply to both of us instead of just me.

To Hell with Poetry

Reading it now, my oddly stilted, written-in-the-third-person description of the night is stupidly ambiguous.[5] But compared to what had gone up on IHJ and The Sarsgaard Soiree, it was a wealth of specifics. I explained about the e-mail from Cantara sharing the news of Ramona's birth, my return e-mail asking for permission to publish, Just Jared's and *US Weekly's* involvement, and how blindsided I'd been by the discovery that there was a problem. I divulged that Susie and I had been working on an official site for Stephen (something we had hinted at but never written openly about) and that despite that, despite the film blog, despite the Q&A, Stephen *didn't know about us.*

"It is *painfully* clear to [Prophecy Girl] that no one has the *slightest clue* about this blog ..."

And on top of that, he wasn't even all that nice.

"[She was] forced into an apology she didn't realize she was making and then told a bunch of stuff that didn't apply to her and made her feel really small and insignificant ..."

And overall, the weekend was so horrible that Jake Watch almost lost one of its fearless leaders(!).

"The experience was so upsetting, she was ready to quit this blog."

The poetry reading incident sparked such widespread disillusionment that the entire controversy, from birth to reading, was later umbrellaed under the term "Babygate." In the following days, the scandal was elevated to legend status, and the general story (if not the accurate details) was known across all of Jakedom.[6]

"This is desperately upsetting ... you were so well meaning, then this," someone wrote.

"Famous people need to understand that without fans they are nothing," wrote someone else. Both comments came from individuals at a rival blog, who hated Jake Watch. *Hated* it.

That! From our enemies!

---

5   http://jakegyllenhaalwatch.blogspot.com/2006/10/pgs-official-poetry-report-recently.html.

6   And it still is. In June of 2009, my Babygate post was linked on both Gawker and Oh No They Didn't (ONTD) as part of a larger story about Cantara. A few ONTD commenters asked about it, and two different people, neither of whom I knew, came forward with amazingly detailed descriptions of what the controversy was all about.

Our regular readers' responses ranged from dispirited to furious. "I'm too mad for words right now," one wrote.

Some tried to organize a campaign to return their copies of *Claptrap* to Cantara. Others abruptly left the fan community, swearing off all Gyllenhaals in the process. Many simply pledged to stick around and read whatever Susie and I wanted to write about. "Find someone else to watch. [Jake's] not worth the effort." And, "I think this blog could make it just fine even without the Gyllenhaals, but it would collapse without the wonderful [writers]."

"Oh, how the mighty have fallen, eh Stephen?" one reader wrote. "We used to make slightly inappropriate comments about your toosh in relation to Jake's. And now you've just pissed us off." Frustration regarding his answers to our questions arose too: "From the answers in the interview, I didn't really like him then; him and his belittling attitude toward fans. Like we're dumb little things kissing his feet." And, "Yeah I felt that too. Glad I'm not alone there. I really had a nasty feeling about his words there … the kind of feeling that this incident portrays, actually. I felt unappreciated and quite insulted …"

"The wonderful, honest, down-to-earth, well-meaning Gyllenhaal-family-world has totally collapsed!!" one fan agonized.

"Could we just pretend it never happened?" another commenter begged.

But no. We couldn't pretend it never happened. There would never be a time when we could pretend it never happened. It was one of those things that, having happened, affected absolutely everything that came after it. We still have two-thirds of the life of the blog ahead of us, and yet it is this point that divides the story in two. There was before Babygate and after Babygate. It would be over a year before Jake Watch would shut down, but even then, as we were saying our good-byes, someone commented that "it wasn't really the same since you met Stephen …"

And that commenter was right. It wasn't the same. Gone were the days when any mention of the name Gyllenhaal was met with childlike wonder. Never again would our idealism reach its former heights. As soon as I was home, Jake Watch underwent a permanent course correction. Starting with Stephen. He was out. The film blog, the official site, anything having to do with him was chucked. "As for pimping his poetry any further—fuck it," Susie wrote me.

Secondly, this was Jake Watch, not Gyllenhaal Watch. Henceforth, we would cover Jake and only Jake. No parents, siblings, or in-laws need apply.

And lastly, our rules of privacy protection, which had been enacted primarily in an attempt to suck up, began their long and complicated journey toward a draconian end. Never forgetting Stephen's desperate claim that "Jake can't do *anything*!" I developed an obsession with protecting Jake's privacy. Regardless of any lingering hurt feelings, I was resolutely determined to never again be cornered and unable to defend my stance on celebrity privacy and the paparazzi.

These were not casual changes that came about over time; these were specific things that Susie and I discussed and agreed between us to implement. We'd never talked about the mechanics of the blog in such technical terms before, but we changed the way we communicated after Babygate. I came home angry and hurt, thinking that Susie had known what I was walking into in New York. But it was soon clear to me that she was just as taken aback as I was. We shared a common frustration; we both felt used. We stopped fighting for Cantara's attention after that, and our loyalty to each other solidified.

If you think about it, I'd been working toward Jake Watch my entire life.

It was part of the natural progression of my long and storied history as a fan, to one day lead others in a fan community. And there I was. Leading Jake Gyllenhaal fans.

My poetry reading post went down as our most commented-upon entry ever. Susie eventually decided to remove the option to leave comments in an effort to get people to move on. That post taught me a lot about the dynamics of a fan community, how its members can come together.

But it was the entry I wrote about Jake that shaped my understanding of the role leaders play. That one received a fair number of comments as well.

"Once you've processed this whole chaotic experience it is going to be a memory you will never forget!" one devoted reader wrote, convinced that the holiness of being so close to him would hit me eventually and cure all woes. The consensus was that Jake had been unable to hear my voice above the din of the photographers because *clearly* if he'd known who I was, he would have stopped and chatted and taken a picture. Even the photograph of the back of his head was a hit: "You know we are happy if we see whatever of him, his thumb, his shoulder, his shoe. But you gave us his NECK! Do I need to say more?"

And, "It's the goddamned most beautiful back of a head in the ENTIRE universe!!"

And my personal favorite: "The nape of Jake's neck is delightful—all artfully wet-combed & rather pale & vulnerable-looking."

Vulnerable-looking?

We shut down the comments on that entry too.

But it was there that regular reader "Girl Friday" offered up her words of wisdom, which I cheerfully pilfered and split into two chapter titles: "Never sit too close to the stage at an opera," she wrote sagely. "It spoils the illusion."

Someone else agreed, "Something dies in a moment like that ..."

During my tenure at Jake Watch, a negligibly small number of fans tried to meet Jake. But those who did fell neatly into two categories: the ones who thought every encounter was special and the ones who understood that none of them were.

The comments I got on the blog, some expressing sympathy, most expressing delight that I'd managed to get so close, stood in stark contrast to the e-mails. Because for all the Stephen chatter in my inbox, there was a fair amount being said about Jake too:

"People will make up excuses for Jake saying 'maybe he didn't hear you' etc," one e-mail read. "And hey maybe it's true but I know you can't help but feel 'blown off.'"

"I have been feeling that Jake isn't too happy with his fans (ie: not walking red carpets anymore, not showing up to charity events, being slightly rude and uninterested to one fan) ..." read another.

"Have any of us ever received a thank you from him or his PR?"

"I personally have lost much respect for Stephen *and* Jake ..."

"The Gyllenhaal family is far too proud and think just because they've got a bunch of vowels in their name that they're above everyone else ..."

And, regarding another fan's encounter:

"I feel like if I really posted what happened people will lose faith in Jake and think he doesn't like his fans. I do not want that to happen (although I'm not sure where he stands on that subject) ..."

Apparently people had encounters like mine all the time, swarming paparazzi or no. It was shocking. And then they lied about it later! Even more shocking!

But the clincher was that every one of the six quotes above came not from ordinary fans, or even from Jake Watch readers, but from *people who ran fansites.*

I'm in no way suggesting there was a vast conspiracy to cover up unpleasant run-ins with Jake, or even that there weren't rare genuinely moving and meaningful encounters with him. I'm saying it was implicitly understood that it was in all of our best interests that Jake Gyllenhaal be as loveable as possible. The nicer he was, the more likely it was that people would retain an interest in him, and thus keep coming to our websites. The image of Jake and his family as accommodating to fans, that I had so wholeheartedly bought into, wasn't just skewed; it had no basis in reality at all. It was the product of fans like Sex and the City Girl, who were overcome by the most fleeting of exchanges, combined with fans like me, who were usually too polite to admit disappointment. There was a lot of frustration from the people who ran Jake's websites, but an outsider never would have known. I hadn't known. Looking back, I was exceptionally lucky that public support was with me after I wrote what I did about Stephen. Had I been as harsh to Jake, the backlash against me would have likely sunk Jake Watch.

After reading those e-mails, I thought back to my naive wish to apologize to Jake in person, and I realized that would never have happened. Ever. If I had jumped in front of him, like Sex and the City Girl had, and said, "I'm sorry!" I would have gotten a smile ... a nod ... move on ...

Those girls who had gotten their picture taken with him before he entered Cipriani that night had gotten a smile ... a nod ... move on ...

Even Ally's story of meeting him at the *Jarhead* premiere ... there just wasn't that much to it. As I sifted through fan pictures and fan stories, there was no escaping the truth. People who ran into him on the street got as much interaction as the girl who ran his biggest fansite.

Yet there I'd been, thinking that my status in the online world somehow translated into social currency in the real one.

It was the biggest change to come from Babygate, and it wasn't announced or even overtly discussed. It just was. The change was in us, in Susie and me, because we now knew that we were nothing outside of Jake Watch. No one was going to thank us. No one was going to seek us out. No one was going to recognize us as anything more or less than two individuals lumped into the generic category of "fan." We weren't special. We weren't anything.

And knowing that, understanding that nothing we did was going to impress the people we were trying to impress, we stopped trying to impress them.

We didn't think smaller after New York, we thought bigger. More than ever, we pushed each other to come up with new and better ideas. We weren't professionals. We didn't have the credentials to procure jobs doing the types of things we did for the blog. We used Jake Watch as an excuse to experiment.

We had been weighed down before by the censoring influence of feeling "watched." But that was gone. No one was paying attention. Jake Watch was stripped down to its most basic elements: a supportive community and an atmosphere of creativity. We thrived in it. It allowed us to bridge the gap between wondering if we could do something and actually trying it. I don't think it's a coincidence that the two posts our readers would later rank as their all-time favorites, one from each of us, both came within three weeks of the poetry reading incident.[7]

Even as people were asking how we could possibly keep going after New York, we had a stauncher resolve than ever. We needed Jake Watch. It was the most productive creative outlet either of us had ever had. And now that the other projects were gone, now that we knew no one was going to sweep in and offer us something better, we threw ourselves into it like never before.

Not that Stephen was affected by any of this, of course. His poetry career slowly petered out after that, and considering the number of books we'd already sold for him, he undoubtedly never had any idea he'd lost support. But the outrage toward him bled from one Jake site to the next, and from then on there was a stigma attached to those few brave fans who attended his remaining readings.

Cantara fared even worse. Though we continued to have contact with her for years to come, her reputation in the fan world was irreparably damaged. Like anyone with ties to a celebrity, she never stopped attracting people who wanted to connect with her in hopes of getting access to the family. But her credibility had taken a hit, and her motives thereafter were always regarded with deep suspicion.

As for us, as necessary as it had been to explain what happened at the reading, Susie and I didn't waste any time moving on. By God, we still had a blog to run.

---

7   "Jake Watch Election Day Special" by Prophecy Girl (http://jakegyllenhaalwatch.blogspot.com/2006/11/jake-watch-election-day-special.html) and "The Mother of All Exclusives," by britpopbaby (http://jakegyllenhaalwatch.blogspot.com/2006/10/mother-of-all-exclusives.html).

Anger is a great unifier, but it has a short shelf life. When two days had passed and our readers switched from venting their anger to pleading, "Do what you do best, WATCH JAKE. Make us laugh again. PLEEEEESE," we did what they asked. We picked ourselves up and kept going.

But, as mentioned earlier, not everyone stayed with us. A year later, in October 2007, an anonymous commenter dropped by to write, "It amazes me that you all are still here writing about Jake after the whole poetry reading situation. It made me not as interested in Jake. I know it didn't have anything to do with Jake and that his dad was the mean one, but still, after all the effort you put into this blog it was a slap in the face. I'm just saying that whoever Brit or Prophecy are they seem to be talented writers. They put a funny spin on anything. I think their efforts would be better spent on someone who appreciates them."

Regular reader "Xenia" jumped in immediately to respond: "Anon, please don't be amazed…for what I know BPB and PG ARE spending their efforts for someone who appreciates them, WE appreciate them! :)"

Well, After All That, What the Hell Are We Going to Do for Jake's Birthday?

JAKE: Yeah, I've been in a lot of movies. I don't want to brag, but I was nominated for an Oscar. I won a BAFTA, too, which is pretty sweet because everyone was like, "Oh, George Clooney! You're so wonderful!" because he was nominated with me. But he came over to me afterward and was, like, "Dude, you are so much hotter than me, so much more talented than me, like, basically I just need to quit the movie industry if I'm gonna be up against you for awards and shit." And he hasn't done a movie since.
—from the script *The Day After Tomorrow Never Dies*

Who? Why? What the Hell?

AssociatedContent.com describes itself as "an open content network."[1] And no, I don't know what that means either. When they say they "[enable] anyone to participate in the new content economy by publishing content on any topic," it makes a little more sense. Or at least it makes sense that if you're in the business of publishing anything about anything, then you might wind up publishing an interview with the girl who started the internet's premiere Jake Gyllenhaal blog.

Toward the end of November, Susie was contacted by a person at Associated Content (let's go with "Associated Content Person") about that interview.[2] I don't know how or why she was chosen, and what Associated Content Person had in mind wasn't particularly groundbreaking, but I thought it sounded impressive that she'd been sought out by someone in

---

1   http://www.associatedcontent.com/company.html.
2   http://www.associatedcontent.com/article/85585/blog_spotlight_an_interview_with_britpopbaby.html.

the business of interviewing. And neither of us was going to complain about free publicity.

Unfortunately, Associated Content Person didn't put a lot of effort into her job.

"BritPopBaby [*sic*] is the owner of JakeGylenhaalWatch.com [*sic*], a blog dedicated to 'stalking' red hot actor Jake Gylenhaal [*sic*], as the owner likes to call it. In fact, her devotion even led to her meeting and interviewing the actor ...," the finished article started.

Clearly, Susie had neither met nor interviewed Jake (I totally would have worked that into the story by now if she had), but the misinterpretation remained, and Associated Content Person asked her to describe the experience: "So you got a chance to meet Jake Gyllenhaal! How was that? Was he everything you ever dreamed of?"

Susie answered in her typical tongue-in-cheek manner: "It was fantastic, he thanked me for all my hard work and said he was not the slightest bit freaked out by the whole thing, then he asked me on a date. Okay, not really. The closest we ever came was meeting Jake's dad in October, but that didn't quite turn out as planned!"

The follow-up question was, "That must have been a really awesome perk of running such a popular blog. How did the opportunity come about?"

Ah, Associated Content Person. Points for effort, but a serious failure on the follow-through.

"You guys obviously have a following," the interviewer blathered while asking what set Jake Watch apart from other fansites. That part was actually accurate. We did have a strong base of supporters. Which brought up an interesting question.

Who *were* all of these people?

No, seriously, who read Jake Watch? They were Jake fans, obviously, but where did they live? How old were they? Why did they keep coming back? If you'd asked me at the time, I would have guessed our typical reader was a non-American in her midtwenties. And I would have been very wrong.

In the early days, before I came on board, one of Susie's biggest undertakings was Jake Secret, a Gyllenhaal variant of the popular Post Secret art project.[3] She asked that people come up with secrets about their love of Jake, illustrate them via digital art, and e-mail her the results.[4] All

---

3   Post Secret is the brainchild of Frank Warren. By his own definition, "PostSecret is an ongoing community art project where people mail in their secrets anonymously on one side of a postcard." http://postsecret.blogspot.com.

4   http://jakegyllenhaalwatch.blogspot.com/2006/05/jake-secret-project.html.

told, she received over fifty entries, the contents of which spanned from sexual fantasies (actual card: "Fantasizing about sex with Jake makes sex with my husband tolerable") to confessions of motherly, er, affection ("I'm old enough to be his mother … and that excites me"), giving a good general idea of the spread of his fans.

But Jake Secret only revealed how people thought about Jake; it didn't tell us much of anything about who was doing the thinking. Not long after Susie's interview, the two of us were having one of our "who *are* these people?" discussions (as we were prone to doing), and the idea was hatched to simply ask our readers what their favorite Jake movie was. I agreed to put all the answers in a spreadsheet if Susie wrote the post.

I was left a bit speechless when I clicked over to the blog later that day to see what Susie had put up. From our minimal concept, she had generated a comprehensive thirteen-question survey that covered everything from age to geographical location to "favorite charity that Jake supports." And thus was launched the accidentally epic "2006 Official Jake Gyllenhaal Fan Survey as sponsored by Jake Watch."

Over the course of five days, we collected 166 responses from thirty different countries.[5] Some of what we found wasn't surprising, like that 63 percent of respondents listed *Brokeback Mountain* as their favorite movie. But age-wise, it turned out that Susie and I weren't exactly writing to our peers. The two of us were twenty-three and twenty-four, respectively, at the time of the survey. A full 56 percent of our respondents were thirty or older. Twenty-one percent were *fifty* or older. And six people (almost 4 percent) fell into the sixty-plus category. In contrast, only 13 percent were teenagers, and those of us in our twenties didn't even make up a full third.

So, that was interesting.

Also interesting was that Americans made up a healthy 45 percent of our readers. And that more non-Americans than Americans listed Rock the Vote (an American get-out-the-vote initiative) as their favorite charity of Jake's.

I could go on, but I don't think anyone cares. No one cared at the time, either, but they humored me as I posted meaningless statistics in list form,

---

5   http://jakegyllenhaalwatch.blogspot.com/2006/12/hey-jakes-pr-im-billing-you-by-hour.html. Due to the unscientific nature of this project, there were no margins of error and undoubtedly loads of sampling bias. But still interesting!

along with pie charts and graphs, and generally acted as if I'd just tallied up a mid-decade census.

"Let's make this an annual (semi-annual?) event. Now that all the non-responders have seen how cool it is, they'll surely want to participate and be represented!" one commenter wrote after the results were posted. Alas, the Official Jake Gyllenhaal Fan Survey was not to be a recurring event. Interesting though it was (to me), it was a lot of work. Once was enough.

And not knowing exactly what to do with the information, Susie and I moved on to the next thing.

And seeing as how it was December, the next thing happened to be an occasion which we were, by default, obligated to celebrate: Jake's birthday. Which was the nineteenth.

I'm Wincing Already in Anticipation of This Story

You know in the last chapter when I was waxing philosophical about moving on, and I wrote things like "we threw ourselves into [Jake Watch] like never before"?

Underneath the anger and disappointment from New York, there was embarrassment. I was embarrassed that I hadn't done better. Worse yet, it wasn't clear to me why I hadn't done better. In the end, I seemed to subconsciously decide that the reason I'd frozen in front of Stephen and the reason I'd let Cantara walk all over me and the reason it hadn't been me to stop Jake in his tracks instead of Sex and the City Girl was because I wasn't working hard enough. Even as I attempted to think of things outside of school terms, I couldn't help but compare the New York trip to failing a test.

And what do you do when you fail a test? You study harder for the next one.

Which brings us to Jake's birthday. Now Jake's birthday was something that had been on the minds of the Jake Watch community for a long while already. Obviously, a group of sock lovers such as ourselves would have high standards when it came to birthday gifts. So in order to trace the origins of the original plan, we'll have to go back. Back to before I was writing for the blog. If I had to pinpoint a specific date, I would put it at June 28, 2006, as that was the day that I formally put forth a motion on the message board to write a movie script.

Jake Watch went through quite a few creative transitions during its lifetime. The time period in which I concocted the movie idea was our James Bond phase. There were a lot of in-jokes about Jake Watch being a top-secret spy organization and Jake being helpless in the world without our guidance and protection. It was mostly the product of Susie's self-conscious efforts to subtly mock the concept of being a fan. In my mind, it also happened to be a *spectacular* framework for a screenplay.

It probably goes without saying that when I presented the idea of writing a script, I did so without any experience or knowledge of what was involved. Nor did I have any specific ideas for a plot. To make up for my many shortcomings, I decided this should be a collaborative project. Anyone who wanted to participate could.

My proposition was met with unguarded enthusiasm, and when ideas for a story line started coming in faster than I could keep up with them, I let my imagination run away with me. "Think we could pull this off by December?" I asked my fellow readers. "And give Jake the craziest birthday present he's ever received?"

The overwhelming response was *yes*. It was a *great* idea to write an entire movie script *about Jake* and then send it to him for his birthday. That wouldn't be weird *at all*.

Okay, so what did we need? We needed a movie poster. We needed a soundtrack. We definitely needed writers. Lots of them. Everyone who worked on the project wanted a part in the script, so we also needed lots of characters and lots of plot intricacies to absorb the number of people involved …

Six weeks passed. Susie took that trip to Italy, I started writing for the blog, and the time I had to devote to the script was drastically reduced. After Susie came back, I sifted through all of the plot suggestions and came up with a basic outline. I then asked for volunteers to fill in the missing pieces. One by one people came forward, and with a deadline of September 1 for scene contributions, it seemed as if we might actually be able to pull this off by our December deadline. In August, regular reader "joycedavenport" gave us the final piece of the puzzle when she suggested the title *The Day After Tomorrow Never Dies* (which I am going to italicize as if it were the title of a real film). It was all coming together quite beautifully.

Next thing I knew it was October … and I was in New York … and reality set in that it was probably an absolutely *terrible* idea to write Jake a movie script and give it to him for his birthday. God. What had I been *thinking?* Just to make sure I wasn't overreacting, though, I pulled together all of the scene submissions and read through them to see if perhaps there was something salvageable to the idea.

I described to Susie the process of reading them: "First there was hysteria and then there was aching pain ..."

Scene 17–INT. COFFEE SHOP - MORNING
HENCHMAN 2: Fucking Gyllenwhores! What have you done to him? He needs his penis back. His ex-wife is multiorgasmic!
HENCHMAN 1 tries to mitigate his genital pain getting some ice cubes from a big mug on the counter table and crying mumbles:
-My ex won't come back with me after this castration
JAKE WATCH AGENT 1: For Pete's sake, it's only been a kick in your balls. You'll survive. (The four girls burst into laughter and the rest of the coffee clientele too)
HENCHMAN 1: At least my ex is not a "Gyllenwhore" like you.
HENCHMAN 2: (nods) Yeah!
JAKE WATCH AGENT 2: I'm a proud Gyllenheart, you bastard!
HENCHMAN 2 retaliates grabbing JAKE WATCH AGENT 3 by the hair. JAKE WATCH AGENT 3 screams and falls to the ground (zoom of her legs).

No, no. I had been right to think that that should never come anywhere near Jake. And you probably read that thinking it didn't make a lot of sense because you don't know the story we were telling. But I can assure you that even if you did know the story we were telling, that still wouldn't make a lot of sense. I could just imagine Jake getting that scene in the mail. For his birthday. With my return address (since undoubtedly I'd be the one to mail it). He'd likely have me arrested.

And while I sincerely appreciated the participation of each and every person who contributed, English was not the first language of five of our eleven writers. Even for those who did speak English natively, writing wasn't necessarily their forte. Not all of the scenes were as off-the-wall as the one quoted above, but even among the ones that were viable, most of the writers had made up new characters or plot developments or sometimes even entire scenes that had nothing to do with our story. Prior to *The Day After*

Tomorrow Never Dies, I hadn't come up with any truly bad ideas for Jake Watch. But I had really outdone myself with the terribleness of this one.

Unfortunately, somewhere between my suggesting the idea and surveying its current state of disarray, a sizable portion of the community had gotten involved. People kept bringing it up, asking when they would get to read the script and what else they could do to help move the project along. It wasn't just the writers, or the many, many people who had contributed to the story line either. There were quite a few who had signed on to do jobs that they hadn't yet gotten to do (editing ... creating movie posters ... someone had mentioned a story board). One girl had even been retyping all of the existing scenes into a script-formatting program to make it look official ... Lord, I couldn't even think about how much time she must have spent typing. I felt so *guilty* for getting so many people involved in my mess. Because that was the only way to describe our half-written, nonsensical movie script by eleven amateur writers from four different countries: a mess.

So it was December. I was still smarting from New York. And now I had to break the news to everyone that, despite months of work, we didn't have a birthday present for Jake. I had failed. Again.

A more practical person, perhaps, would have quietly buried the movie script idea and moved on before any more time and energy could be wasted on it. But *not* looking at the situation practically and instead clinging to some masochistic desire to prove my worth, I went back to the message board, opened up a discussion on the future of the project, and allowed myself to be swayed by public opinion, public opinion being that the entire script should be published on a separate website for the enjoyment of all those who participated. So instead of walking away from it, I did the exact opposite. I made the decision to keep going. I would finish the movie.

No, wait ... I would finish the movie, and it would be *awesome*.

I did a lot of things in the month and a half that followed. I created a movie poster. And a second one. And a third one. I created the website where I would be publishing the script.[6] I set up a MySpace Film profile for advertising purposes.[7] I even sent the script to a script editor who had offered her services months earlier.

---

6   http://prophecygirl922.livejournal.com.
7   http://www.myspace.com/tdatnd. Susie also made a MySpace Music profile for the soundtrack, but it was later deleted by MySpace without explanation.

The script editor, after receiving the screenplay, promptly disappeared off the face of the earth for two months. She later claimed that she had a family emergency, and that very well may have been true, but I would not blame her if she'd just been avoiding me on account of the atrocity that I had sent to her.

For all the other things that I was doing involving the script, I wasn't doing anything with the script itself. I really didn't want to do it. But I promised everyone that I would do it, and now it was clear that no one was going to do it for me, and the more time that passed, the more questions I was getting about my progress on it. So in January, I gave myself an arbitrary deadline and did the best I could.

And now I will tell you the story of *The Day After Tomorrow Never Dies.*

The Story of *The Day After Tomorrow Never Dies*

Our tale opens with our heroine, Kitty Fangirl,[8] sitting in class. She is naught but a lowly college student at the fictional Bubble University ... *until* the crack team at Jake Watch tracks her internet activity (for no apparent reason) and notices she seems to have a healthy interest in a certain actor. Kitty is accosted by several Jake Watch agents in a dark alley after school and blindfolded. She's then led to the Los Angeles Jake Watch Headquarters, where she's asked to become part of a high-tech spy organization geared at watching (and protecting) Jake Gyllenhaal:[9]

> *JAKE WATCH AGENT 1 opens the door and KITTY is met with the exciting bright and modern world of the Jake Watch Headquarters. KITTY gasps.*
> *KITTY: Is this the CIA?*
> *JAKE WATCH AGENT 1: Better. It's Jake Watch.*
> *KITTY: Jake Watch? The blog? You're kidding me. You mean ...?*

---

8   "Fangirl" is a mildly mocking term referring to a female who is overly enthusiastic about whatever fan circle she participates in. In many situations, the term denotes a certain level of hysterical, blind, naive devotion. The character Kitty Fangirl was actually remarkably observant and resourceful. Her name, though, was recycled later on Jake Watch as one of my blogging aliases. As a blogger, she lived up to her surname.

9   Parts in italics are from the finished script.

JAKE WATCH AGENT 1: It's all real.
KITTY: No.
JAKE WATCH AGENT 1: Yes. We're agents. We protect Jake, and have a helicopter. All true.
KITTY: Unbelievable. How? And why?
At this, everyone stops what they're doing and replies in unison:
EVERYONE: Well, somebody needs to keep a damn eye on him.
KITTY smiles painfully and everyone goes back to their business.
KITTY: That was borderline creepy.

After her in-depth tour of the facilities, Kitty requires further convincing that Jake Watch is the choice for her. This allows for more script contributors to be worked into the plot while she is repeatedly approached by a bevy of Jake Watch agents.

Meanwhile, Jake (who for some reason wound up being slightly dim-witted in our story) is dealing with life-altering issues of his own when his poor puggle Boo is kidnapped by Ben Stein while Jake is eating dinner with Peter Sarsgaard.

JAKE: He totally took my dog! The little one!

The mastermind behind this devious kidnapping plot is none other than a fictional gossip columnist who *just happens to be* the archnemesis of Jake Watch. The nefarious columnist, though, has barely begun; he plots to also kidnap Jake himself at the NASTIE Awards (i.e., the Non-descript Acting/Screen/Theater International Entertainment Awards).

With so much excitement going on around her, Kitty makes the emotional decision to join Jake Watch.

KITTY: Ok, whatever. I'm in.

Next come many fight scenes with henchmen, some of whom steal Jake's socks and others who are armed with *exploding pennies*. Clueless, Jake escapes from harm time and time again, even at the NASTIE awards, where he wins the award for "Best Jake Gyllenhaal in a Jake Gyllenhaal Film."

JAKE WATCH AGENT 2: And finally tonight, the winner, as voted by the International Community of Non-descript Actors in the Entertainment Industry, the Best Jake Gyllenhaal in a Jake Gyllenhaal Film is ... Jake Gyllenhaal!
Audience erupts in approval and JAKE stands up grinning humbly as he walks toward the stage. He goes up to the mic.
JAKE: Wow, guys. I just ...
Cut to outside the theater after the awards show. Media is everywhere. JAKE is walking down the red carpet; he's being interviewed.
JAKE: ... can't believe that I won. I never, ever in a million years would have thought. Especially up against that competition!

After the interview circuit, Jake spends some time chatting with Kitty, who has been assigned to keep an eye on him.

JAKE: You're in TV, right?
KITTY: Actually that was a lie. I haven't been in anything. My whole appearance at this awards show was an elaborate illusion.
JAKE: Whose wasn't? Are you from LA?
KITTY: Wyoming. I'm out here for school.
JAKE stops and looks at her thoughtfully.
JAKE: I can't think of any more questions to ask you.

But alas! The disreputable-though-wholly-generic henchmen do not stop their kidnapping attempts after the awards show. They show up again at a coffee shop, where they are chased off by the employees (i.e., *agents*) as Jake naively buys his coffee.

And yet *more* henchmen appear on the Pacific Coast Highway as Jake, Matthew McConaughey, and Lance Armstrong go bike riding. Again and again, Jake Watch comes to the rescue, allowing the celebrities the illusion that nothing is wrong ...

JAKE WATCH AGENT 3 is pushing past the other bikers.
LANCE: Jesus, man! Slow down, will ya?
Shot of LANCE out of breath.
JAKE: Where did you learn to ride like that?

JAKE WATCH AGENT 3: I was in military-like training for ... something. Very intense. I guess I'm still in shape.
LANCE (panting): I'd say.
They continue on the ride.
LANCE: Come on, you guys! Livestrong!

But then! Just when it seems that Jake Watch can never be outsmarted, Jake *is*, in fact, kidnapped! But that is quickly remedied when a double agent inside the gossip organization hands him back over to the good guys. (Whew!)

Now in Jake Watch custody, Jake flies across the country and winds up at the New York Jake Watch Headquarters. Which happens to be in Rockefeller Plaza. And happens to be right next to the *Saturday Night Live* studio. So he hosts *Saturday Night Live*.[10]

And then it is revealed that the kidnapping scheme was all because the gossip columnist was trying to blackmail Jake into testifying to his credibility as a journalist because the gossip columnist was being sued by (who else?) Heath Ledger. Poor Heath had been accused, by the columnist, of running an illegal koala-breeding ring.

GOSSIP COLUMNIST: I busted him for leading an illegal koala-breeding ring. And it turns out, he's not even Australian.
JAKE collapses in a fit of laughter.
GOSSIP COLUMNIST (protesting): It's all true!
JAKE (still laughing): No, it's not. Points for originality, though. (thoughtful) Although he did give me that koala for my birthday last year ...

When the case gets to court, britpopbaby and Prophecy Girl are already in the courtroom, ready to tell the judge about the gossip columnist's reprehensible kidnapping activities. The case is thrown out, and the gossip columnist gets one final tongue-lashing:

PROPHECY GIRL: You don't want to mess with us. Of all celebrities, you had to choose the one that had an elite team of professional secret agents protecting him.

---

10 Jake really did host *Saturday Night Live* on January 13, 2007 (http://jakegyllenhaalwatch.blogspot.com/2007/01/as-it-happens-snl-recap.html). That part of the script was us trying to be timely.

GOSSIP COLUMNIST: But it was Jake! He's just so …
BRITPOPBABY: Likeable?
PROPHECY GIRL: Admirable?
BRITPOPBABY: Blog-able?
GOSSIP COLUMNIST (sadly): Adorable.

The story ends with Kitty flirting with Jake in a G-rated manner and britpopbaby and Prophecy Girl being kidnapped by the gossip columnist.

Lieutenant Dan and David Boreanaz guest star.

"I know it had potential to be great," Susie lamented. "I couldn't get into it at all and help out with writing. I wish I could have but I hit a complete wall with it." In reality I wasn't sure if, with the story line in question, there was ever any potential for greatness. But strange things can happen in the throes of editing. As I sank deeper and deeper into the story, I thought maybe, just maybe, it wasn't quite as bad as I had originally thought. Maybe it was *secretly brilliant.* I had only meant to spend a little bit of time cleaning things up, but as the weeks flew by, hours and hours and *hours* went into it. *Surely* all of that hard work had had a beneficial effect on the final product. By the time I was ready to start publishing, I was, dare I say it, excited about it.

I posted the script in four segments, one every Friday in the month of February 2007. I had a couple of volunteer editors who saw each section a week in advance. They were usually complimentary and didn't offer too many suggestions, so again I thought perhaps I had been exaggerating the extent of its badness.

But no.

Maybe you didn't know that a fake movie can bomb, but *The Day After Tomorrow Never Dies* proved that it is possible. Because it bombed.

Oh, and it wasn't that I hadn't hyped it enough. I had done well with the hyping. I had posted a teaser scene on Jake Watch, solicited lots of MySpace friends for the film profile, and showed off the movie posters everywhere I could think to. Several readers volunteered to help me promote and talked it up elsewhere on the internet. One even made a trailer for us and put it on YouTube.

No, it bombed because no one read it, and no one read it because it was awful. And I could do nothing but take full responsibility for that because by the end, 90 percent of what was posted had been either written or rewritten by me. On "opening weekend" fewer than one hundred people clicked over to read the first part. At a time when Jake Watch was pulling in two thousand readers a day.

> *Jake Gyllenhaal arrived in Los Angeles Thursday night for the premiere of his new movie,* The Day After Tomorrow Never Dies. *Gyllenhaal's appearance was a surprise as he is spending time in Morocco filming his next movie,* Rendition. *When asked about his unexpected appearance, Gyllenhaal said, "Oh, I wouldn't have missed it. I really wanted to be here for Prophecy Girl and britpopbaby. It's so sad that they've been mysteriously kidnapped and are missing the release of this absolutely true documentary about their extremely adventurous daily lives. I didn't think I was going to be able to make it until the very last minute which is why I'm wearing the same clothes as from the* Jarhead *premiere."*
> —"Jake Takes Time Out of Busy Shooting Schedule to Make Jake Watch Premiere," Jake Watch, February 2, 2007

In an attempt to retain those few who had read the first week, I did everything I could to entice them to come back. A new reader, who hadn't been around when the plot was being hashed out, requested a scene for the final act. Despite the looming deadline, I wrote it and worked it in for her at the last minute. The only comment she left was, "That was really … long."

The script crashed and burned, sunk by its creepy fan fiction feel and not-quite-satirical-enough sanctimonious portrayal of our community. It was mocked mercilessly on another Jake blog and ignored most everywhere else. A peaceful devastation set in by the time the fourth and final segment went up (the only one cowritten with Susie, who graciously offered to help when she saw me flailing). My internet service at home was intermittently down that February, and I was without access the Thursday before the conclusion was published. I came home from work, drove my laptop to a nearby apartment complex, sat hunched over in my car, and stole a wireless connection while shielding my screen from oncoming traffic. I sat there for an hour fine-tuning that week's script so all I had to do was hit "publish" when I got to work the next morning. I did that knowing that if I didn't publish right on time, it was possible (if not likely) that no one would care, or even notice. But it was my project. I owned its failure as I would have liked to have owned its success: wholeheartedly.

Of the forty or so who read it through to the end, several inquired about a sequel. But when that last segment went up, three weeks after the first portion, eight months after I proposed the idea, and twelve hours after nearly being rear-ended as I idled on the side of the road, I knew I couldn't do it.

I said no. No sequel.

That was the end of my career as a fake-script writer.

Speaking of Kidnapping

During this exact same time period, Susie was experiencing a creative meltdown of her own.

The two of us were alike in many ways, but on two points we differed drastically. One, Susie started Jake Watch with the clear goal of writing, and as such, her definition of its success was based on writing. Cantara's interest in the blog had been a dream come true for her, what with Cantara being a publisher and Susie wanting to be published. Unfortunately, Cantara had not proved to be the surefire career launcher Susie was hoping for, and no one else with professional credentials had approached us so …

Susie started to flag. I had already made the deep and introspective decision to be okay with Jake Watch even if it didn't technically "go anywhere," but Susie never made any such promises.

Secondly, though I had (and would continue to have) very personal blog-related experiences in the "real world," Jake Watch didn't exist outside of the internet for her. Being in England, it wasn't feasible for her to take weekend trips to New York, or anywhere else in the U.S., the way I did.[11]

For me, there was an ameliorating effect to going out and meeting people in real life. The more people I met, the easier it was to separate Becky from Prophecy Girl. But for Susie, as time wore on, the opposite problem emerged. She felt confined by the happy-go-lucky persona she had created in britpopbaby and hated it when people confused her for her character. She hated it so much that she grew to hate britpopbaby herself.

---

11 Later I'll talk about another fan from England who did manage to repeatedly journey to the United States. But that fan was older, had plenty of money, and was motivated by different things than Susie was.

In fact, by January 2007, britpopbaby was such an irritation that Susie wanted to kill her.

But in the end, she settled for having her kidnapped.

She first presented me with the idea in December, and I disliked it so much that it took her that entire month and most of January to talk me into it.

Having grown tired of readers assuming they "knew" her through her online alter ego, Susie decided on the radical step of getting rid of her alter ego altogether. Her idea was to "depersonalize" Jake Watch and shift the focus away from britpopbaby and Prophecy Girl as characters. Instead, we would concentrate on writing better posts. Her argument was that Jake Watch's prime attraction should be its content and not our aliases.

And God, did I hate this idea. I'll tell you why. I didn't like it because I thought our content ranked pretty highly as an attention getter already, and I didn't like it because I thought the affection our readers had for the two of us was one of the best things we had going. People were emotionally attached to the blog, but I couldn't imagine they'd stay that way if the leaders they'd come to love vanished without a trace.

And yes, it would be leader*s*, as in plural, who were doing the vanishing. If brits went, PG had to go with her. If all Susie did was change her blogging name, and Prophecy Girl remained intact, everyone would still know who was who.

Which brings us to what I saw as the worst part of Susie's plan: she didn't want anyone to be able to distinguish between the two of us. britpopbaby and Prophecy Girl would "die," and Susie and Becky would continue to write Jake Watch under a single name. Our new character would be an ambiguous, gender-neutral creation with no known history or distinguishing personality of any sort.

Susie called him/her/it "Number 6."

"I think it would give us more freedom to write what we want," she insisted.

We had many long and drawn-out discussions about the possible ramifications of enacting this scenario, during which time I protested that I was already writing what I wanted and, furthermore, I was quite fond of Prophecy Girl. She came in handy. When I went to New York, all I had to say was, "I'm Prophecy Girl!" and a room full of strangers knew who I was.

I tried to imagine what it would be like if there was another trip to New York, what the reaction would be if I announced, "I'm one-half of the genderless, personality-less blogger alias Number 6." I didn't foresee a reaction as welcoming as that in the original scenario.

But Susie's heart was set on it, and Susie hadn't rained on my parade when I'd had the asinine idea to write a movie script, so after two months of being lobbied, and after she agreed to reduce our fates from "dead" to "kidnapped," I relented.

And that's why britpopbaby and Prophecy Girl are kidnapped at the end of *The Day After Tomorrow Never Dies*. Because they'd just been kidnapped on Jake Watch during a mock heist in late January that Susie staged by temporarily hiding all of our old posts and covering the blog with distress signals like, "INTRUDER ALERT" and "THIS IS NOT A DRILL."[12] Rightfully, people were scared and confused.

She gave it a day to sink in, and then the community was introduced to their new leader: "Hello agents, I am Number 6, the acting commander of Jake Watch."[13]

From that point forward, the story was that britpopbaby and Prophecy Girl were being held indefinitely in a prison cell in the jungles of Mexico, captured by the fictional gossip columnist from the movie script.

Jake Watch had some difficulty adjusting to Number 6. No one was sure what he (she/it) was or why he was there. It wasn't clear if the two of us were still writing, or if one of us was Number 6 and the other had left the blog, or if Number 6 was someone completely new to Jake Watch. "So who is Prophecy Girl? Number 6? Britpopbaby? Real names? Locations? When did you all start/form?" someone e-mailed to our new joint e-mail account, from which we composed messages that were signed simply "JW."

The lack of a familiar name at the bottom of each post drove a few readers away. Among them were my friends in real life, almost all of whom stopped reading once it became impossible to distinguish what I had written and what I hadn't.

Further complicating matters, Number 6 was soon joined by even more unfamiliar names. Susie also started writing as "Madame Swiss" and "Terence the Office Dog," and I occasionally posted as *Day After Tomorrow Never Dies* alum Kitty Fangirl. Susie and I were the only ones

---

12   http://jakegyllenhaalwatch.blogspot.com/2007/01/intruder-alert.html.

13   http://jakegyllenhaalwatch.blogspot.com/2007/01/initial-status-report. html.

who ever knew who had written what, though that didn't stop people from guessing.

"Yesterday's Madame Swiss post was brilliant!!" a reader e-mailed, complimenting me on a post that Susie had written.

Despite the above quote, Madame Swiss, an elderly Southern woman with a penchant for gossip, was a source of confusion. Susie created her as a means to mock the gossip we had so carefully removed from Jake Watch, and while her posts were far from tabloid-ish, the subject matter was nonetheless occasionally mystifying. "I get 'Madame Swiss' even less than I do 'Number 6,'" one longtime reader confided in an e-mail. "I've only read one post from 'her' so far, but wasn't the point that JW shouldn't be about gossip?" I didn't know how to respond. Even when satirizing it, where was the line between denouncing gossip and encouraging it?

I like to think of the Number 6 months as our experimental *Sgt. Pepper* phase, except instead of revolutionizing pop culture, we mainly just confused a small, internet-dependent group of Jake Gyllenhaal fans.

In the end, the changes remained. It was obvious that Susie was a lot happier.

But I was miserable.

Anyway, back to the portion of the story where it's still December and we haven't yet been kidnapped and *The Day After Tomorrow Never Dies* is a disaster so Jake will not be receiving a script from Jake Watch for his birthday ... back then, Susie was hatching (yet another) plan ...

So excited was she about her plan that she actually proposed it to Cantara before she proposed it to me. For despite the strained relationship between Cantara and the fanbase, courtesy of Babygate, she was still the only person we knew who had access to anyone whose last name was Gyllenhaal.

Susie wanted to hold a charity raffle in Jake's name, and she wanted Cantara to help us out by finding a way to get Jake to autograph things we could give away to our winners. We got as far as deciding to give the money to Livestrong before Cantara wrote back to suggest we instead go with the American Civil Liberties Union. Sensing the ACLU might be a difficult sell to the 55 percent of us who weren't American, we went directly to Livestrong. Who absolutely loved our idea.

So Livestrong was in! Susie was in! I was in! Jake was ... completely unapproachable. As usual. Cantara offered no help, so we wrote his management company, carefully explaining our plan and emphasizing that under no circumstances would he have to have any personal contact with either of us (in case that was a deal breaker).

And that's where the plan died. Where all such plans of ours died. With Jake. We never got a response.

So he didn't get anything from us for his birthday. Except maybe the gift of making it public that he was quite popular with the menopause crowd.

And then it was reported online that his family gave him (of all things) *socks* for his birthday.[14]

I doubt we could have topped that anyway.

---

14 "A pair of cashmere socks, a british [*sic*] tea set, and a hanging garden wooden chime" were Jake's reported gifts, given to him at a restaurant in Hollywood, according to someone who spied on the situation from another table (http://madmegan.blogspot.com/2006/12/stars-theyre-just-like-us-6-days-of.html).

2007 Jake Watch Oscar Coverage

Yeah, there is no Oscar coverage. We're boycotting, because we hold grudges like that. But let us know if Jake shows up! Or if hell freezes over and someone wins an award for portraying a fictional character.

—"2007 Jake Watch Oscar Coverage,"
Jake Watch, February 25, 2007

The Dastardly Uncle Jack Nasty and Other Fake Jake Stories

Hi Jake
I love you!
> —message sent to the Jake Watch MySpace profile
> August 20, 2006

I was wondering if you know if Jake really has a MySpace account. If so, which one it is. I'm sure you get asked this a lot. I have a hard time believing if some of them are really him. Then, just when I think it is him ….. turns out its not!!
> —message sent to the Jake Watch MySpace profile
> January 26, 2007

I didn't really know if UJN was really him, I guess maybe I just wanted to believe it was him considering he made the profile look so believable to a person who hasn't done their homework on him. I just want to know FOR SURE it isn't him because I'm in total denial! I really thought for a while I was talking to him.
> —message sent to the Jake Watch MySpace profile
> December 17, 2006

The Rise and Fall—and Rise and Fall—of Uncle Jack Nasty

A lot has changed in the world of social networking since the days of Jake Watch. Can you believe that when the blog started, Facebook wasn't available to just anyone who wanted to join?[1] Can you believe such a time existed?![2] Crazy!

Back in those days, it was all MySpace. And MySpace, to be fair, did engender a few reservations.

"I just don't feel safe joining," a friend fretted to me once, re MySpace. No amount of soothing on my part could convince her that her underlying fears were ungrounded.

Celebrities, on the other hand, had reason to fear MySpace. For one, MySpace was a breeding ground for new celebrities. To my knowledge, no one ever got a record deal or dating show on MTV because of their notoriety on Facebook.

And secondly, perhaps more importantly, there is a certain rule of behavior that no famous person can escape. I have pretentiously dubbed it The Immutable Law of Celebrity Profiles: if you are famous, then you will be impersonated on social-networking sites. I have yet to find any exceptions to this law (okay, I haven't looked that hard).

The Immutable Law of Celebrity Profiles stands true, improbably, even when celebrities have authentic profiles. But when a celebrity is absent from the scene altogether, his or her online image is essentially offered up for free to the best available impersonator. And best doesn't necessarily equal most accurate.

I'm sure you know where I'm going with this. Guess who didn't have a MySpace profile?

During my tenure at Jake Watch, I saw some pretty bad impersonators have some pretty incredible successes. Accuracy is not an issue when people *want* to believe. "JAKEY JUJU BENJI BEAR … I like nicknames, so if you make one up for me I'll put it on the page," writes "Jake" on one of the fifty-seven profiles that currently show up when you search MySpace for "Jake Gyllenhaal." Are we really to believe that this is the Oscar-

1 Facebook opened to the world on Tuesday, September 26, 2006. The always universally open MySpace (as you may have noticed) was the primary means of social networking throughout the lifetime of Jake Watch (http://www.redorbit.com/news/technology/673143/facebook_now_open_to_everyone_cal_poly_students_frustrated/index.html).

2 I can believe it. I "applied" for a Facebook profile in the dark ages of 2005 when only verifiable college students or alums were allowed to join. My alumni e-mail address ended in ".net" instead of ".edu," which I suppose seemed questionable, so I had to wait three weeks and appeal twice before I was given the okay to create a profile. And now they just hand out profiles to anyone. *What the hell.*

nominated Jake (a.k.a. Benji Bear) himself? The girl who wrote, "You are super amazing because you're like the shizzle in hollywood and i got mad love for you …" seems to have fallen for it.

Even the Jake Watch MySpace profile attracted the occasional grammatically confused fan: "Ok so there are a lot of jake's on myspace so as a fan i hope this is you cuz if not i may cry lol no really it's dumb two be a fake but if this is you love all your moves well have a good day." (I love Jake's "moves" too.)

Boo's profile, as already mentioned, had its fair share of hopefuls writing in. It's a profile for a *dog*, and there's an explicit disclaimer stating the site has no affiliation with Jake. Imagine the damage you could inflict if you were actually trying to deceive people.

Uncle Jack Nasty (UJN)[3] was among the deceivers. Head and shoulders above his peers, he (or she) redefined the standards for Fake Jakes on MySpace. Months earlier, when my participation with the blog was in its infancy, Susie let one of her hopes for Jake Watch slip. "Now only if I could make it into Uncle Jack Nasty's Top 8 …" she wrote.[4]

Ah. Dreams do come true sometimes.

In November, to our gleeful surprise (for neither Susie nor I had ever had any contact with UJN), Jake Watch's MySpace profile inexplicably rocketed to the number one spot on his Top 8. For the hundreds, if not thousands, who thought UJN was really Jake Gyllenhaal, this move made it look like Jake himself had personally endorsed our blog. Embracing this unexpected, and free, form of advertising, we did nothing to correct the misperception.

UJN was fascinating for precisely two reasons: (a) he was a monumental success in an arena with much competition, and (b) he was possibly the lamest impersonator in the history of MySpace. Height? Wrong. Dates Jake was in school? Wrong. List of upcoming movies? Wrong. He also exhibited questionable behavior, such as leaving Boo (i.e., me) messages to schedule walks on the beach, claiming to be in New York when paparazzi pictures put the real Jake in L.A., and pilfering profile pictures from the

---

3   "Jack Nasty" was in reference to a line in *Brokeback Mountain*. The "uncle" part was, presumably, referring to Jake recently becoming an uncle to Ramona.

4   On MySpace and other social-networking sites, you can request the "friendship" of other people by sending "friend requests." Many sites allow the options of listing "top friends," which the user chooses and showcases on his or her profile. MySpace made famous the concept of the "Top 8," referring to a person's top eight friends.

"Fan Encounters" section at IHJ. And he *never put spaces after his commas* (i.e., "me,boo and atticus").

He had over six thousand friends. He was so notorious that Cantara even brought him up during brunch in New York.

No good fake is without "proof" of legitimacy, and UJN's weapon of choice was his MySpace blog. Three days after her birth, he posted a blog entry that he claimed was the first announcement on the internet regarding the arrival of his niece, Ramona. Those of you who remember the events of Chapter 5 may have already guessed that I took extreme personal offense at that particular claim.

He also wrote a blog entry about his plans to play Lance Armstrong in an upcoming movie, a piece of news that had been circulating as an internet rumor for some time and had already been proven false by the time he published it.

And yet the legions of believers could not be dissuaded. To fans the world over, UJN *was* Jake Gyllenhaal.

Well, until he wasn't.

Within weeks of Jake Watch becoming associated with UJN via MySpace friend placement, his profile was deleted. Gone, without a trace. One day it was there, and the next there was only a white screen and the words "Invalid Friendship ID."

"What happened to your sweet loving blue eyed daddy?" one concerned fan wrote Boo.

"I hope all is well with Jake. Jake are you okay?" lamented someone else. Boo had no answers to give. Boo followed the lead of Fake Naomi and put up a bulletin telling people not to panic and that UJN would soon be back in business.

"Fake Naomi?" you ask. Why yes, gentle reader. The Immutable Law of Celebrity Profiles extends even to the *mothers* of celebrities. Naomi Foner did, indeed, have a profile, and though there was a time when there was some debate as to whether it was legitimate, that particular question was settled for Susie and me as soon as "Naomi" started posting bulletins about UJN.

Naomi, while not offering any explanation as to *why* UJN's profile had disappeared, did seem fairly confident that he would be returning to MySpace very, very soon. I took a closer look at her profile and found that, lo and behold, she *never put spaces after her commas* (i.e., "My extremely talented family. Stephen,Maggie And Jacob."). Either there was a secret Gyllenhaal family coalition for the use of rogue punctuation, or the profiles of Naomi and UJN were being run by the same person.

Boo, curious as to how all this would play out, kept his eye on the situation and offered his assistance by sporadically issuing placating messages to the distraught masses. "Jake will be back! Minor complication …," wrote Boo (though I can assure you Boo didn't have any idea what he was talking about).

And sure enough, Uncle Jack Nasty reappeared a week later, as mysteriously as he'd gone, with a brand-new profile and all the same tricks, though he did manage to use the correct school dates this time. What he did not give was an explanation as to why he had gone away.

Up again went Jake Watch onto UJN's top friends. Up again went UJN's friend count. Up again went the number of unread messages in Boo's inbox from people so, so glad to see "Jake" was back online. (It was then that Boo stopped responding to people on MySpace.)

It seemed all was back to normal. Until December.

In December, UJN decided that Jake Watch was no longer worthy of being his Top Friend. He bumped us down to the second slot and replaced us with a profile labeled "Celebrity Awareness Project," a listing of "authentic" celebrity MySpace profiles. UJN was its most recent verification.

As in, UJN had been listed as authentic.

As in, against all laws of human rationality, UJN had been certified by this site as the one and only, real, true Jake Gyllenhaal.

According to the Celebrity Awareness Project (awareness? really?), a profile was admitted onto its list only if it could be conclusively confirmed by the celebrity in question or his representation.

I was pretty sure UJN hadn't been able to fake anything as sophisticated as an identity verification because he couldn't even properly work the spacebar on his computer. But regardless of how he'd done it, Susie and I decided on the spot that Uncle Jack had crossed a line. Impersonating Jake was one thing; taking the deception to such lengths as to make it onto an official listing was another. We wanted him off of that list.

The Celebrity Awareness Project, as we would soon find out, was helmed by a woman named Barbie, who had no professional credentials and had set up her site as a vigilante response to a story she'd heard about a young girl being raped by someone who had impersonated a celebrity on MySpace. Her site was part of a wave of celebrity-authenticating sites that popped up on MySpace mid-decade. Such sites, almost always run by unauthorized civilians, were attractive because the owners, in compiling their lists, had presumably legitimate reasons to contact celebrities. And that's always exciting.

The first time I wrote Barbie, I was merely fishing for information. I explained that I ran a fansite for Jake and was interested to know how UJN had confirmed his identity as I had been told by a friend of the family (Cantara) that he was a fake. Barbie promptly responded that Jake hadn't submitted anything personally, but that his identity had been "confirmed from his Mom Naomi." She further offered that UJN's first profile, the one that had strangely vanished, "got hit by the 411 virus, it was a tabloid produced virus, mostly celeb sites went down. Naomi kept me in the loop that Jacob (as she calls him 'smiles') was working on it."

Okay. Let's back up here. The "tabloids" produced a virus that took down Jake's MySpace profile and while he, personally, was re-creating his site, he had his mother write someone who ran an unofficial profile listing site to keep her updated on his progress? Call me crazy, but I was skeptical.

Barbie ended with some advice: "Ask Jake first what he prefers to do, and if he prefers his readership not know [that the profile is real], just respect that and do as he directs." Her theory was that the profile was for Jake's "private" use and that I had been told it was a fake to mislead me, so that I wouldn't alert other fans to the fact that he was online. Yes, it was because Jake was interested in keeping a profile for "friends and family only" that he was having his own mother aggressively contact a random stranger to make sure he made it onto a celebrity-authenticating website. Also, yeah, if I had a way to ask Jake personally about this, then I probably would not be writing Barbie on MySpace.

Bizarre backstory aside, Barbie had provided the information I was looking for regarding UJN's confirmation. It all went back to Fake Naomi. The real question, then, was how did *she* manage to convince Barbie she was the real deal? But Barbie changed her story several times when pressed on that issue, so that one remains a mystery …

Back in the fan world, UJN's new "legitimate" status had not gone unnoticed. After making it to the top of his friends list, Susie and I experienced a spike in inquiries about our association with him. We had always maintained that he was a fake, but our judgment was called into question now that we were at odds with the Celebrity Awareness Project.

Barbie seemed … okay maybe "rational" isn't the right word. But I thought she could probably be swayed to remove UJN's name from her list if we approached her delicately enough. While sincere in her efforts, she was clearly not immune to the thrill that came from communicating with famous people. Or famous people's mothers. I could tell from my brief correspondence with her that she *truly believed* she was talking to

Jake Gyllenhaal's mom. We just needed to calmly explain to her that UJN really was a fake, and so was Naomi, and we'd all be better off if Jake wasn't on her list.

Unbeknownst to me, however, Susie had taken things into her own hands: "Okay so I logged onto the Jake Watch MySpace and there was some dumb message from some 12 year old about how do we know UJN because he writes on our wall and could we put her in touch with him. For fuck's sake. So I messaged the Barbie woman."

Susie had written Barbie not from her personal MySpace profile (as I had) but from the Jake Watch MySpace profile. In said message, she challenged Barbie's authority, demanded UJN be taken off her list, and signed it "Jake Watch." Because Barbie had already been in contact with me, and because she knew I ran a site called "Jake Watch," I was pretty sure she would think that *I* had written the message. Alarmed that I might lose what fragile trust I'd already built with her, I wrote Barbie to explain that I had *not* written the message, my co-blogger had, but that it really would be in everyone's best interest to remove UJN from her list.

What I didn't know is that *before* I wrote Barbie this explanatory message, Barbie had already written *Susie* back, thinking she was writing *me*.

It was terribly confusing.

It was made more confusing when Barbie mistook the message I had written to be a sign that I was on her side of the argument (i.e., that UJN was really Jake) and that together we were working against Susie. Susie, meanwhile, was miffed that I had written Barbie to explain the identity mix-up and also accused me of taking Barbie's side.

Further confusing matters, Barbie changed her story when Susie asked her to again explain how UJN came to be on her list. "I verified this Jake through a mutual friend who knows [Jake's] dad Stephen," she wrote. So the confirmation hadn't come through Naomi? Or was Barbie now referring to Jake's mother as a "mutual friend" of Jake and his father? Really, it's anyone's guess. Regardless, her advice was that Susie and I "have [Jake] take the time to verify that he does not [have a profile] ... I would be doing the real Jake a disservice to delete him out of hearsay."

In other words, the only thing that would persuade Barbie to remove UJN from her list was word from Jake himself. And since it would be a cold day in hell before anyone from Camp Gyllenhaal took the time to send us verification of Jake's MySpace status, I became quite discouraged.

Susie, on the other hand, became quite angry.

Forty-eight hours and countless e-mails later, Barbie was referring to Susie as a "Nazi Cow" and accusing her of running a smear campaign against Jake, and Susie was publicly posting Barbie's e-mails and exaggerating the number of fans who had come to us crying when they found out Celebrity-Awareness-approved UJN wasn't real. The fight did nothing but strengthen Barbie's resolve to leave his name on her list.

Still inexplicably caught in the middle, I was receiving messages from both of them almost hourly. ("At first I thought she might be doing that 'project' from the goodness of her heart but turns out she is a black-souled bitch," Susie wrote.) Neither had any intention of backing down, so the only hope for resolution came from whomever it was behind UJN's profile.

Because UJN, you see, hadn't signed into MySpace *once* since the argument began. After months of playing the star, he chose that particular week to take some time off, meaning he was unaware of the drama unfolding around him. Unless he showed up to either defend himself or fold, it was simply Barbie's word against Susie's. So the e-mails continued and the insults got more personal and then …

… Barbie threatened to file harassment charges.

Of the many things we had faced over the months (personal ridicule, unwarranted anger, stinging rejection), we had not yet had the privilege of being criminally prosecuted. Susie all but ignored the threat. Being on the same side of the Atlantic as Barbie, I was slightly more fearful, even though Barbie assured me that she would not press charges against me personally. (In general, I preferred my Jake Watch–related correspondence to be free of phrases such as "press charges," regardless of whether or not I was the intended target.) Barbie wrote that she was keeping a file of all of her correspondence with both Susie and me and requested that I "please ask [Susie] to cease and desist from any further communication with me."

And suddenly I, too, knew what it was to fear MySpace.

Susie, neither ceasing nor desisting, challenged Barbie to come up with Ramona Sarsgaard's middle name, as that was something that wasn't public knowledge at the time; Susie and I knew only because Cantara had let it slip during brunch. The theory was that Fake Naomi and/or UJN would be unable to give Barbie the correct answer, thus proving their illegitimacy.

Barbie's response was almost immediate: "Nazi Cow. Ramona's whole middle name is 'Kierkegaard' you ass."

Well … actually … no. That was not the answer we were looking for, though Barbie was no more willing to take our word on that than she had been about anything else we'd told her. "Write away for the birth certificate!" she snapped when I relayed the news that "Kierkegaard" wasn't right.[5] Her growing hostility toward me did little to calm my fears about the harassment charges.

Another twenty-four hours passed, the tension unbearable, and then, somewhere between Susie's defiant "You can't do anything to us!" and Barbie's "I'll give you the name of my lawyer!" the subject of all this, the man himself, the substandard-by-any-definition Uncle Jack Nasty, logged into his MySpace account.

He promptly deleted his entire profile.

And then Barbie stopped talking to us.

At least we didn't have to hire an attorney.

Barbie did take UJN's name off of her celebrity list, but she kept Naomi on until the Celebrity Awareness Project was deleted in early 2008. Around that time, sites like Barbie's became obsolete as MySpace started its own official list of celebrity profiles.

Naomi didn't make that list.

MEANWHILE ...

As news of our MySpace crusade spread, Susie and I became unofficially known as the people to go to when trying to debunk the poorly forged profiles of *Brokeback Mountain* stars.

A complete stranger (we'll call her "Complete Stranger"), who had gotten my name from a Jake Watch reader, wrote me for my guidance regarding a certain "Heath Ledger." Complete Stranger had befriended "Heath" (whom we will call "Heath Plus" for reasons soon to become apparent) for a laugh after finding his impersonation attempts to be subpar. Heath Plus had several hundred friends, most of whom were young women, most of whom periodically wrote love letters on his wall trying to outdo each other in proving their devotion. Complete Stranger jumped in to alert these women that they were wasting their time wooing a faker. In response, several of the women angrily lashed out at her and demanded that Heath Plus remove her from his friends list.

Much to Complete Stranger's surprise, Heath Plus reacted instead by writing to her personally. "Despite the numerous requests," he wrote, "I will NOT delete you as a friend."

---

5   Although maybe that really is Ramona's middle name. *Who knows*?! Honestly, by the time this whole thing played out, I couldn't say with certainty what the hell her middle name is.

He had difficulty when it came to spelling ("the umpcoming [*sic*] release of 'Candy'"), seemed a little clueless about the internet ("I will also join www.yahoo.com in promotion on certain charity questions"), and ended his message with the unlikely signature "Heath +" (hence his nickname), but his response was enough to make Complete Stranger have second thoughts. She forwarded the e-mail to me and asked, "Because I respect your opinion, did I just do a HUGE oopsie?"

Like many before her, Complete Stranger was quick to suspend her disbelief. She *wanted* Heath Plus to be real. So before she even got an answer from me, she wrote him back, and next thing you know, they were chatting about *A Knight's Tale*.

It's no big secret that before he died, Heath posted on message boards devoted to him and even kept in cell phone contact with at least one administrator of a fansite. Because of this, I had an authority to turn to. I wrote someone I thought could provide an answer and got a quick response. Heath didn't have a MySpace profile.

I dutifully relayed the message to Complete Stranger, but she wasn't wholly convinced: "I will assume it is not him, but just in case, I will try not to insult him." Complete Stranger and Heath Plus continued to correspond at a feverish pace over the next twenty-four hours. She was finally convinced of his fakeness only after a suspicious post on his wall from (no lie) Fake Ryan Phillippe.

Heath Plus's profile was deleted shortly thereafter.

MEANWHILE …

I opened up my inbox to find I had been forwarded an e-mail from none other than "Jacob Benjamin Gyllenhaal." Jacob Benjamin had not written me personally, mind you; rather he had written a Jake Watch reader, who then passed the message along to me. "I'm sure it really isn't Jake, but I wanted you to read it …," she wrote.

Jacob Benjamin had "accidentally" sent an e-mail meant for "David" (as in David Fincher, director of *Zodiac*) to the e-mail address of our reader:

"David, I still havent [heard] back from you, i had thought you wanted to speak to me, perhaps your busy on set. Id apreciate it if you could reply to me asap. Thanks. J Gyllenhaal"

As if the sheer oddity of that message wasn't enough, Jacob Benjamin's e-mail address was "jacobbenjamingyllenhaal@yahoo.co.uk." Dot co dot uk? So Jake was British now? (In my typical overly literal manner, I replied to the sender, "I mean, if you're going to go to all the trouble of impersonating someone, at least do your research! You can tell from the time stamp that it was sent from a computer in Greenwich Mean Time.")

When the Jake Watch reader replied to Jacob Benjamin to let him know he had e-mailed the wrong person, he wrote back with an apology and a friendship offer. Fake celebrities are notorious for claiming computer ignorance while simultaneously asking to be e-mail buddies. "Im sorry if i caused you any inconvenience, Im not a computer whizz, haha … if you wanted to chat sometime, id be happy to, I always enjoy meeting new people," Jacob Benjamin wrote, illustrating my point perfectly.

What they lacked in skill, Fake Jakes made up for in sheer numbers. In private, Susie and I halfway hoped for a challenge, a faker who would require some effort to prove the illegitimacy of.

Jacob Benjamin was not it.

He gave up disappointingly easily, admitting to me that he was fake after only two e-mails: "people want more than anything to speak to jake, its never going to happen, im a fan too, and by making someone think they spoke to jake, it makes them so happy, im not here to be mean, im here to give people their dreams."

What grand aspirations.

Susie wrote him the day after I did to say that (a) we'd contacted Jake's management (not true), and (b) we'd informed yahoo.co.uk that he was "using their e-mail service to fraudulently act as someone you're not" (also, not true … we so did not have those kinds of connections).

We didn't hear from Jacob Benjamin again.

Imagine being us (scary thought, I know). We are powerless. Jake's management ignores us, the Gyllenhaals don't acknowledge us, and even among Jake fansites we rank second behind a site run by a sixteen-year-old (not that IHJ wasn't worthy of its first place standing … but there were pride issues). We are two intelligent, creative, and competent people who don't even have the pull to sway the opinion of a woman like Barbie. Barbie, who was gullible enough to believe that the tabloids create computer viruses to take down MySpace profiles, but refused to acknowledge that the two of us might know how tall Jake Gyllenhaal is.

And yet there we were, donating our time and energy to warding off Fake Jakes (and Heath Pluses) at the request of fans everywhere.

This was not our responsibility. We had a blog to run. And it's not like we had any soft feelings toward Jake's management such that we were eager to step in and do a job that probably should have fallen under their jurisdiction.

So we could either continue to battle the posers one by one, or we could go to the root of the problem.

We chose option two.

All we wanted was a disclaimer on Jake's official website, a disclaimer that clearly stated that Jake did not have a MySpace profile. (Or e-mail fans out of the blue from Greenwich Mean Time.) Then no one could argue with us over fake profiles; in fact, no one would even have to come to us to ask our opinion because the answer would be written in plain view for everyone to see.

It was flawless, really, as far as plans go.

Definitely, in my mind, worth the two days of more time and more energy it took to track down the man who maintained Jake's official site. When I found him, I briefly explained the situation and asked for his help.

Twenty-four hours later, he wrote me back: "Thanks for your message. Jake only has one official site at www.jakegyllenhaal.com. He does not play online so anyone claiming to be Jake and answering their [*sic*] fan mail is an imposter."

Again, imagine you are me. You are already kind of pissed off about the situation. And then you get a jackass-y answer like that.

Well, *no shit* Jake didn't "play online." Therein was the problem.

Also, that had nothing to do with putting up a disclaimer.

Not above being a pest, I wrote him back, reiterating the need for a disclaimer and adding, "Oh, by the way, are you planning on updating Jake's movies soon? I noticed that [the site] looks like it hasn't been updated since 2005."[6]

He didn't write me back.

Which brings me to my next story.

Our Personal Crusade to Take Down Jake's Official Website

Look, a person can only take being ignored by so many people in a single family's circle of associates before something snaps. And that damned

---

6   Ha ha, that was so bitchy of me.

website—that horrible, never updated, graphically inferior website—suddenly seemed like the embodiment of everything that was wrong in our lives.

Did you know there wasn't even a reliable news page on Jake's official site? Can you *believe that*? We couldn't. We looked on in disgust at the newsfeed that stood in its place, doing nothing but generating an unfiltered list of every "article" on the internet that popped up with Jake's name in it.

We were a more accurate source of news than the official site. And we just made shit up half the time.

And the site was always at the top of Google searches for Jake's name. Which meant *our site wasn't*.

And this guy, this dude who did nothing except sit around all day and ignore my e-mails, well, Susie and I presumed he was getting *paid* to let Jake's site deteriorate.[7]

Oh no. We would not let this stand. We were going to take action. Even if it took *waging a war*, we were going to put www.jakegyllenhaal. com out of its misery.

We started with a petition.[8]

> *You know how Prophecy Girl and I are crusaders of Gyllenrights? Vigilantes if you will. Well, we got bored and made a most awesome petition.*
> —"We'll Fight Them on the Beaches, We'll Fight Them
>   at the Smoothies Stand," Jake Watch, April 13, 2007

Susie wrote it and set it to be sent to the webmaster and people of importance within Jake's management as soon as we collected 500 electronic signatures. Fans complained about the official site all the time. Five hundred was nothing. We had four times that many people visit our site every day, and Susie and I spread out and hit up other Jake sites to ask for their help too.

---

7   There was an ironic injustice to the thought of the webmaster being paid for his services while ignoring our requests for a disclaimer. Especially as we remained unpaid for our work dealing with the fallout from not having that disclaimer.

8   http://www.petitiononline.com/jakefans/petition.html. The petition included, among our complaints, this threat: "If britpopbaby and Prophecy Girl discover someone is being paid inordinate amounts of moolah to maintain this site they will switch their allegiance to Orlando Bloom, or, if they're really upset, Chad Michael Murray."

And you know what? We did get a lot of sympathy. We really did.

It's just that most who agreed with our cause did so without actually signing our petition.

After two weeks, only 144 people had signed, and our angry enthusiasm was replaced by the familiar glow of feeble discouragement.

Sensing that 500 may have been an overambitious goal, Susie changed the send-off number to a less-impressive 250, though it soon became obvious that even that was asking too much.

The campaign could have died a valiant death, but instead it limped along for months. A few die-hard supporters created new e-mail addresses so they could sign under multiple names. Others did some digging online, hoping to inspire new signees with what they found regarding the webmaster's other internet offerings (all of his sites were about as well taken care of as Jake's). And then there was the find on Yahoo! Answers, a site where you can post any question about anything, and anyone can answer you. Contributed by the webmaster himself, and posted to the internet, under his real name, for the world to answer, was the question: "What are some good things to talk about to a girl? I like this girl but I keep on running out of stuff to talk to her about and there's always awkward silences. Help? Anyone?"

In the end, we wound up with 246 signatures, a pitiful 4 supporters short of our goal. It was a slow and mournful defeat. We never got a disclaimer. The site was never updated. The webmaster bested us simply by ignoring us.

Or maybe he didn't respond to my e-mail because he locked up on account of me being a girl.

MEANWHILE ...

In February, like a phoenix from the ashes, Uncle Jack Nasty rose again. Though he had rechristened himself with the improbable screen name "Nobody_Wants_U_Like_I_Do" (we will continue to refer to him as UJN as NWULID is entirely too cumbersome), we knew he was UJN because *he never put spaces after his commas*. And in true UJN form, he had thrown together a slightly schizophrenic "About Me" paragraph, where he included information about his love of cooking bacon (?) and a solicitation for female companions for his dogs ("I've got two cool dogs named Atticus Finch and Boo Radley who are looking for love,so,if you got a lady pup,send her their way ;-)"). Already he had several hundred friends, most of whom were convinced they were socially networking with the one and only Jake Gyllenhaal.

> *An alarming spate of "Jake Fakes" have surfaced to wreak mild havoc on online Jakedom. If there is one thing Jake Watch will not stand for it is dopplegangers ... and Paris Hilton ... and camel racing. Today I bring you the horrific news that Uncle Jack Nasty has once again reared his fake lame fake retarded head but this time it's WORSE!*
>
> —"Worrying Times,"
> Jake Watch, February 8, 2007

Susie and I surveyed the mess. And grimaced at the pathetic attempt. "'I fuckin' love the West Wing', 'War movies are awesome'—aaarrrggghhhhh! NO EFFORT!!" Susie wrote. "And the Photoshopped 'proof' pic? Too far dude, too far."

For it was true. As "proof" of his authenticity, UJN had upgraded from his standard wildly inaccurate blog entries to photographic evidence. Identities on MySpace are often confirmed by what's called a "salute," which MySpace defines as "a current photo of yourself holding a handwritten sign containing your MySpace account ID." In the days before MySpace's official celebrity profile listing, sites like the Celebrity Awareness Project encouraged celebrities to post salutes on their profiles so the public could see they were the real deal.

UJN "proves" he's real. Devil horns added by Susie.

133

UJN's salute was about par for the course when it came to his impersonating skills. The picture was tiny, grainy, black and white, and showed a seemingly shirtless Jake Gyllenhaal "holding" a piece of paper on which was written his MySpace URL and the word "Jake." Except the quality of the picture was so bad that the web address was illegible, so it looked like he was just holding up a sign with his name on it. Which was completely stupid.

Under this stunning piece of graphic art, UJN apologized for the low-quality photo, explaining that he didn't have a good camera (what!?). By the time we discovered his new profile (two months to the day after we discovered he had made it onto Barbie's list), he had *pages* of comments assuring him that his identity was not in question and that he didn't need to prove anything to anyone.

Not having the energy to bother with him a second time, Susie and I simply put up a disclaimer of our own on MySpace stating that Jake did not have a public social-networking profile. But UJN's shelf life the third time around proved the shortest yet, and he disappeared for the final time not long after. To the best of our knowledge, Uncle Jack Nasty's MySpace days have ended.

Fake Naomi, however, lives on.

The next great Fake Jake ("The Official Jake G") didn't arrive on the scene until near the end of Jake Watch. More technologically advanced than UJN, The Official Jake G still claimed computer ignorance ("Yes, it's really me; but I'll be the first to warn you that I'm still extremely new & not very computer savvy when it comes to this whole MySpace experience."). He also claimed to have made all the graphics for his page himself, a claim that might have gone over better if he hadn't stolen something that I, personally, had made for Jake Watch. After only accumulating a few hundred friends, he disappeared randomly too, but as of writing this, is trying to rebuild his site.

And so the tradition continues, as it will as long as there are people willing to believe. The lesser fakes come and go, and few notice. But the great ones? The great ones inspire felony charges. And embarrassingly ineffective internet petitions.

Even if they never do get that height thing right.

Zodiac: A Disaster on Many Levels (For Me, It Was Personal)

> *Our very own Cindy did Jake Watch proud last night. So successful was she acting in her undercover role as "Fan on the Red Carpet at the BAFTAs," she was written up by the BBC (no, really, she was). Brilliant maneuvering, Cindy. And what the hell, BBC? You act as if it's unusual for people to be willing to impale themselves for The Gyllenhaal. Um, clearly you do not realize the dedication required by the agents of this fine institution. What kind of news agency are you running there, anyway?*
> —"Jake Watch Agent Awarded Red Carpet Merit Badge," Jake Watch, February 12, 2007

Meet Cindy

Cindy, a native Brit, was a regular reader of ours who had risen to internal Jake Watch fame after she stood on the red carpet in London, in the rain, for twelve hours, awaiting the celebrity arrivals for the 2007 BAFTA Awards.[1] She was rewarded for her efforts with an autographed copy of a magazine. Jake held one side while he signed; Cindy held the other. "Ecstatic" doesn't begin to describe her euphoric response, and seeing Jake in the flesh must have awakened something in Cindy because she was quick to decide that she wanted to see him again.

For those of you who weren't keeping up with the trials and tribulations of getting *Zodiac* ready for public consumption (i.e., all of you), it's difficult to convey just how tremendous the confusion was over the movie's release date. *Zodiac*, being Jake's first film appearance post–*Brokeback Mountain*, was eagerly anticipated by fans, but it also had a certain notoriety about it. There were whispers of agonizing shoots, with ninety-plus takes per scene, and excessive editing in postproduction. It had taken Jake several

---

1 The British Academy of Film and Television Arts Awards.

months to commit to a new movie after *Zodiac*, and though he was filming *Rendition* as this chapter unfolds, he hadn't signed on to do anything after that.

It was a dirty little behind-the-scenes secret that Susie and I didn't want Jake to attach himself to any new projects after *Rendition*. We had a theory that he was going to quit acting for a while. We based this theory on several things, like the inanity of his website, and all the disappointing fan encounters we were still covering up, and the way he kept mentioning in interviews that hey, he might want to quit acting for a while. We didn't see much evidence that he was enjoying what he was doing, so while the rest of the fan community was in a low level of panic about his empty schedule, Susie and I kept our fingers crossed that he remain uncommitted.

It was precisely this sort of detachment between what we thought and what we wrote that was starting to wear on us. We still put on a good show for the reading public, but Susie and I were finding it increasingly difficult to maintain our enthusiasm for an audience we could not always relate to. We had racked up quite a few failed Jake Watch ventures between the two of us by this point. We were tired. And disillusioned. And it was hard to write for people who were neither tired nor disillusioned. Part of the adventure of the early days of the blog was that it was overrun by people who didn't really know anything about Jake. But as the months wore on, many of those people grew disinterested in him and left, leaving behind an ever more obsessive audience.

"I can't WAIT until *Zodiac* so we can get some fresh people who haven't gone psycho after spending the last year online obsessing over everything Jake does," I wrote to Susie. A good solid performance in *Zodiac* would hopefully lure in some new prospects. As much as we enjoyed speculating on Jake's career in the future, we were stuck covering it in the present. If the film was successful, it might revitalize the whole Jake Watch community, and us along with it. For that reason alone, we *really* wanted *Zodiac* to do well.

And then the movie kind of tanked, and we didn't get any new readers.[2]

---

2   *Zodiac*'s domestic box office take was just over $45 million (http://www.boxofficemojo.com/movies/?id=zodiac.htm). Though it was a smash hit compared to *Rendition* (under $10 million domestically [http://www.boxofficemojo.com/movies/?id=Rendition.htm]), the movie did not have nearly enough cultural impact to drive hordes of (or any) fresh new Jake fans into the willing arms of Jake Watch.

Anyway. Back to the release date ...

First it was a generic "late 2006." Then it was an equally generic "early 2007." Then it was finally nailed down as February 2007.

Cindy decided that the Los Angeles premiere of *Zodiac* would be as good a place as any to see Jake in person (again), so after waiting through several false premiere dates, she booked her international flight for February. Sadly for Cindy, by the time she was ready to board her flight, the date had been pushed back again. To March.

Despite this setback, she flew to Los Angeles anyway. She had a friend in L.A., so she met up with her, and the two did a little research. A week later, upon her arrival back in England, Cindy announced to Jake Watch that she had been able to confirm that *Zodiac* would be released on March 2, 2007, and she knew the time and place of the public premiere.

There's a telling line in *The Day After Tomorrow Never Dies* when Kitty Fangirl announces that she'll be joining the ranks of Jake Watch. "Why not?" she asks as she accepts her new position as an agent. "I can't imagine where this is going to lead me, but it's gotta be more interesting than what I'm doing with my life right now."

Kitty thought that because *I* thought that, not just about Jake Watch, but about meeting Jake. Why, you may ask, would I contemplate attempting to meet him again, knowing the difficulty involved and the (most likely) frosty reception I would receive if successful?

Even I can't be sure of the complex thought patterns dominating my brain back in early 2007, but I can say with certainty that pursuing a meeting was more interesting to me than not pursuing a meeting. As I've said before, I never put much effort into researching these things for myself, but if someone else was willing to give me a time, a place, and a specific date, then hell, I'd show up. And that was my thinking with the *Zodiac* premiere. Jetting off to Los Angeles was more exciting than sitting at my desk at work. So L.A. it was. It took me all of twenty-four hours to make the decision and book my flight.

In the same e-mail in which I informed her of my intent to go, I proposed a promotional scheme to Susie: "Dude, I've been thinking about this! I want something to pass out to people [in front of the theater]. I think I want to make Jake Watch buttons."

She wrote back, "How on top of things are you!! We just need little badges with 'I'm Stalking Jake!' on them ..."

Twenty-four hours after *that*, I had finished designing the button, ordered 150 of them, and decided to mail a few to a couple of late-night talk show hosts who were interviewing Jake the week before the movie came out.

If Things Seem to Be Going a Bit Too Smoothly …

The First Sign of Trouble came via the aforementioned talk show rounds. Almost every day (i.e., every day after I had bought my plane ticket) brought a new interview announcement.

An interview that Jake would be taping on the *East Coast*.

The Second Sign of Trouble came when IHJ creator Ally found herself in the audience at MTV's *Total Request Live* while Jake was guest hosting. While making his rounds during commercial breaks, Jake talked to Ally for about five seconds, during which time she tried to apologize for the baby-name fiasco and he acted like he had no idea what she was talking about. And then he called I Heart Jake "awesome." Uh, way to steal my thunder there, Ally.

The Third Sign of Trouble came when I mocked up a schedule of all of Jake's television appearances, complete with the Los Angeles premiere penciled in, and posted it on Jake Watch. An anonymous tipster commented, "No Jake in LA … after flying to NY next week for media events he's back to Morocco to continue filming [*Rendition*]. He won't even be at the LA Premier next week."

Usually I ignored anonymous comments touting "insider" information, as they had a tendency to be supremely stupid and inaccurate, but this one carried an air of authority about it. I was fairly certain that I had just bought a plane ticket and used up three vacation days to go to a premiere that Jake wasn't going to attend. This fear was amplified when rumors began circulating that all of his talk show appearances after Wednesday would be pretaped.

I did something then that I really didn't ever foresee myself doing: I called Cantara. Cantara asked Stephen. Stephen confirmed. Cantara called me back.

No Jake in Los Angeles.

I talked my parents into taking me to England when I was sixteen, and our family spent six nights in London and one in Liverpool. The one night that we were in Liverpool, Sir Paul McCartney held a memorial service for his late wife Linda, in London, and for the first time in nearly thirty years, the surviving Beatles were together in public. The first time. In almost *thirty years*. And they were *in London* the night I was *in Liverpool* ...

That is a tragic story of unfortunate timing.

In the grand scheme of popular culture, missing Jake Gyllenhaal by being on the wrong coast when *Zodiac* premiered is not a tragic story. It's not even particularly noteworthy.

But Jake Watch had a way of siphoning away my perspective. So entrenched was I in my pursuit to ... what? Meet him? Get a story for Jake Watch? Have an adventure? Whatever it was I was going for, I was so wrapped up in my own little world that Jake's absence felt a lot like devastation. I was gutted. I wanted to know why he insisted on *torturing me* like this.

"Don't tell anyone I did this for you!" Cantara warned. "I don't want this to get out. I only asked Stephen because it's an emergency." I had made it sound like an emergency by shrieking into the phone that people were flying in from as far away as England to see Jake, and I needed to let them know as soon as possible if he wasn't going to show. For Cindy, she of the BAFTAs and apparently endless means, had made the decision to go *back* to Los Angeles (the second time in less than six weeks) to try her hand at making the premiere. As it turned out, though, it was a little late for any warnings; she was already on her way. The only other person I could conclusively confirm flying in was me.

A small number of people had expressed interest in driving in though. Hoping to circumvent widespread disappointment on the day of the premiere, I e-mailed a few people and quietly took down any mention of the premiere on Jake Watch. But taking Cantara's words to heart, and not wanting a repeat of Babygate, I made sure no public announcements went up regarding where the information had come from.

And then I started noticing "tips" from anonymous commenters on other Jake sites. Tips that started, "A source close to the family tells me ..." and went on to explain that Jake would not be attending the *Zodiac* premiere in L.A. Considering the timing, I would imagine the "source" in question was me, though I don't think anyone would accuse me of being particularly "close to the family."

A Quick Aside to Address This Issue

The problem with following our Mr. Gyllenhaal, a private celebrity as far as celebrities go, was that he bred inherent competition among his fansites.

He didn't mean to; he just didn't give us a lot to work with. He didn't have a functioning official site (see previous chapter), he didn't talk to the press much outside of promotional blitzes for movies, and he never responded to tabloid rumors. When information did appear, then, it was left to the discretion of fans to determine what was true and what wasn't. Rarely was there a consensus across the board and, as a result, every site followed a slightly different Jake.

Fans were always looking for signs that an insider was watching them, hoping to confirm that their version of him was the "real" one. Susie and I pretended to be above it all, failing to see the irony of mocking others for interpreting his every move while we adamantly declared in private that Jake surely was getting tired of acting and gosh, he'd be so much happier if he just took a little time off to get away from Hollywood …

While Jake Watch was known for embellishing the facts, we certainly weren't the only site to stretch the truth in the name of self-promotion. And all of that goes a long way toward explaining why instead of simply openly sharing the information about his schedule, *all of us* hastily scrambled to pass it along in secret, each doing our best to make it look like we were a little more connected than the rest of the rabble.

God, I'm so depressed by our pathetic-ness right now …

And We're Back

Susie was upset. Not about the "source close to the family" crap, but about Jake not showing up to his own premiere. "Argh! Why must he suck on so many levels!!!!" she asked.

That was the eternal question, but my reaction focused less on anger and more on drowning in self-pity.

It was two days before I left. I had mailed 5 "I'm Stalking Jake!" buttons each to Conan O'Brien and Jon Stewart, packed the remaining 140 buttons in my suitcase, taken off work, paid a premium spring-break price for a plane ticket, and booked a nonrefundable hotel reservation.

For the Fourth Sign of Trouble had come when I found out that neither Greta nor Crystal (you may remember them from Chapter 3) would be able to put me up the first two nights I was in Los Angeles. So I had to find a hotel room. So I was looking at two nights. Alone. At the Best Western off of Hollywood Boulevard. With a suitcase full of now-worthless buttons.

It was pretty much the worst vacation ever, even before I left home.

Susie, not one to let me dally in misery, suggested that I forget everything else, go to the premiere anyway, and focus on finding an opportunity to give *Zodiac* costar (and presumed premiere attendee) Robert Downey Jr. an "I'm Stalking Jake!" button. "Maybe a positive attitude will produce some overdue karma and then good things will happen," she wrote optimistically.

Cindy and I, along with her friend in L.A., had planned to go to the premiere together from the beginning, and those plans did not change after the glaring omission on the guest list came to light. Cindy took the news of Jake's absence at the feature event better than I did. She seemed happy enough to hang out all day in front of the theater regardless. We e-mailed back and forth a few times to coordinate our schedules, and in one of her messages, Cindy mentioned something that she had assumed I already knew. Her friend in L.A., whose name was Maureen, was also a Jake Watch reader.

I had thought that Cindy and Maureen were longtime friends, and that they were my age, and that they were part of that original group of readers who were in it for the fun and nothing else.

I have no idea why I thought any of this, because it was all wrong.

Turned out, they were not my age. They weren't even my generation.

They hadn't known each other for long. They knew each other the same way I knew both of them: through Jake Watch. Cindy's earlier trip to Los Angeles was the first time they had met face-to-face.

The basis of their friendship, and the impetus for repeated transatlantic travel, was Jake Gyllenhaal and only Jake Gyllenhaal. These were not casual fans. These were the opposite of casual fans.

And that disclosure was the Fifth and Final Sign that my *Zodiac* trip was *doomed*.

At Least Things Couldn't Get Any Worse
Tuesday night, the night before I left, I stayed up to watch Conan O'Brien to see if he wore an "I'm Stalking Jake!" button while he interviewed Jake. He did not.

By the time I boarded my plane that fateful Wednesday morning, the entirety of my hopes for coming out of the trip with some sort of tangible victory was contained within an *Esquire* magazine with Robert Downey Jr. on the cover and a Sharpie in my purse. I still had that. I could still get an autograph, and I could still give Robert an "I'm Stalking Jake!" button.

But when I touched down in Los Angeles, I had a voice mail from Cindy.

"Becky, it's Cindy here. I'm sorry to tell you this, but the premiere's been canceled."

Canceled.

Fucking *canceled*.

And just like that, there went Robert Downey Jr.'s chance at a button.

I was just about to delete the offending message when my phone rang—Cindy again. She recapped her voice mail and added a little more detail. Maureen, who had not been able to find anything online verifying the public premiere, had called Paramount Studios earlier that day to make sure everything was a go.

But it wasn't a go. *Nothing* was a go. No public premiere. No red carpet. No reason for me to be in L.A. for the next forty-eight hours.

"Then *why* did they advertise that there was going to be a premiere?" I seethed into the phone. "I mean, you found that information, like, a *month* ago, and it said there was going to be a premiere."

Cindy didn't know. She thought maybe the studio had simply changed its mind. She was very calm too, despite having traveled a significantly greater distance for this event than I had. She asked if I still wanted to hang out the next day, and I told her I had already reserved the day for her anyway so, you know, why not?

I hung up, deplaned, got my luggage, and headed outside.

What followed was a horrendous hour-long shuttle ride to my hotel, during which time the driver yelled at me for trying to eat a granola bar ("*No eating in the van!*"), and Greta called me twice, the second time becoming so concerned about my mental well-being that she insisted on meeting me for dinner.

My hotel was the last stop. The driver decided it wasn't worth maneuvering through traffic to take me to the door.

"See?" he said, pointing in the general direction of the Best Western sign. "It's down there. You can get out here. Go."

Dejected, I plodded miserably down the sidewalk and checked in. I had half an hour to kill before meeting Greta, so once I was in my room, I plugged in my laptop and logged into Facebook. Danielle, of The Sarsgaard Soiree, had written on my wall. I was expecting some expression of sympathy (news of my ill-fated trip had traveled quickly over the past few days), but instead, I read:

"i … i met him and got a pic with him. i will … tell you more later. i gotta go to class/have more heart attacks. GAHHHHH. my heart is with you though … i still cant believe your LA situation!!! *HUGS* I REALLY wished you were with me today!"

Sputter … sputter … seriously?! She *met* him? As in "Jake" him!?

Okay, so fuck the internet. I could always watch *The Daily Show* when I got back from dinner. Maybe the buttons I'd mailed to Jon Stewart would have more of an impact than those I mailed to Conan O'Brien.

I looked up Comedy Central in the channel guide. 62. Up the channels I went. 59. 60. 61. Static. Static. More static. I wanted channel 62, and I will be *damned* if that television didn't receive any channels past 61. It was actually starting to feel conspiratorial at that point.

On my way out to meet Greta, I stopped by the front desk and asked about the Comedy Central situation. The woman behind the desk frowned at me and said she'd never heard of Comedy Central.

"It's a television station!" I said, my eyes watering.

"Are you okay?" she asked, understandably concerned that I was crying over the cable lineup.

I cried the whole walk down Hollywood Boulevard. And then I saw Greta standing outside the subway station. Familiar, happy Greta. She gave me a hug and said the nicest thing anyone had said to me all day: "Come on, let's go to IHOP."

I cried through most of our meal too.

"I'm really happy I'm going to get to hang out with you and Crystal this weekend," I told her. She didn't look convinced. It was probably the sobbing. People were starting to stare.

"So what happened?" she asked quietly. I filled her in on the whole story as best as I could, starting with the anonymous comment that changed the course of the trip and ending with the television in my hotel room.

"It's fucking Comedy Central! It's basic cable, for God's sake!" I blubbered, stuffing pancakes into my mouth.

I could tell she was struggling to understand why I couldn't stop crying, and that just made me feel worse.

No, *Really*, Things Couldn't Get Any Worse

When I got back to the hotel, *The Daily Show* had already aired on the East Coast. I checked online to read up on what I was missing. The buttons (of course) got zero airtime.

I then opened up my inbox to find that Susie had e-mailed me to say that Jake possibly had a new girlfriend ("The New Girlfriend" was a class of rumor we always dreaded because of the likelihood of mass hysteria). And she was a redhead. As I am.

"Yeah, that would happen now, wouldn't it?" I noted dryly.

"I'll assess the redhead situation," Susie wrote back. "My first thought was, 'Hey! She stole Becky's whole image!'"

The next morning before I headed out, I made my internet rounds and reported back to Susie: "I posted something on the message board [last night] about the redhead honing in on my territory and I wake up to see she's been identified, thoroughly researched, and cautiously dismissed as a risk. I am very scared by these people."

And then I threw a few "I'm Stalking Jake!" buttons in my purse and went down to the lobby to call a cab because I had a date to meet one of those people.

The pound was doing mighty well against the dollar, and Cindy was staying in a nice hotel. Nice enough that someone opened the cab door for me when I pulled up. It was a step up from being dropped off down the street.

Cindy had given me her room number, so I guardedly made my way through the lobby and into the elevator. Once at her door, I gave a tentative knock, and she swung into view almost immediately.

"Oh, you're here! It's so good to meet you!" she exclaimed before the door had fully opened. She grabbed my arm and pulled me into a hug, ushering me into the room after she released me.

"Come in! Come in! Have you eaten? I thought we could go to breakfast at a café down the street where Jake likes to go, as long as you don't mind a bit of a walk."

I told her that sounded wonderful and sat down as Cindy finished getting herself ready to go. I'd somehow imagined her to be a stereotypical British-motherly type, maybe a bit plump with graying hair and dressed in drab colors. She was none of those things. She was full of energy, rushing around as she filled me in on our options for the day. She told me there was going to be a private screening of *Zodiac* on the Paramount lot that evening. How she knew this was beyond me.

"Yeah, I think that's why they canceled the public premiere. So they could have this private party instead." She looked thoughtful at that.

"But we could still go, right? We couldn't get in, but maybe we could see the celebrities or something?" I asked, getting more excited by the second at this possibility, mentally noting that I needed to go back to my hotel at some point to pick up that *Esquire*, just in case. The Sharpie was in my purse.

"Yeah!" Cindy said, also clearly tempted by the idea. "Or, I have a friend who might be able to get us tickets to see *Zodiac* tonight. There's a sneak preview, and he thought he might be able to get three passes."

This was looking better by the minute. We actually had options, as in more than one *Zodiac*-related activity from which we could choose and then about which I could write for Jake Watch. It was as if a weight had been lifted.

"I'm up for whatever," I told her truthfully.

We both decided we could make that decision later, and then Cindy mentioned Maureen, saying she was looking forward to the three of us hanging out. "She lives outside the city, so she's going to drive in this afternoon. She cried for days when she found out Jake wasn't going to be in town for the premiere," Cindy said, sadly shaking her head. "I think tonight will really cheer her up. I keep telling her we don't *know* that Jake's not here."

I frowned a little at that but didn't say anything.

"So Jake eats here?" I asked when we made it to the café.

"Yeah," Cindy said, pausing for just a fraction of a second before adding, "he's photographed here all the time."

I stopped dead in my tracks.

"Oh, right," I said, trying to sound as if I knew that but panicking just slightly at what I'd revealed.

She was holding the door and watching me.

Dammit.

She was going to know. She was going to know that I was a fraud, a fraud who ran a fansite but didn't know where Jake liked to eat breakfast. Who wrote about him every day but hadn't even seen all of his movies. It would be another month before I ran across *Lovely and Amazing* on sale at Target. I wouldn't watch *Highway* again if you paid me.

I stood there while she waited for me to walk inside, knowing with complete certainty that I wouldn't have been in Los Angeles right then, wouldn't have cared about *Zodiac*'s premiere, and sure as hell wouldn't have been meeting up with another Jake fan were it not for Jake Watch. But I knew just as surely that she *didn't* know that. She was the real deal, in it for Jake. And she thought that I was too.

"Well, you know, Susie and I are usually so intent on looking for stuff in pictures to poke fun at that we sometimes miss the obvious, like the location. We try to focus on the unusual," I explained, trying to recover.

And that was the truth. We really *didn't* pay attention to where pictures were taken. Cindy smiled back at me, but my heart sank a little. Last night it had been Greta, freaked because I was in too deep. Today it was Cindy, dissatisfied because I wasn't in deep enough. Cindy wasn't eating breakfast with me because she wanted to hear Becky's philosophy on Jake Watch; she was here because she wanted to talk Jake with Prophecy Girl.

So Becky slipped away for the time being and let Prophecy Girl take over. After all, Becky had been very disappointed in this trip so far; she didn't want Cindy to be disappointed in her.

As Cindy and I dug into our meals, she shared with me a theory, which she had obviously put much thought into, that Jake was secretly in Los Angeles *at that very moment.* Cindy, like so many of us, wondered why Jake wouldn't show up to his own publicity event *and* why his interviews set to air over the weekend had already been taped.

"So he must have already left New York," she concluded, "or else why not do the interviews live? And if he's not in New York, he's probably here *right now.* Why wouldn't he show up for his own movie?" Becky wasn't so sure about this theory. Becky had word from both an anonymous commenter and Stephen Gyllenhaal that Jake had hopped on a plane to Morocco the night before to continue filming *Rendition.*

But Prophecy Girl wasn't going to spoil anybody's fun, so PG excitedly nodded her head, said that it was just as good a theory as any and, after all, why *wouldn't* Jake be in the city? Cindy thought our best course of action would be to walk around to some of Jake's favorite haunts in L.A. that day. Prophecy Girl thought that was a wonderful idea.

The problem with Prophecy Girl, though, was that she was used to being wheeled out for a few blog entries a week and then disappearing. She was also used to playing her part from behind a computer screen, where there was plenty of time to edit and perfect what she was going to say before it became public. Playing her in real time, in real life, had exhausted me by the end of breakfast.

By midday, I'd lost my resolve completely. I heard myself saying things like, "I'm actually more into Jake *Watch* right now than Jake" and "I have some issues with the way a lot of these fans blindly attach themselves to Jake, like he can do no wrong." I would then mentally slap my hand over my mouth and guiltily look over at Cindy, watching as she politely went on with the conversation as if I hadn't just insulted her.

Hours went by.

We walked by Jake's doctor's office. We walked by the hospital where Jake went when he cut his finger with a carving knife. We walked through the farmers market where Jake had bought produce. We walked by Sprinkles cupcakes. We walked through the parking lot where Jake had once lost his car, and then we looked on Cindy's handheld media device at some paparazzi pictures of Jake looking for his car, and then we talked about how we were standing in the same place that Jake had stood in those very pictures while he was looking for his car. We had lunch and talked about Jake. We got smoothies and talked about Jake. We went into a Nike store because Jake likes Nike sneakers (does he?) and talked about Jake. And his Nike sneakers.

"I can't believe I'm here, in L.A., with *the* Prophecy Girl," Cindy mused aloud as she browsed the shoe collection. Not with Becky. With Prophecy Girl.

Back in Cindy's room, my outwardly placid smile was covering my growing apprehension about another fan joining us for the evening. Cindy again brought up the option of going to the advance screening of *Zodiac*, saying that she had heard back, and the tickets were ours if we wanted them. Maureen showed up minutes later, before any decisions had been made, and proved to be much more externally calm than Cindy. She was also dressed nicely, in contrast to Cindy and me, who had walked miles in the sun in our jeans that day. I wondered if I should go back to my hotel and clean up a little ...

Cindy was online checking her e-mail. "There *is* a private party tonight. And it's at the Paramount lot," she confirmed happily after scanning a message. She checked her watch and turned to Maureen. "Do you think we could get down there?"

"You mean instead of going to the sneak preview tonight?" I asked.

"We can always see the movie tomorrow," Cindy said. "This says," she paused, then started reading, "they're having 'a private VIP celebration for *Zodiac* at the Paramount lot tonight.'" She looked over at me. "I *really* think Jake might show up. I'd just be *devastated* if he was there and we weren't there to see him. I think we should try."

We didn't have a lot of time. And I didn't have my *Esquire* with me. But I did have a Sharpie and ...

"Oh, guys! I almost forgot! Do you want an 'I'm Stalking Jake!' button?" I asked. Cindy and Maureen were visibly delighted that I had come prepared with giveaways. I quickly told them about our failed attempts to get them on television and then darted into the bathroom to throw some water on my face. Good enough.

And then we were off.

Maybe it was the addition of the third person to our party, maybe it was the tantalizing pull of possibly seeing famous people, maybe I was just delirious from trying to split my personality all day, but as we cruised toward Paramount with Maureen behind the wheel, I started to feel optimistic. I didn't think we were going to see Jake—no amount of positive thinking from the front seat was going to convince me of that—but maybe, just maybe, this night could be fun.

Though the party wasn't until seven, and it was only then just past five, I could feel the tension emanating from the other two as I sat in the back and slowly became contaminated by it. By the time we rolled around to Paramount Studios, I was as nervous as they were. On our drive over, Maureen told us her story of calling the studio to ask about the premiere. She was put through to someone of seeming importance who confirmed the public event was not happening but then asked suspiciously, "Who is this?" The call was rather coldly ended when she told the man that she was "just a fan."

At a stoplight, Maureen pulled down her sun visor and revealed two pictures of Jake taped underneath. "So I can daydream when I'm sitting in traffic," she told us. "He's always with me."

"Oh, that's fantastic," Cindy raved.

"Wow, that's dedication," I offered.

At the first set of Paramount gates, we were allowed in ... but only to turn the car around. A friendly guard directed us to a second set of gates farther down the street.

"Your party's down there," he said. "They probably won't let you in. *I'd* let you in, but I don't know what's going on at that gate."

The security guard at the second set of gates was not so personable and rather harshly told us the public *wasn't invited*, and if we wanted to stand outside, we could, but we were going to have to park down the street.

So that's exactly what we did, and by the time we'd walked the quarter mile or so back to the gates, there was a line of people standing on the sidewalk. The closer we got, however, the more evident it became that every person in line was a photographer. Not a fan among them.

But *Surely* Something Good Will Come From This Trip

From our vantage point at the end of the (then short) line of photographers, we could see a red carpet set up outside the studios, just beyond the guard shack. I snapped a couple of photographs from the sidewalk but then decided I could get a better shot from the driveway. I had taken no more than two steps onto the drive when a security guard menacingly charged toward me, shouting that I was *not* to be on the driveway but *only* the sidewalk and *no, I could not take a picture.*

Mortified, I slunk back over to my place in line (where several people were now staring at me as if I'd just been tagged as a security threat …, which, okay, maybe technically I had) and eavesdropped. The favored topic of conversation was celebrity treatment of the paparazzi.

"She's terrible!" a man several people ahead of me was saying. "I went to an event where she actually turned away from all of us and refused to have her picture taken! What a bitch!"

The bitch in question was Oprah Winfrey. Like most Americans, I feel it's unpatriotic to insult Oprah, so I turned to the man immediately in front of me and tried to judge if he could be of any help to me. Before I could think of something appropriately clever to say, he turned and asked who I was hoping to see. Apparently it was obvious I was not there in a professional capacity.

"Well, I guess technically Jake Gyllenhaal, but …" I started.

"Oh, I don't think he's going to be here," he interrupted me. "His name isn't on the list. His wife's name is on there, though."

Maureen, Cindy, and I shot him three shocked stares. He also earned a scandalized "He doesn't have a wife!" from me. He looked appropriately contrite and quickly backtracked, "Oh, well, I don't know. Her last name is Gyllenhaal."

That would be his sister Maggie, we told him. I'm sure it's a mistake he never made again. And I'll save us the effort of dragging out the suspense and tell you that she didn't show up either.

I spent the next ten minutes smiling a lot and asking dumb questions before he told me, "I wish I could help you get in, but I can't. I'd tell them that you're my assistant, but security's tight, and they won't let anyone in if their name isn't on their list."

Was I that transparent?

Also, dammit.

At last the guard shack opened, and the procession of photographers started to move. When I got to the door (quickly, since we were near the front of the line), I stopped and held the door open for all those behind me. By that point there were lots. Hundreds. Half of the people completely ignored me, about a quarter said, "thank you," and the remaining quarter either looked at me curiously, asked if my service was complimentary of Paramount, or offered to let me go in ahead of them. To the latter I always sadly replied, "I'm not allowed in," which inevitably led to some variation of sympathy but nothing that was of any value in aiding me in my quest for entrance.

One man stopped and dramatically shouted at me, "Stay right there! The sunlight is beautiful in your hair!"

And then he laughed as he walked through the door.

I overheard one woman say as she walked in, "I can't believe he's not going to be here! I mean, he went to the one in Tokyo." She caught my quizzical look and then turned to her conversation partner to amend, "Oh, that was the *Spider-Man 3* premiere!" (Which it was not, because *Spider-Man 3* would not premiere in Tokyo until over a month later.[3])

Knocking Oprah, making fun of my hair, confusing Jake for Tobey Maguire in movies that hadn't even been released yet—these are the people who brought you the photographs of *Zodiac*'s VIP-only premiere event.

When the last photographer had gone in, I looked back and saw that Cindy and Maureen had moved down the sidewalk, slightly less comfortable with my brazen pleas for access than I was. I made my way to where they were standing, and minutes later another fan showed up, a guy around my age who wanted to see Chloe Sevigny (also in *Zodiac*). We'll call him "Chloe Sevigny Guy."

"She's hot," he explained.

"You want a button?" I asked in return.

I dug an "I'm Stalking Jake!" pin out of my purse and handed it to him.

"Jake Watch?" he asked, squinting at the fine print. "Oh, that's you?" I didn't really see him as the Jake Watch type, so I figured he was just being polite, but it was nice that he at least pretended to recognize our site.

"So we can't get in," he stated after a moment.

"No," I said. "They're going to make us stand out here, and you can barely see the red carpet." I pointed over to where the photographers were

---

3   *Spider-Man 3* premiered in Tokyo on April 16, 2007 (http://news.bbc.co.uk/1/hi/entertainment/6559933.stm). Americans could see it in theaters in May of that year. The *Zodiac* event was March 1, 2007. I have no idea what that woman was talking about.

now setting up alongside it. And then I looked over the four of us. Making a decision, I headed for the guard shack.

So ...," I said after I opened the door.

"Your name has to be on this list," a guard sitting behind the desk told me, his sentence punctuated with a hard stare.

"Right. Well, I figured it didn't hurt to ask."

In return, he gave me a tight smile and an apology that, to my ears, lacked conviction.

When I walked back outside, Cindy and Maureen had moved even farther down the sidewalk, leading me to believe that I was possibly embarrassing them. Chloe Sevigny Guy walked with me down to where they stood.

Then a man came stomping out of the guard shack and told us we couldn't be on the sidewalk.

"They want you across the street because you're blocking the entryway for *invited guests!*" he told us, before whirling around to exit Stage Right.

And that's how we came to be kicked off the Paramount lot. After I was kicked off the driveway at Paramount and essentially kicked out of the guard shack at Paramount. We were made to stand outside the gates like common ... moviegoers.

I refused to cross the street. Luckily I didn't find any protesters to my suggestion that we instead remain on the sidewalk just beyond the gates, though even from that vantage point we were much too far away to see anything. The sun was starting to set too, and it was getting cooler. The guests would start arriving soon, and though we would be able to watch their cars drive up to the party beyond where we stood, we scarcely dared to hope anyone would slow down long enough to acknowledge us.

Two middle-aged women and two geeky twentysomethings, banished from a movie lot, hoping someone might roll down a car window. It was pathetic. I knew it was pathetic. I had previously been looking forward to *Zodiac*, but I was starting to feel the first twinges of resentment toward it.

Before the first car pulled in, another guard came out and told us no, really, we'd have to cross the street once the VIPs started arriving. As soon as he left, we made a group decision to ignore him. After all, it was still just the four of us.

And then there were five of us. A girl a couple of years younger than me walked up to where we stood. She was there for Jake too. Ever the unnecessary PR person, I reluctantly relayed the news that Mr. Gyllenhaal would not be attending the screening this evening and I was sorry for her disappointment. Cindy quickly jumped in to say that she was still not convinced that Jake wasn't going to show and then engaged our new friend in conversation.

Her name was Rachel. Rachel had met Jake on the set of one of his early movies, *Moonlight Mile*. She was an aspiring actress, and he had told her at the time to look him up if she ever made it to Los Angeles. She'd been living in the city for a while, but this was her first opportunity to see him. She'd written him a letter in hopes of giving it to him that night. It was a much better story than I could offer as to why I was there. I didn't even *know* why I was there. But I knew then that there were going to be people even more disappointed with the evening than I was.

Cindy asked Rachel if she'd heard of Jake Watch. She had; not only that, she'd participated in the 2006 Official Jake Gyllenhaal Fan Survey.

"Well, that's Prophecy Girl," I heard Cindy say, pointing at me.

I watched out of the corner of my eye as Rachel's mouth dropped open a little. "*The* Prophecy Girl?" she asked.

Cindy nodded proudly.

"Wow," Rachel said.

Pretending that I hadn't been eavesdropping, or secretly thrilled by her recognition, I casually sauntered over to where they were standing and asked her, "Would you like a button?"

A few more people filtered in. In the end, there were about fifteen or so Jake fans, including a group of teenagers with handmade signs. Outnumbered, Chloe Sevigny Guy left our group to mingle with the lone Mark Ruffalo fan. I made the rounds, handing out buttons and apologetically explaining that Jake would not be coming that night. Cindy went around behind me, telling everyone that wasn't necessarily true.

And then the guests began to arrive.

Car after car after car sped by us. Finally, *finally*, one vehicle stopped, and a woman leaned out of her window to ask us who we were waiting for. One of the girls with the signs yelled, "Jake Gyllenhaal!" The woman shook her head and said that Jake had already flown back to Morocco to continue filming *Rendition*, as I had been telling everyone all evening.[4]

---

4   For the purpose of historical accuracy, I feel it necessary to point out that, despite having now heard this message from three separate individuals, Jake was *not* in Morocco. But he also wasn't in Los Angeles. The *Zodiac* event was held on Thursday, the day he supposedly left the country. The following Saturday, Danielle of The Sarsgaard Soiree, having already met him once that week, ran into him a second time in Central Park in New

Cindy didn't believe her, either.

"I still think he'll show up," she told the teenagers.

A man who identified himself as Mark Ruffalo's brother walked down from the red carpet area. When one of the girls with the signs asked him about Jake, he told us that Jake *was* going to be there later (what?! shut up, Mark Ruffalo's brother!) and then got the teenagers to pose for a picture "to give to Jake." I wasn't sure why he was saying these things, so I kept my distance, though later I would regret not thanking him for being the only person to come down to greet the fans that night.

When the last of the cars pulled in, without a single celebrity sighting all evening, some of the group started to leave. But not our group. No, Cindy was still hoping Jake might make an appearance.

"Or maybe he's already here," she said, squinting in the direction of the red carpet setup. It was completely dark by then, and we could see lights off in the distance. Sometimes we could even discern vague humanlike forms walking down the carpet. But details, identification, determination of gender—none of these things were possible from where we stood.

When the photographers started to leave, those on the sidewalk left in droves. But not our group. No, Cindy theorized, "Maybe Jake is going to show up late because he wants to avoid the photographers."

Soon it was just the teenagers and Cindy, Maureen, and I. Chloe Sevigny Guy had long since disappeared. The stream of photographers passing by us was getting larger. One of the teenagers asked a passing paparazzo for his press badge, a little laminated piece of cardstock with a *Zodiac* graphic and the word "press" at the top. The man she asked handed it over without a word and walked off, leaving one very happy girl and five jealous ones behind.

The next photographer who came out was accosted from two different angles, by me and another of the teenagers.

"Can I have your press badge?" I asked.

"Can I have your badge? Tomorrow's my birthday!" the girl asked right after me. I turned to glare at her. It had been a long night, and I was getting a little sick of girls shouting out "It's my birthday!" when they wanted attention, so I opened my mouth to ask her if she was just making that up.

York. He did finally go to Morocco the following week, though why I was told otherwise and why he pretaped his interviews for Friday and Saturday remains unknown. At any rate, it appeared he never had any intention of making the Paramount event in L.A.

But the man looked back and forth between the two of us and started taking off his badge. I closed my mouth and grabbed it as soon as it was free. He looked at me, surprised.

"I'm sorry, but it's her birthday tomorrow," he said, nodding toward the teenager.

I must have looked really upset because the girl shook her head quickly, "No, no, it's okay. You can have it."

So that was my big accomplishment for the night. Stealing a press badge out from under a girl a decade younger than me. Who was probably having a birthday the next day.

But considering that the first two photographers who had been asked had willingly given over their badges, it seemed highly unlikely that anyone would be going home empty-handed.

"You know you can't get in with it," one sneered at Maureen before walking off, badge still securely around his neck. Some of the photographers apologized and said they collected their badges. Most of them walked by us without acknowledging we were talking to them. There were a few who laughed at us, and others who just barked, "No!" and kept walking.

No one else got a press badge.

"I can't believe I held the door for those assholes," I said to Maureen, a little too loudly, after she was rebuffed yet again.

As the last of the photographers scurried past us, Cindy came to the conclusion that maybe Jake wasn't going to show up after all.

"Or," she asked, "do you think he went in a back entrance and we missed him?"

I gave her a long, silent look and then turned to walk in the direction of Maureen's car.

The ride back to my hotel was quiet.

"Maureen and I are going to see *Zodiac* tomorrow, Becky. You're more than welcome to join us," Cindy said as I hopped out of the car.

"Thanks, but I think I'll wait until I get home to see it," I said.

Processing

I spent the rest of the weekend with Crystal and Greta doing decidedly non-Jake-related things, including going to PaleyFest[5] and meeting the cast

---

5   PaleyFest is an annual festival put on by the Paley Center for Media. Cast and crew of various television shows host forums that include a question-and-answer session and screenings of their work.

of *The Office*. The contrast between *Office* night and *Zodiac* night could not have been more striking.

"I can't get over how nice they all were!" Crystal said as we walked back to the car.

We were in the standby line for tickets when Jenna Fischer and Angela Kinsey came out to greet the crowd before the show started, just in case those of us in line didn't get a chance to come in (though the three of us did make it inside eventually). After the program, while fans swarmed Steve Carell for his autograph, he found each person in the crowd and looked them in the eye as he handed the signed merchandise back to them.

"They are *literally* making me leave, guys," Jenna Fischer had said, as a security guard *literally* dragged her away from autograph seekers.

"Yeah, see?" I said, angrily stepping onto my soapbox as we climbed into Crystal's car. "That's the television industry for you!" I ranted for most of the drive about how television audiences are based on the number of viewers, but movie attendance is measured in dollars. "We're not individuals to them, so they don't care. You ever see someone win an Academy Award and then thank their fans? Or even the people who saw their movie? No! And why the hell not? Like movies aren't made for audiences just like everything else in the goddamned entertainment industry?!"

I'm guessing that Crystal and Greta enjoyed my company more during these little Hollywood vacations *before* I started writing for Jake Watch.

Zodiac grossed a paltry $13 million its opening weekend. However many individuals that represented, I wasn't among them. The Tuesday after I got home, a friend passed through town for the night. He had wanted to see the movie and thought it would be fun to see it with me. So at his suggestion we went. Two nights later my mom called to say she and my dad wanted to see it … and thought it would be fun to see it with me. So at their suggestion we went.

Friday, Megan and I drove up to Indiana to see Kara at grad school. Our plans for Saturday night?

"Well, you might be a little *Zodiac*-ed out, but …," Megan said.

"We were thinking it'd be really fun to see it with you!" Kara finished for her.

As I walked out of the theater for the third time in five days, I asked them if they'd liked the movie. Both thought it was great. Both complimented me on Jake's performance as if it reflected upon me personally.

"He did a seriously good job, Becky," Kara said.

"Thank you. I'm glad you liked it," I replied. And I was glad. I genuinely liked the movie myself.

"But you know what?" I continued calmly. "I'm *not* going to see it again. And I'm *not* going to buy it when it comes out on DVD. I'm not spending another *fucking dime* on it, and anybody else I know who wants to see it can go without me."

And I didn't see it again. Before *Zodiac*, I saw one to three movies a week. Every week. But after that last viewing, I didn't step foot in a theater for months.

I was kind of sick of the movie industry.

"I Think Jake Would Smell Sort of Like Apples," and How That Quote Relates to the Business of Selling T-Shirts

Oh PG that was a great post it really really was. I know u must feel like its all a waste of time, and i mean all of it, all of this Jake stuff... but i do think he would appreciate everything your doing and if he knew he would try but i just think he doesnt 'know' Thank you for everything u do for us, and even tho it doesnt feel worth it it totally is!
—comment left in response to my Los Angeles post,
"Prophecy Girl Reports From the Red Carpet ...
Or At Least Down the Street From It!"
Jake Watch, March 2, 2007

This Would Be So Much More Tolerable If I Was Getting Paid

To recap, after eight months of blogging, I had gotten no further than outside the gates of Paramount scrapping over a void press badge with a teenager.

Susie and I were still writing under the Number 6 alias, but I wrote my Jake Watch account of the *Zodiac* fiasco as Prophecy Girl. The reaction was so enthusiastic ("PG!!! You're back! Words cannot express—man, so great to have a post from you again ...") that Prophecy Girl came back permanently. Susie reinstated britpopbaby shortly thereafter. We never explained the reasons for our disappearance, or reappearance, and everyone carried on as if nothing had happened. Considering how hard she'd

Becky Heineke

campaigned to get rid of britpopbaby, Susie was surprisingly accepting of her return. If she had any misgivings, she never let on.

So maybe the names we were writing under weren't the problem.

I went out to lunch with a friend of mine the week after I got back from L.A., and I remember the exact tilt of her head as she sat across the table from me and pondered, "*The Little Mermaid* ... The Beatles ... *Buffy* ... Jake ... I wonder what your next obsession will be ..."

As far as lunchtime conversation starters go, I suppose hers was innocent enough. My life up to that point had, indeed, featured a series of very public pop culture fascinations, and I'm sure she wasn't the first of my acquaintances to wonder what I'd latch onto next.

But me? *Obsessed with Jake?* I had to physically control my anger as I explained that I saw people every day who were obsessed with Jake. I *knew* what it was to be obsessed with him, to have a fan say to me (while we're on the subject of The Beatles) that she had once had a conversation with Paul McCartney, but that didn't come close to the thrill of just *seeing* Jake walk a red carpet in front of her. To have complete strangers lash out at me for being "disrespectful" or "mean to Jake" over the most insignificant things. To watch as people wasted their lives away searching the internet for any mention of his name so they could pin down his location, map out his travels, and guess where he was going next and who he was spending his time with.

Running a fansite (at least the way Susie and I did it) had *nothing to do with obsessing over Jake.* I wasn't like that, I had never been like that, and why the hell was she sitting there acting like I was like that?!

Swept up in a sea of restaurant-inappropriate emotion, I lost her, much as I'd lost Greta at IHOP. And my lengthy, convoluted reasoning did little to help my argument that I wasn't "obsessed." I conceded that I was probably too emotionally invested in the blog, but it had been such a productive creative outlet that I had learned to take the good with the bad. I was involved with Jake Watch not because I was obsessed with Jake, but because it was fun. Right? This was fun. This was really fucking *awesome*, all this fun I was having ...

Right?

It occurred to me, as I replayed my rationale in my head, that it was possible I had gone slightly insane while in Los Angeles because very little of the past few months of Jake Watch could be considered "fun."

158

Our readers had complimented Prophecy Girl on her publicly cheerful handling of the *Zodiac* trip, but the truth remained that Prophecy Girl *wasn't real*.

Jake blogs still sprang into existence regularly, but they also died off at an alarming rate. Of all the ones that had cropped up a year earlier when Jake Watch started the trend, only one of our competitors was still active. One lone blog that had weathered a full twelve months along with us. And that blog veered off topic so frequently it barely qualified as a fansite half of the time.

He was just so damned hard to write about ... Jake, who was aloof and inaccessible and, let's face it, not exactly a font of pop culture input after *Brokeback Mountain*. Coming up with ways to make him seem wholesomely interesting day after day, month after month, was like pulling teeth. Calling Jake Watch fun without putting any qualifiers on it was denying the effort it took to make it work.

Not that there wasn't *any* fun involved. There was still the thrill of coming up with a good idea and then running with it. That was always a good time. Okay, so Los Angeles had been terrible. That was one long weekend. Really, only a day and a half out of that weekend. Out of *months* of other experiences. Any way I looked at it, the good still outweighed the bad, but ...

... how long could I keep going? Susie had been fading for months. Already I feared the day when britpopbaby would check out and I would be left to run the blog alone. I didn't even know if I *could* do it alone. Right then and there, sitting in my car in the parking lot of that restaurant, I decided I needed to do something to save Jake Watch for both of us.

We just needed a source of motivation ...

There are few greater motivators in life than money.

Like most fansites, Jake Watch generated no income. We had a "piggy bank," a PayPal account that people generously donated to for no reason— leading a U.S. PayPal representative to once call Susie in England to ask what kind of racket she was running—but the piggy bank was limited to such duties as buying "I'm Stalking Jake!" buttons in bulk.

Susie, back in Chapter 3, had opened the marketing doors when she designed the first Jake Watch T-shirts. We checked into a few online retailers at the time, but in the end she wound up using a local company in England that required a minimum order of twenty-five shirts. Even in the blog's heyday, it was difficult to find a minimum twenty-five people willing to commit to buying a T-shirt at exactly the same time. And once the shirts were ready, Susie had to hand address the envelopes and stand in line at the post office to mail each individual order to whatever country its owner inhabited. In the end, she didn't even make any money:

"I caused a right scene in the Post Office with my 30 packages to 30 different countries. I think I balanced out at +3 pence or something lame like that," she reported.

It seemed to me that neither the T-shirt idea nor the Jake Watch Piggy Bank was living up to its full potential.

Two weeks after I got back from L.A., I presented my plan to Susie, a plan that primarily consisted of opening an online store and watching the dollars roll in. We already had a built-in base of customers; in fact, we regularly received requests from readers for Jake Watch merchandise. Demand, meet Supply.

"People are practically begging us for stuff," I wrote. "Hell, we wouldn't even have to do much since we've got tons of images floating around just waiting to be put on sellable items."

I had been able to convince myself that this was a venture worth pursuing by rationalizing that the amount of work involved would be minimal. Over the months, I had created many memorable Jake- and Jake Watch-related graphics, so I theorized that the most difficult part of the process was already done. All we needed to do was stick those images onto something that people would pay us for.

Susie didn't take much persuading. "Would we be better going down the sticker/mug route rather than clothing?" she asked. "I mean, definitely have one or two T-shirts for sale but perhaps stick to the smaller things so people buy more?"

A viable suggestion, perhaps, but I was averse to the word "smaller." Oh no, I told her. People will want T-shirts. So we should make T-shirts.

In addition to providing motivation and income, there was a third reason the time was right for a store. Our muse, as you may recall from the previous chapter, was in Morocco filming *Rendition*, and rumor had it he was going to be gone for five months. That was a significant amount of time if, say, one was responsible for a blog of Jake-related content, whose primary audience was anxious fans mourning his prolonged departure from the paparazzi scene. (Actual reader comment: "Why are there no paps in Morocco??? Why?") A major distraction, such as a large and colorful Jake Watch store, filled with brilliantly designed shirts and other paraphernalia, seemed both timely and lucrative.

From conception to reality, the store took one week. But after that week, mere hours before we were ready to unveil our work to the public, the online vendor deleted our entire store. Apparently they didn't want us to use any images of Jake, not even artistic renderings, and they just didn't bother to tell us that until, you know, I'd spent seven freaking days working on it.

Drawing on the knowledge I'd picked up during my one semester at art school, I wrote what I believed to be an extremely thoughtful and legally sound argument about my right to sell my own artwork under the fair use doctrine.

I got an automated response to my protest letter telling me that if I wanted to lodge a complaint I should … write a protest letter.

And by this point, I'm not telling you anything new because we all know what happens when Becky and Susie are blown off in an e-mail: they get really angry.

"Fuck them," I wrote Susie.

"Fuck 'em big time," she wrote back.

So we switched companies. And started over from scratch.

The Goddamned Jake Watch Store, Goddammit

The new company was more difficult to navigate and didn't ship to quite as many countries as the old, but they had no problems with our graphics and, well, what can I say? We had tried the easy way and failed, and now we had a clean slate. There wasn't much we did half-assed, and when it came right down to it, goddammit, this was the Jake Watch Store. The Jake Watch Store needed to distract thousands from the fact that a man was in Morocco for five months. The Jake Watch Store needed to be *spectacular*. Fuck these silly "existing" graphics. If we were going to do this, we should do it right.

Susie: "If we can make more general Jake fan stuff rather than Jake Watch fan stuff, we should shift a load. Can we make a stamp like image of Jake's head?"

Becky: "I'm right with you on the general stuff. Like a *Donnie Darko* shirt that says, 'Grandma Death: Somebody oughta write that bitch.' I'll work on a stamp of Jake's head."

Susie: "We have tonnes to go with! That Grandma Death one is class … We need an 'I was a gay cowboy before it was cool' T-shirt."

Becky: "Ha! I'd buy one of those myself."

Back and forth we went, for days, until we had more ideas than we knew what to do with. Every night for a week, I came home from work and stationed myself at my computer until I went to bed. One new T-shirt design had morphed into two and then four and then six, along with two existing designs, and then there were buttons and bumper stickers and even a mousepad. No question about it, Susie and I had our enthusiasm back.

"Seriously, when can we quit our real jobs and go into T-shirt production full time?" Susie asked as we surveyed our finished store, roughly two weeks after I had proposed the idea. We had never unveiled something this large without any advance warning to our readers. We could barely contain ourselves thinking about their reactions. We *knew* we had done something big.

On March 26, 2007, the Jake Watch Store officially opened for business.[1] We had our first sale by the end of the day.

"I wonder what the order is!!!!" I shrieked to Susie, heady with the thrill of entrepreneurial success. "It's probably like a button or something ... but still! No matter what, we're at least a dollar richer!!"

When our commissions statement was updated at the end of the day, we found out we were actually *three* dollars richer, thanks to the sale of a T-shirt and a package of buttons. We'd done it. We'd made money!

When I asked readers for feedback on which designs they liked best/worst, one reader e-mailed to say she wasn't interested in a Team Gyllenhaal shirt because she thought I'd made Jake look too much like Hitler. You be the judge.

---

1   http://jakewatch.spreadshirt.com/.

And we were going to make more money because our readers were talking among themselves about what they were going to buy and which designs they liked best. That first day, no one was talking about anything but our store. We were a hit! An unequivocal success!

It was too good to be true.

"Watch," I predicted to Susie. "He'll show up tomorrow in L.A. or something."

And guess what? The next day, Jake showed up in L.A. He always did that. Without fail. We'd work on something long and hard, and then he'd pop up in some paparazzi pictures and distract everyone. Moroccan filming schedule or no, having put as much effort as we had into our store, it was inevitable that he would somehow disrupt our launch.

And he did. Like Old Faithful, that Jake. He was nothing if not predictable.

I broke the news to Susie.

"He's back in L.A.? That's just too stupid for words," Susie wrote.

"I'm so annoyed. I say we ignore him for at least today," I replied.

But we couldn't ignore him because he was Jake, dammit, and we were Jake Watch, and since these photos were completely unexpected and came at a time when people thought it would be months before they saw him again, they incited wide-scale bliss. And euphoria. And as if Jake himself was defying us to try to turn our backs on him, he was prominently displaying a pair of very, very white shin-high ribbed running socks.

Damn him.

Susie caved before I did. She put up a Sock Watch at the end of the day.

On the third day, Jake, still in L.A., did something even more destructive to our enterprise. He took some of his old clothes (clothes that reportedly still held a whiff's worth of his cologne, no less) and put them up for sale on eBay for a charity auction.

"To recap," I wrote on the blog, "Jake Watch opens a store and two days later Jake's selling the clothes off his own back."[2]

"For someone who is so patently oblivious to your existence, he sure does have a tendency to follow your lead, doesn't he?" regular reader "Call Me Cherita" noted.

No one could stay focused on our clothes when Jake's were being offered so enticingly. "Not to get too gross on y'all, but I think I'd buy his pee-stained underwear," one commenter wrote.

---

2   http://jakegyllenhaalwatch.blogspot.com/2007/03/jake-decides-to-sell-clothing-too.html.

"I think Jake would smell sort of like apples …," someone else fantasized.

Despite the loss in momentum, sales weren't horrible our first week. Or at least not by my minuscule profit standards. "Holy fucking shit!" I announced to Susie. "Someone placed a HUGE order and we're up to $24.50 in commissions!"

I don't recall if I was legitimately excited to be approaching the $25 mark or if my enthusiasm was just an attempt to revive us as we watched Jake unknowingly wreck our attempts to make money off of him.

Probably a little of both.

More, More, More, More, More

Determined not to let our efforts completely fall prey to cologne-spritzed jeans, I Photoshopped Jake into an "I Was a Gay Cowboy Before It Was Cool" shirt to compete with the eBay story.

Months later, I ran across that very photo on two different blogs. On one, the picture was being used as definitive proof that Jake was not only gay but completely open about it. On the other, the blogger noted how hip and cool Jake was to wear such a thing in public.

Unfortunately, neither claim helped us sell any T-shirts.

As for the gay cowboy himself, Susie had other news, "Did you see Perez? Says he's had it confirmed by a secret source that Reese [Witherspoon] and Jake are definitely on."

Jesus Christ. There was a time when we were checking PerezHilton. com for Jake news? I am so ashamed.

Perhaps more importantly … Jesus Christ. Jake in an unconfirmed relationship with his *Rendition* costar?

Oh God.

Not that I was surprised. The second that casting had been announced for the movie, gossip bloggers had started speculating about the inevitability of the recently single Reese and the not-so-recently single Jake hooking up in a stereotypical Hollywood, met-on-the-set-of-a-political-thriller romance. In fact, the rumors (which we ignored, naturally) were so—what's the word—*boring* that from a purely clinical standpoint, I was disappointed that Jake had apparently succumbed to the predictable.

And in spite of myself, there was another standpoint from which I couldn't help but be disappointed.

"I can't see it myself," Susie admitted.

"I'm not sure I believe it," I agreed.

Denial. It's the first stage of grief.

As mentioned before, The New Girlfriend was unmatched among rumor categories. It alone had the power to invoke elation and/or depression, to make some question their loyalty, to cause others to create new blogs in celebration.

And God help us, we had just proven ourselves unable to distract our audience from socks and (fictional?) pee-stained underwear.

Deep down, I think I knew we were in trouble at that point. I knew that we weren't going to make any money, and I knew that our brand of no-gossip coverage would wither and die as Jake's love life flourished. And I knew Susie wasn't happy but was avoiding talking about it. I wasn't happy either. I didn't want my personal success to depend on a person who didn't know me, but that was exactly the corner I'd painted myself into.

Then, almost as if in response to that very predicament, a reader, out of the blue, sent me Jake's agent's e-mail address.

We'd been seeking an interview opportunity for months already, but seeing as how this was the first time we had the means to formally request one, this is the first time it's popped up in the narrative. For that is precisely what I thought we should do with the agent's address. Use it to ask for an interview with Jake.

Our gingerly constructed request for a Stephen-style Q&A (no personal contact required) went through no fewer than three rewrites before being sent on its way. Susie and I spent hours perfecting the wording, knowing full well that we were going to be denied. "Jake has a massive online fanbase and while this kind of interaction might be unprecedented for him, we cannot stress enough how much it would mean to his supporters," we wrote. And it was true. And we knew for a *fact* that no one on the other end cared. And yet we asked anyway.

Back in the clothing world, business was failing. Miserably.

After Jake showed up in socks, we started getting requests to sell Jake Watch socks. And Sock Watch T-shirts. And after painstakingly working around the Jake Watch brand to create products we thought would appeal to general Jake fans, we found that the requests by and large were for just the opposite. People *wanted* Jake Watch merchandise, so much so that when we didn't give it to them, some of our readers began making their own Jake Watch T-shirts and selling them to each other. It was a nightmare.

Sales tapered off as the days wore on. As did my patience.

"I just saw there [is] no shipping to Israel! Can you fix it please?" (I could not.)

"How come your description says 'Lightweight cotton T-Shirt by Fruit of the Loom,' but when I look at their product at their website, the men's T-shirts say 'Heavyweight cotton T-Shirt'?" (As if I was in any way responsible for Fruit of the Loom's product descriptions.)

"So, is it possible for you to take [this] Jake pic, and grow the width of it from 6.7" that it is now, to the 10.2 inches that [this other] Jake picture is already? The way I thought you could do this is by slicing very narrow strips of the picture off the end and replicating it over and over, 1.63 inches on the left end and 1.63 inches on the right end ..." (And this person was our best customer. By far.)

We made $78 our first week, which averaged out to just over $2 an hour for the work I'd put in. While that was better than the $0 an hour I'd gotten for all the other work I'd put into Jake Watch, I knew there was no way we could sustain that sales rate. I just needed some time to sit back and think about things ...

But there wasn't time. There was never time with Jake Watch. One crisis bled into the next. I had no sooner tallied up our profits for the week than Susie was writing me in a panic: "Shit! Our one year anniversary is like, next fucking week. What the shitting hell are we going to do? I got nothing."

"Basically all we've got is the interview," I sent back, "and that's not exactly the kind of chances of success we want to be banking on. I have no idea. Maybe we should have waited to launch the store."

Jake Watch's six-month anniversary had coincidentally fallen on the day Ramona was born, and what with the birth and far-reaching scandal that followed, our standards for marking the blog's milestones were depressingly high.

Convinced that an interview with Jake was the only event truly worthy of our one-year anniversary, I followed up with the agent, asking if our request had been received. Amazingly, I got a response almost immediately. But it wasn't from the agent. It was from his PR firm. In it, I was rather curtly told that Jake would not be participating ...

Of course Jake wasn't participating. Jake *never* participated. I hadn't expected Jake to participate. And yet I was upset. Like, *really* upset. Upset on a scale that was comically disproportionate to the negligible hopes I had had that it might work out. I actually cried over that stupid e-mail.

It was such a definite refusal, such an ungracious reinforcement of our insignificance. I knew then, unequivocally, that we would leave Jake Watch without giving our readers any sort of interaction with Jake Gyllenhaal. Unlikely as achieving that may have been, until that moment, I hadn't accepted it as unattainable.

I mean, for fuck's sake. He was just some guy. Asking him a few questions hadn't seemed like an unreasonable thing to try for …

Or maybe it was. We (and by "we" I mean mostly "I") would later be criticized for even asking for the interview. Many in the fan world considered Jake far too high above the rest of us to ever talk to his fans. The boldness of our actions was discussed as far away as IHJ: "I don't think someone can just start a blog and get an interview with Jake," a commenter wrote. "The people who do get interviews with A list actors work in TV, magazines, etc. If a blog was all it took I'm sure about 400 new Jake blogs would pop up each day. lol."

It was a common sentiment. People had no idea how hard we worked; they looked at what we'd done in a year and classified it as "just starting a blog." They looked at Jake—who had never headlined a blockbuster, who was still unknown enough in the mainstream that when he hosted *Saturday Night Live* in early 2007, NBC misspelled his name on their website—and called him an "A list actor." And people *did* start Jake blogs every day, but Jake's fanbase was neither big enough nor outgoing enough to ever inundate him with interview requests. Susie and I were almost positive that none of our contemporaries had ever asked. Or ever would ask.

He was held in such high regard that some fans felt he should be defended against people like us: "I've read funny things [on Jake Watch], but in the end, you were making fun of him, so that would explain why you were never granted that interview you were after, that and the fact that actors only give interviews to people in the business, to promote what they do, to reach thousands at once, so I don't think this blog ever fell into any of those categories."

Susie and I ranted endlessly to each other about comments like that. We *did* reach thousands. We promoted what he did every single day. And we did so to a very specific audience: *his* audience, the people who were most interested in what he had to say. There was such a disconnect. Those same fans at IHJ who rolled their eyes at our "naivety" spent hours on their message board coming up with questions to post under the topic "If You Could Ask Jake Anything …"

On another site, which catered to an older audience, I read talk of how Jake would likely never be happy romantically because he would never find anyone as perfect as he was. This was a serious discussion. Among adults.

As time wore on, we were overrun with fans with views like this. Susie and I looked at an interview as a nice, fun thing, for us, for our readers, maybe even for Jake.

But what people saw was the two of us crossing some invisible line, insulting him by asking him to come down to our level. I had personally never experienced anything like that. It was new and unpleasant to have someone tell me I wasn't worthy of someone else's attention. And to have it come from people I worked hard to entertain every day … Disappointing as the expected rejection from his management had been, the reaction from fans hit me like a slap in the face.

Happy Birthday to Us

Jake Watch's one-year anniversary was a somewhat low-key affair, dampened by both the loss of any hope of an interview and the precipitous drop in T-shirt sales after our first week. Business slowed to a halt in the weeks that followed.

> *OH! Has it been a year? It feels like only weeks, nay months, since the good ship Jake Watch left the port of sanity to sail the turbulent seas of online fandom. We've achieved er, little and Jake hasn't been with us for all the ride (fuck you Morocco) but still, we had fun didn't we, chums?*
> —"It's Our Birthday and We'll Photoshop Ridiculous
> Images of Jake If We Want To,"
> Jake Watch, April 3, 2007

And just when it seemed like things couldn't get any worse, Cindy defected and started her own Jake blog.

Cindy, a devoted reader if ever there was one, hadn't mentioned anything in Los Angeles, but in her e-mails to me, she sometimes indicated she wasn't as happy with Jake Watch as she'd once been (join the club, right?). She'd grown weary of britpopbaby's and Prophecy Girl's increasing hostility toward Hollywood and thought of our crackdown on gossip as "censorship."

Jake Watch was not a democracy. Two people did all of the work, and those two people set all of the rules. When Cindy branched out on her own, she was neither the first nor the last to leave us in hopes of creating something better tailored to her own interests.

She *was* the first, however, to experience breathtaking success while competing against us. Dumbfounded by the number of comments she received on her first posts, I inquired about her traffic numbers and discovered, to my devastation, she was pulling in more readers a day than Susie and I were.

I couldn't understand it, because I couldn't understand the person Cindy was writing about. She was writing about some other Jake Gyllenhaal. He was like a god straight out of Greek mythology. He was the embodiment of physical perfection, the zenith of talent among men. His mind was as sharp as his wit, and when he wasn't making the world a better place simply by existing, he was making it better by gracing those around him with his gentle kindness and unyielding benevolence … (I could go on, but I don't want you to throw up.)

All in all, he was a distant cry from the "just some guy" we knew at Jake Watch. "He's not bloody Gandhi," Susie grumbled after reading through Cindy's first few posts.

Cindy's success seemed a mandate on the future of the fan community. That her Jake was preferable to ours spoke volumes about the mindset of the average fan. There was also the great unspoken truth that there simply weren't as many fans as there had been a year ago. Struggling for a long while against a pattern of decreased interest among casual fans and increased intensity among the less casual ones, Susie and I were rapidly losing relevance. People couldn't always find humor in the way we poked fun at their devotion, and while we had a loyal base, it still felt like betrayal to watch the less loyal leave us for greener pastures.

Within one two-month time period, it seemed that everything I touched had fallen apart.

The Day After Tomorrow Never Dies? Bombed.

Trip to L.A.? Disastrous.

Attempt at an interview? Failed.

T-shirt business? Flagging.

Jake Watch traffic? Steadily dropping.

It's safe to say that in April 2007, I hit my Jake Watch rock bottom.

"Why don't you just quit?" my mom asked as I lay crumpled in the fetal position in my parents' living room one weekend.

"I can't go out like this!" I wailed melodramatically.

The "can't" in that sentence was annoyingly literal. I had put so much of my time and my effort and *myself* into the blog that leaving it at the drop of a hat wasn't an option. It was part of me now, and if I was going to walk away, I had to do it on my own terms, and not during a low point.

To tell the truth, I already knew exactly when I was going to quit. I just hadn't told anyone yet. Looking up at the ceiling from the floor in the living room, I spoke aloud something I hadn't admitted even to Susie:

"I'm going to quit after *Rendition* comes out," I said. "I think I should see it through until then, but I can't do it after that. He's not even signed on to do any more movies. What if he moves on with his life and does something else? I mean, who could blame him? He's probably as sick of his fans as I am."

To be fair, I had connected with some incredibly intelligent, thoughtful, and caring people through Jake Watch. Most of our readers were far too normal and kind and supportive to ever garner a mention in this book. Several lifelong friendships developed between people who found each other on the blog, and for many more, the site was a comforting and healthy escape from reality. I knew Susie would not want to continue on her own, and shutting down the blog meant arbitrarily disbanding a community of thousands. It was not a decision I took lightly, and it was for the people who made the work worthwhile that I wanted to keep going.

But there weren't enough of them. I resented the crazy ones and the mean ones, and I resented the constant brush-offs from everyone associated with Jake himself. I was tired of being told "no" or "you can't" or simply being ignored every time we tried something. Sick of half of the people I was writing for and sick of the person I was writing about, picking a stopping date was the only sane thing to do.

And *Rendition* seemed a fair end point. It was the only movie Jake had signed onto since the start of Jake Watch, and there was a certain symmetry in having its release mark the end. That gave me six months.

I could survive anything for six months.

Onward

It wasn't easy going as April progressed. News slowed to a crawl, Susie's e-mails to me got shorter and shorter, and our traffic continued to be diverted to Cindy's blog. In response to systemic apathy, I decided that Jake should run for president of the United States.

I threw together a post, in letter form, informing him of his impending political campaign, and gave him a catchy slogan, "Jake in '08." Lo and behold ... it was a hit!

> *I see only one minor flaw in this scenario and that is that you are not technically eligible to be President. According to lawkids.org, the President must be a) a natural-born citizen; b) at least 35 years of age; and c) have lived in the U.S. for at least 14 years. It's that second qualification that might prove difficult ... Hey, I'd totally be willing to vouch that you were born sometime in the early 1970s. I'm known in some circles to be at least semi-trustworthy. Look, if you don't tell, I won't tell. I really don't think we should let the Constitution slow us down on this one ...*
> —"OMG, I Have the Best Idea Ever!"
> Jake Watch, April 25, 2007

"Is there any age limit on VICE President???" a commenter asked. "Because I think Jake would make a better Vice than a President at this particular time."

I never knew if comments like that were meant to be funny or if the writer genuinely had not understood that what I had written was satirical. Regardless, everyone else loved the idea. New paparazzi pictures of Jake showed up that day, and (if you can believe it) most of our commenters *ignored them* in favor of talking about the Jake in '08 campaign. It was unprecedented. Prophecy Girl even made the short list during the ensuing debate over who should be his running mate.

"Next time I lose all faith in Jakeness, just tell me to do a political post," I boasted to Susie.

Many more Jake in '08 posts followed, by both of us. There were campaign posters and a politically themed MySpace profile. The real presidential candidates for 2008, on both the Democratic and Republican sides, had MySpace profiles of their own, so I spoofed aspects of as many of them as I could. The end result was a MySpace page even more popular than the Jake Watch posts about the campaign. Shockingly, my Jake in '08 profile collected MySpace friends at a rate faster than Boo had in the early days. And then came the T-shirts and the buttons ...

On the days we weren't rewriting the American political landscape, we took on other projects. Susie, in an effort to get to the bottom of a mystery that had been bothering her for months, attacked the disappearance of

Jake's dog Boo. Boo, though still active on MySpace, rather suddenly disappeared from paparazzi pictures late in 2006, and the dog's well-being and whereabouts were of immense concern to her.

"If Jake has dumped Boo, dear God, that would be a serious crisis of faith for me. I've always liked Boo a bit more than Jake at the best of times," she wrote me. In pursuit of the truth, we mocked up a postcard with Boo on a milk carton on the front and a facetious plea to Jake's agency for answers on the back. Both sides went up on Jake Watch, and we asked readers to print them off, glue them together, and mail them.[3]

Dear Mail Opener,
It has been brought to my attention by Jake Watch/counsellor/senator/hot dog vendor that Boo 'The Puggle' Gyllenhaal has disappeared. Where the freakin' hell is he? I'm sending this card because (check one):

☐ A. I am Jake Gyllenhaal. Dude, where is my dog?

☐ B. I had an extra stamp that I wanted to use before postage goes up.

☐ C. I'm crazy. No, seriously.

☐ D. I'm an active member of the International Puggle Federation and I demand to know why our most prominent public representative is MIA.

Signed _____
(real name optional)

Place
Stamp
Here

Jake Gyllenhaal's Fanmail
Department
c/o Creative Artists Agency
2000 Avenue of the Stars
Los Angeles, CA 90067

A few of them actually did.

But that was more of an exercise in being annoying than anything else. (They deserved it.)

It didn't get us any closer to figuring out where Boo was.

"If you didn't know better, would you not think this was Jake Gyllenhaal?" my friend Melissa asked in an e-mail around the time Creative Artists Agency was likely throwing our postcards directly into the trash. Melissa worked for the Pittsburgh Parks Conservancy (PPC) and was

---

3   http://jakegyllenhaalwatch.blogspot.com/2007/05/theres-special-place-in-heaven-for.html.

referring to a photograph that had been used in a 2001 PPC brochure. It showed a man on a bike, and the angle, the helmet, the sunglasses ...

"It's NOT him? Wow," Susie responded when I forwarded it to her.

Carefully omitting any mention that the cyclist in the picture was Jake, I posted the photo as an "exclusive" and asked readers to guess when and where the picture had been taken.

You will ONLY see this picture on Jake Watch. I'm not even joking. Try looking for it. You won't find it. A Jake Watch gold star to the agent with the best guess as to when and where this was taken and how we were able to snatch it.

—"Jake Watch Exclusive!"
Jake Watch, May 19, 2007 [4]

"You cannot mistake those fine calves with anyone else's. They are definitely Jake's!" someone wrote in one of the over one hundred comments we accrued over two days. France ... New Jersey ... California ... the guesses kept coming.

"Bloody hell, he is on the left hand side, err, presence of Fir trees and mountains makes me hazard a guess at Scotland."

"The gloves actually look like they might be the Livestrong brand. I can only guess that this photo was taken somewhere other than Southern California ... he looks gorgeous no matter where it was taken."

One person did quickly express suspicion: "The weird thing is, he's not riding his usual bike, wearing his usual helmet, or even wearing his usual shorts. Something is definitely amiss."

"The bike helmet has been worn before," someone authoritatively protested.

---

4   Photo by Abbie Pauley. Used by permission of the owner, Pittsburgh Parks Conservancy.

Melissa, up in Pittsburgh, laughed for days.

When I finally revealed the truth, a few people came forward to offer their expert opinions ("This guy has bigger thighs. Jake's thighs are slimmer and more muscular and toned.") but for some, the exercise was a devastating lesson in human fallibility:

"There isn't anyone who ever lived who looks like Jake. Jake is absolute perfection. Truly. How could I look at some random picture of some random cyclist and just assume it's Jake??? HOW? I'm crushed. I'm really depressed. This whole experience makes me very sad and uncomfortable. As if I was tested and found wanting."

The person who wrote that comment encompassed quite perfectly what was left of Jake's fanbase a year and a half after *Brokeback Mountain* hit theaters. It was nothing but die-hards.

Well, die-hards and britpopbaby and Prophecy Girl. And those two threw their hands up in exasperation after their innocuous guessing game wound up causing psychological torment.

That was the first and last time we pulled a prank on our readers.

And as for the T-shirts? Sales never stopped completely, so we left the store up indefinitely (it's still there; buy things!). After nearly a year in business, our profits added up to exactly $150.50. The money sat in my PayPal account, untouched, until Heath died. And then we donated it to charity.

Dear Jake,
Just a quick note to keep you updated on your campaign for
Presidential victory …

We've been working on a few ideas, y'know, the usual—
global warming, Iraq War, Paris Hilton—when we thought,
wait! This is Jake Gyllenhaal's election mandate and what
says 'Jake Gyllenhaal' more than STRAIGHT OUTTA
LEFT FIELD. So, we present to you now a proposed policy
we concocted in preparation for the July 4th celebrations:

Friends, Romans, countrymen, lend me your ears:

When in the course of human events, it becomes necessary
for two people to dissolve the creative restrictions which have
bound them to lesser websites and to assume the powers of the
internet, the unified international achievements to which the
Laws of Blogger entitle them, a decent respect to the opinions
of Jake Gyllenhaal fans requires that they should declare the
causes which impel them to reverse the separation as set forth
by our forefathers on July 4, 1776.

Four score and seven weeks ago, britpopbaby set forth
upon this internet a new blog, conceived in jest and dedicated
to the proposition that Jake Gyllenhaal is hot shit.

We hold these truths to be self-evident, that not all men
are created equal, that some are endowed by their Creator
with certain unattainable hotness, that among these greater
men are Jake Gyllenhaal and Jake Gyllenhaal alone. — That
to secure his station as object of our affection, websites are
instituted among men, deriving their just powers from the
consent of the people who read them … [legal crap] … as to
them shall seem most likely to effect their online enjoyment
of Jake's sexy body and stellar acting career.

We, therefore, the Representatives of Jake Gyllenhaal,
assembled under the power of the Google web search, appealing
to the Supreme Judge of the world (i.e., Jake) for the rectitude
of our intentions, do, in the name, and by authority of the
good People of Jake Watch, solemnly publish and declare, that
the united Colonies of America will reinstate Allegiance to the
British Crown under the Rule and Guidance of britpopbaby
(of the Crown) and Prophecy Girl (of the Colonies) so that

henceforth the two nations, conceived in liberty, and dedicated to the proposition that all men are created equal (except for Jake), shall join as one to share duties on the site known as Jake Watch.

That this blog, under Jake, shall have a new birth of freedom, and Jake Watch, as a unifier of the people, by the people, for the people, shall not perish from the earth. A-fucking-men.

Sources: The Declaration of Independence, the Constitution, the Gettysburg Address, Mark Antony's speech from Julius Caesar, *and my ass.*

—"Jake Watch Reverses 231 Years of American Independence," Jake Watch, July 3, 2007

This Chapter Is Basically Just Susie and Me Working through Some Shit

Jake Watch is going back to its roots and by roots, we mean the drunken idea britpopbaby had for an ironic fansite after spending a night on the beach with Liquid Cocaine, not what actually made it on to Blogspot originally. Honestly, some of you may not like it, others will love it.

—"The All New JW.com Means Business,"
Jake Watch, June 1, 2007

Spiraling toward Entropy

Susie kept starting new blogs.

Really, I couldn't blame her. We were all starting to lose it. First Jake was in Morocco. And then he wasn't. And then we didn't know where he was. And the readers were freaking out over Reese. And I was melting down in my parents' living room.

And Susie was just going stir-crazy.

Throughout the first half of 2007, she spent a lot of time on new blogs. She'd create them, write a few entries, and then walk away from them. Sometimes she didn't even get as far as writing anything; she'd stop after she created the layout. Usually I was involved in some way, but none of them lasted long enough to turn into true joint projects.

I think she resented the fact that none of her other ideas had the success of Jake Watch.

"We are TALENTED, BABY! And Jake Gyllenhaal is holding us back," she wrote to me. She was always on the lookout for stories of other bloggers—who weren't writing about Jake Gyllenhaal, who weren't working half as hard as we were, but who were getting book deals and/or making six figures in advertising revenue.

The cruel irony was that none of Susie's other ideas attracted an audience the way Jake Watch did. She was stuck with Jake as long as she cared about her hit count, and now that our hit count was dropping, she felt trapped by him. MTV contacted us about hosting an ad on our site, saying they'd pay us a flat rate for every click we gave them. But the ad was only up for two days before MTV yanked it, citing poor traffic as an excuse.

So, yeah. No ad revenue for us.

Susie once told me in an e-mail that not even in the early days did she consider herself a "fan" of Jake's. I didn't understand that until I watched her try out different blog ideas and then drop them, one after another. If Jake Watch hadn't experienced the instant popularity that it had, I have no doubt she would have dropped it too.

Except it *was* popular, and she hadn't dropped it, and now, over a year later, it had taken on a life of its own. It was successful enough to make it tough for her to walk away from, but not successful enough to always justify the energy it took to keep it going.

So she kept looking for something else. First came the blogs, but there was also a website design business, an online entertainment magazine, and a host of blogging alter egos that were used once, twice, or sometimes not at all. None of it got off the ground. No one was interested. And in between new ideas, she worked on perfecting old ones. She changed the look of Jake Watch every few months, sometimes just tweaking it, but more often than not completely overhauling the design. We went through no fewer than nine layouts in nineteen months. Twice we went through a prolonged design process but the finished product didn't make it to Jake Watch because by the time she settled on what she wanted, she'd moved on to the next thing.

I never forgot that the blog was her creation. I was only where I was because she'd allowed me in, so I yielded to her even when I was happy with the way things were. The constant changes were frustrating and exhausting, and yet I understood them. Jake Watch was one of the few things we had control over in our lives. We didn't know where we were going. We weren't in school; we weren't looking to get married. We were in our midtwenties and we needed to pay the rent, so we got up every morning and went to mundane office jobs where we made copies and typed letters.

And then we came home at the end of the day and got to be different people. We were people who were well-known and well-loved and had a whole community following our every move.

As mentioned before, Jake had been dropping more than a few cryptic hints during this time that he was contemplating exploring his options outside of acting. When I was feeling really self-indulgent, I'd imagine that I understood where he was coming from … because he, too, was in his midtwenties and knew what it was to play a role for people and seemed to be wondering what came next. I also imagined he might have an idea of how intoxicating popularity can be, and how it's easier to think about walking away from something than to actually do it.

So in June, when Susie wanted to yet again redefine the blog, I offered her my support. We would keep writing as britpopbaby and Prophecy Girl, but she also wanted to introduce a new cast of characters that we could write under. She wanted fewer but better posts, and, of course, the blog would get a completely new design.

The banner I made for the top of the page was my greatest artistic work to date. I Photoshopped Jake's head onto the bodies of The Beatles, Marilyn Monroe, and a few other famous people (caricaturing our regard for him as the most important celebrity in our world), stuck the word "Jake Watch" at the bottom, and set it all against a white background. It was perfect. It was the best thing I'd ever done.

Or at least I thought it was.

Susie promptly sent it back to me, hacked to pieces, and told me it needed to go on a gray background.

And I snapped.

I don't remember when it was that I stopped trying to relate to Jake Gyllenhaal, but he never seemed more irrelevant than when Susie and I fought over that banner.

Becky: "I know this is late in coming and I should have just flat-out said it after the last design fiasco, but the reason I waited so long to even start on this design is because I spend SO MUCH TIME creating this stuff and nothing I do is ever good enough! Not a SINGLE banner that I designed has gone up on JW exactly as I gave it to you. Not one … I feel so incredibly out of control 95% of the time … I feel like the escape I was getting via Jake Watch has just turned into another portion of my life where I can never do anything right."

Susie: "I feel like I do consult you on everything I do but you have to tell me if I've done something you don't agree with or aren't happy with. And I'm sorry if I fly about the place with ideas but I'm trying desperately to get my enthusiasm going again and it's just the way I work … My job bores me to tears but also manages to be taxing and poorly paid, all my best mates are away at Uni … I never thought of JW as the one area of my life where I had some control and power but now you've pointed that out …"

Becky: "I mean, if you think about it, it's amazing we've accomplished as much as we have speaking only via e-mail and we're on the same track so much of the time that I really do enjoy most of the stuff we've done."

Susie: "You're right, we do spend so much time communicating that I forget I've never met you and you're perhaps not fully aware of my idiosyncrasies and vice versa."

In the end, we did what we always did. We compromised. The essence of the piece stayed the same, but Susie got her gray background and she rearranged my celebrities. I never liked the end result, and I'm not entirely sure she did either.

And that was the last time we redesigned Jake Watch.

Through a much less emotional process, we also changed the subtitle of the blog that June. We went from "Jake Watch: Well Somebody Has to Keep a Damn Eye on Him" to "Jake Watch: Stalking Jake Gyllenhaal Daily," an ironic title since a passerby was less likely to find accurate information about his whereabouts on our blog than any other Jake site on the internet. Not to mention we no longer updated daily.

Alas, not everyone understands irony.

We always had a fair number of anonymous commenters dropping by to announce they were going to New York or Los Angeles and asking if we would tell them where they could find Jake. As if we knew. As if we would tell if we did. The inquiries, which we usually deleted, increased with the name change.

I would get irrationally angry at those people, nobodies who dropped into the comments section and expected us to give them directions. Interrupting us to demand answers. I hated that. I especially hated when they asked where he lived. *As if we knew. As if we would tell if we did.* I had no idea where the hell he lived.

Until one day, I did.

Meet Marcia

Marcia had e-mailed me a few times before, but that summer, between postcards and presidential campaigning, she and I struck up a regular correspondence. She liked *Buffy the Vampire Slayer* and Jake Gyllenhaal, so the two of us got along great.

I first knew of Marcia because of the role she played in a story from the previous summer. In August of 2006, she went to Stephen's poetry reading in Martha's Vineyard, the one Jake had gone to. She came back with the astonishing information that Jake had a large tattoo down his forearm. It was a word, but she couldn't make out the lettering.

News of Jake's tattoo spread quickly across the internet. When Susie heard, she scrounged up a picture of him with his forearm exposed, typed "britpop" on the photo in an Old English font, and posted it on Jake Watch as a joke.[1] Somehow her photo wound up on IMDb, and for a while, there was a raging discussion over there about who this "britpop" was, why Jake had tattooed her name on his arm, and if she was his new girlfriend. A short time later, a paparazzi picture of Jake surfaced with the tattoo visible but almost completely worn away. It had been a temporary one.

We called that controversy "Tattoogate."

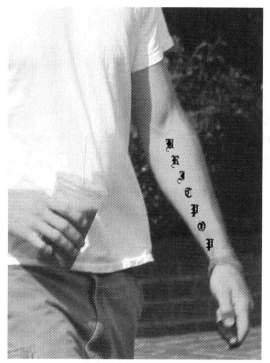

People thought this picture was real. People will believe *anything*.

---

1 http://jakegyllenhaalwatch.blogspot.com/2006/08/to-be-honest-im-little-disappointed.html.

Jake Watch was not Marcia's Jake site of choice, but she was a reader during the Tattoogate era, and she stopped by to personally describe the tattoo to us in as much detail as she could, prior to the pictures of it showing up. After the revelation that it was fake, she faded back into obscurity. It was close to a year later that she started writing me regularly, initiating contact by sending me the news that Cindy had just started a blog.

Marcia always had information. She also flew a bit under the public radar, saving most of her opinions for private messages. She knew more about Jake than most anyone else I knew, save Cindy, and she knew something that no other Jake fan that I knew of did: she knew where Jake lived. She also knew where Heath Ledger and Michelle Williams lived, and where Jake's parents lived, and where Maggie Gyllenhaal and Peter Sarsgaard lived. And she was *very* careful about whom she told.

There were a couple of Gyllenhaal residences that were relatively well-known within the fanbase. I knew of two girls who staked out the family's summer home just for the hell of it, fleeing only after an oblivious Stephen walked out the door. ("SOMEONE EXITS THE HOUSE. Who is it? Oh, just mothereffing Stephen Gyllenhaal. I FREAK out and start RUNNING …") The other parental abode, in Hollywood, was practically a staple of Gyllenhaal tourism. I'd even been invited to meet up with someone in L.A. just to scope out that house. (I politely declined.)

But Jake's house? He spent half his time on the East Coast and the other half on the West, and God only knew where he stayed in either place. As with so much in Jake's life, it was the *not knowing* that drove people crazy. It wasn't just fans, either. A relatively well-known gossip columnist once wrote Susie and me, asking us to spill what we knew: "Do you know if he lives in SoHo or the West Village? Or another NYC neighborhood? The door he's been going into the last few days must be where he lives, right? So at least the paparazzi know where he lives, you think?"

I told him, quite honestly, that we didn't know where Jake lived. And that fact remained true even after one reader sent me more than one multiple-page Word document deconstructing paparazzi photos in an attempt to locate his house.

Marcia had taken a much more practical, public, and legal route to find the answer everyone sought. I never came right out and asked her, but I suppose I seemed trustworthy enough because by the next time somebody asked me where Jake lived, I was lying when I said I didn't know (on one coast, at least).

"Are you going to go to his house?" Megan asked me during a morning run. I felt a bit burdened by this new knowledge and wanted to share it with someone outside the bubble.

"God no!" I said. "This just makes it easier for me to send people in the wrong direction if they come too close. Jesus Christ, I'd never go to his *house*. I'm not an *actual* stalker."

Susie and I had a list of people we thought might be actual stalkers. I'd asked Cantara one time if we should tell someone about it. "Your stalker list is probably accurate, but who would listen?" she replied. "I mean, Jake's PR people?"

Point taken.

Marcia was not on our stalker list.[2] By no means. On the contrary, I respected her greatly for having the information that she did and being so selective in her dissemination of it. By the end of the summer, she was one of my best e-mail buddies. I halfheartedly mentioned to her that I had been thinking about going to New York for the *Rendition* premiere to maybe see if I could atone for the *Zodiac* trip, and she tentatively agreed to come along with me if I went.

But long before any such trip could take place, I was back in New York anyway as a result of my real job. In July my boss sent me to a business conference there. The conference was at the end of the week, but if I stayed the weekend …

Becky: "Dude, you know what you should do? You should fly to New York the weekend of July 14–15!"

Susie: "July 14–15? Might be workable!"

It turned out it was workable. Susie and her friend Anneka[3] made arrangements to be in New York City for a week, and their first weekend overlapped my stay. It would be our first face-to-face meeting and Susie's first trip to the United States.

Meet Susie

I flew into New York on a Wednesday evening. Susie and Anneka were due in on Thursday, so the three of us made arrangements to meet for dinner

2   No one mentioned in this book was on that list. Our tolerance for bizarre behavior was exceptionally high, and it was only the genuinely creepy who caused us any real discomfort.

3   Anneka was the unofficial third Jake Watch writer. She wrote a few movie recaps for the blog, though she never quite got into Jake the way Susie and I did.

on Thursday night. After a day of meetings and note-taking, I planned to skip out on the company group dinner and rendezvous with them in the lobby of my hotel at 5:30. At promptly 5:25, I dropped myself into a chair in the lobby and started watching the door.

Five thirty came and went.

Ten minutes passed.

Twenty. Thirty.

After forty-five minutes, I went back to my room to see if I had received any messages. I hadn't. I thought that perhaps they had gotten the time wrong. Or maybe I had. Maybe they'd be here at six thirty ...

An hour passed. An hour and a half.

At the two-hour point, I called the hotel where Susie and Anneka were staying and found that there were no reservations under either of their names. Something was very, very wrong.

"Did she set you *up*?!" my dad roared. I had both of my parents on the phone, and I doubted that Susie would have survived an encounter with either one of them at that moment.

"I don't *know*!" I cried, already reaching my quota to shed tears at least once during every Jake Watch–related trip. "I don't understand what happened! No, she would *not* set me up. I trust her. I just don't know what to think right now."

My parents tried to convince me to call the airline and switch my ticket so I could come home the following day. I called Kara next.

"Did she set you *up*?!" Kara asked, only slightly less furious than my parents.

"I don't think so," I said, tears slowing.

I went through the story a third time with Crystal. Crystal had, since my last trip to L.A., moved to Washington, D.C. I tried to convince her to come up for the weekend so I wouldn't spend a lonely two days in the city by myself.

"Becks, I want to so bad," she said, "but I just don't have the money right now. I can't find a job, and I'm going through my savings trying to pay my rent ..." She launched into a story about her search for employment, but I wasn't focused enough to give her the proper level of sympathy.

"Crystal, I'm really sorry, but I can't talk about this right now," I told her, and then I abruptly hung up. I checked my e-mail. I ordered room service. I half watched *My Name Is Earl*. I checked my e-mail again.

As a last resort, I posted a desperate plea on Jake Watch asking if anyone could verify that Susie was coming to New York that weekend. I also wrote a friend of hers on MySpace and asked for Susie's cell phone number. It was the middle of the night in England, and I wasn't even sure her phone would work in America (if she was, in fact, in America), but maybe I'd at least have a number to call in the morning.

"How do you even know she is who she says she is?" my mom had asked me.

I didn't know, although I couldn't bring myself to believe that she had deceived me. I had to admit that the nonexistent hotel reservation was suspicious, but I was sure there was an explanation. I must have misunderstood where they were staying ... but if that was the case, I was left with the unsettling option that she had intended to meet me, but something had gone wrong. Distraught, I shut myself in the bathroom for a long, hot shower.

When I got out, I had a message.

"It's from Susie," the man at the front desk reported. "She said her flight was delayed, and she'll meet you at the same time and same place tomorrow."

Oh, the relief.

I had to call everyone back. Then I had to take down that Jake Watch post because Susie and I had agreed to keep our meeting a secret ...

"Is that all she said?" I interrogated the front desk man. "Did she leave a number or anything? Where is she staying?"

"No, just that she'll meet you tomorrow at the same time and place," he repeated.

"Thank you," I said. I hung up. Then I called him right back.

"You don't have caller ID or anything?" I said. "I mean, I just want to know where she called from."

"I'm sorry, ma'am," he said, "she just said she'd meet you at the same time and place tomorrow."

Placated, I made all the necessary calls. I replaced the post on Jake Watch (which had gotten no comments—I couldn't know how many people had read it, but it hadn't been up for long, so hopefully not many), and then I crawled into bed and slept.

The next morning, I was up bright and early for the last of the business conference. The day before, since I was attending alone, I had seated myself at random. By the sheerest of coincidences, the woman in the seat next to me turned out to be the sister-in-law of my academic advisor in college. I sought her out the next morning as we gathered for breakfast. I must have looked pretty bad because the first thing she did when she saw me was ask if I was all right.

I'm not usually one to tell my life story to (almost) strangers over breakfast, but I gave her an abbreviated version of the night before, leaving out the part about crying into a grilled cheese sandwich while watching *My Name Is Earl*. I hedged when she asked me how I knew Susie. "Um, we write a blog together," I said, leaving it at that.

She hesitated and then shook her head slightly. I knew what she was thinking. She was thinking the same thing my parents had thought, the same thing Kara and Crystal had thought … this is what happens when you try to meet someone you befriend on the internet.

"Are you sure she's really here?" she asked, nothing but honest concern in her voice. Suddenly I was tired of telling this story, tired of trying to explain the stupid duality of my life. I couldn't even work up a proper defensive tone because I was sure I'd be asking the same questions if she was saying to me what I was saying to her. "I'm meeting her this afternoon," I promised her. Then a speaker walked into the room, and the conference started for the day.

I was done at noon. I had made reservations for the rest of the weekend at the hotel where I thought Susie and Anneka were staying, so I checked out of the first hotel and hailed a cab for the trek away from downtown Manhattan. At the front desk of the second hotel, I again asked after reservations in Susie's and Anneka's names. Again I was told there were none.

I trudged upstairs, luggage in tow, into a dismal room with a window unit blocking most of my view of the cement wall ahead. I cleaned up a bit and then got ready to go back to the first hotel to wait in the lobby for Susie and Anneka to show up. I took out a map. It was sixty-three blocks. I had absolutely nothing to do. I might as well start out now and just walk. I put on my shoes, checked to make sure I had my key, opened the door, and …

… the phone rang.

"Becky?" Susie's reassuringly British voice asked from the other end.

"Where the hell are you?" I demanded in response, still a little emotionally raw.

She was three floors above me. They were staying at the same hotel after all, but the reservation had been under Anneka's name, and her last name had been misspelled in the register. When the two of them came down to my room a few minutes later, I filled them in on the trouble I'd had trying to locate them. They explained that when they'd checked in, the woman had had some difficulty recognizing Anneka's name, presumably because it was misspelled, but apparently she hadn't corrected the error.

I expressed my relief that everything had worked out but stopped short of telling them how upset I'd been in light of how mildly they were reacting to my story. From the few months I'd lived in Ireland, I knew from experience what it was like to be confronted with hysterical Americans after immersion in the European lifestyle. In the best interest of everyone involved, I took a deep breath, calmed myself down, and asked what the plan was for the rest of the day.

We agreed to go out and find something to eat, and they ran back upstairs to get ready. In their absence, I made my final round of phone calls.

"So what's she like?" Kara asked immediately.

"I don't think I know yet," I replied.

Of all the people in my life at that time—family, friends, co-workers— the only person I talked to every single day of the week, often multiple times a day, was Susie. We used to joke that we were the Lennon and McCartney of the Jake Gyllenhaal blogging world. She was John and I was Paul. Even if one of us had done all of the work on a particular project, we always referred to the end result as a joint venture. "We" did this, or "we" did that. But prior to that trip to New York, I'd never really thought about how little we talked about our lives outside of Jake Watch. We were completely engrossed in the world that we had created and were constantly pushing each other to go further, come up with something better … but whenever we talked about the real world, it fell flat. It was strange when we finally met face to face. What were we going to talk about if not Jake Watch?

And we didn't talk about Jake Watch. Who wanted to while we were free for a couple of days in New York City? We were on vacation, from the internet as much as anything else. The three of us simply hung out for the next two and a half days. We saw *Harry Potter and the Order of the Phoenix*; we wandered Central Park; we went to the Natural History Museum; we didn't talk about Jake or Jake Watch until it was almost time for me to leave, and even then we only talked about how we'd avoided those subjects. We did race by Heath Ledger's house in Brooklyn (courtesy of Marcia's real estate prowess), stopping nearby to eat and joking that we were dining at his favorite restaurant. "I'm sure he comes here all the time!" Anneka snickered. But that was Heath, not Jake.

Before I'd left, I'd written Susie to say, "It'll be weird to hear you with a British accent. When I read your e-mails, it's always the voice in my head, which is distinctly American."

She'd replied, "I know, same here. I keep thinking this isn't a big deal because we know each other so well but then I remember we've never actually met. And just so you know, you're British in my head."

There was an ease to that exchange that we never quite matched in person. She was more soft-spoken than I'd imagined her to be, and less excitable. We took one picture together the whole weekend; it was of the three of us standing outside the Natural History Museum. The passing tourist we asked to take it stood far enough away that our expressions are barely discernible. In the shot, Susie and I are standing a bit stiffly on either side of Anneka. We don't look like britpopbaby and Prophecy Girl. We look like two girls who barely know each other.

I thought Susie might have a list of things she wanted to do in the city, but she didn't. She was quiet and mellow, as was the pace of our sightseeing. After the drama and intensity of Jake Watch, the way in which we wrung every ounce of opportunity from the most menial things, it was surreal to be out in the world and taking it in slowly. It wasn't just the pace; the snappy comebacks, the harsh language, the entirety of how I was used to communicating with Susie didn't translate in real life.

It was as if we didn't have that other portion of our lives, the one that explained how we knew each other. I talked to Susie more frequently than any other person I knew, and yet when it came right down to it, she was practically a stranger to me.

We didn't tell our readers about the trip. We had stopped posting on weekends weeks earlier, and no one noticed our absence, much as no one noticed Susie's absence when I took over the writing upon returning home, while Susie and Anneka remained in New York the rest of the week. Not long ago, it would have been impossible for her to disappear for an entire week without a single inquiry as to where she was. But things had changed.

Though I'd been expecting it, I still dreaded the topic Susie confronted me with once she was back home. "I have about as much interest in Jake as I have in my toaster right now," she told me.

She wanted out. Effective immediately. Meeting me, coming to the U.S.—that was as far as she was looking to take her Jake Watch experience.

"If you did walk away, I'd try to make it until *Rendition*. I've kind of had *Rendition* in my mind for a really long time," I responded.

And from those humble beginnings spawned the worst fight we ever had.

I had my ideas; she had hers—when to quit and how to quit. She was more ready than I had realized. She was ready right then to simply stop posting. I argued that under any circumstances, I wanted to at least give our readers a little warning.

Becky: "I don't have this general loathing for the people that visit our site, and I feel like every time I turn around, you've got another complaint about the readers in general. I almost feel that since the 'new' JW,[4] you've been trying to sabotage the site to give you an out."

Susie: "Fine. What do you think should happen then?"

Becky: "I don't know; I don't have some grand master plan."

Susie: "I'll have to re-evaluate the whole thing then."

We wound up leaving it open. I would continue; she would pitch in when she could. But the floodgates were open, and as we brainstormed on how best to move forward, all of our frustrations poured out, starting with the more recent …

Becky: "Maybe the T-shirts are all shit, or maybe no one really gives a fuck about Jake enough to wear a shirt, or maybe we should have just listened to what people repeatedly asked for and made fucking Jake Watch shirts and then we'd have actually sold something."

And then going back to the earliest days, when Susie was flying solo …

Susie: "One of the Jake Secrets read 'I was raped when I was 15. If it had been someone like Jake, it wouldn't have been so bad'. You think JW is the best place for screwed up shit like that? We're not psychologists or counsellors. Which is why I consider 'writing jokes about Jake Gyllenhaal' a lot bigger, a higher priority, than maintaining an outlet for the emotionally unstable who seem to have invested themselves into Jake Gyllenhaal to act as a barrier to the real world."

Becky: "Well, this should have been the conversation we had when we met because it would have been a lot easier to talk this out …"

---

4   Since the design change and the new subtitle.

Our war-weary bickering was a long overdue acknowledgment of the fact that neither of us had known what we were signing on for when we started. But even when we were snipping at each other, there was still an underlying camaraderie. We were the only two who understood what it really took to keep our site running. It was grueling. "I'm just sick of changing everything all the time," I wrote. "It's too much effort to change; it's too much effort to have to go looking for Jake crap."

We settled on November 1 as our official end date.

And then we pressed ahead as if we hadn't just fallen apart backstage. Our readers never knew.

Three months now.

The Doldrums

Sometimes weeks would go by with nothing to write about. My posts from that era are strange. Desperate. I was lucky to get one in every other day and rapidly fell behind Cindy, who unfathomably came up with nothing short of an essay seven times a week.

In August, Susie went to the Chester Zoo where she had, so long ago it seemed, adopted the red panda for Ramona. She took a picture of the plaque with Ramona's name on it and published it on the blog.[5] Cantara saw the post and promised to pass the picture along to Stephen, thus presumably closing the chapter on that part of the story.

And then Susie lost her internet connection for a month. She attempted to switch providers and in the process wound up with nothing at all. I don't think she minded that much, considering the timing. A few days a week, she would drive her laptop to a corporate parking lot to snag a wireless connection long enough to e-mail me, but other than that, I was completely alone.

At the end of August, I received another blow when, without warning, MySpace deleted my Jake in '08 profile. Weeks of effort expunged from existence for seemingly no reason.

"Can NOTHING go right?!??" I railed to Susie in an e-mail I didn't know when she'd get.

When I asked MySpace for an explanation, I was told I needed to submit a salute.

---

5   http://jakegyllenhaalwatch.blogspot.com/2007/08/anti-climax-of-year.html.

A salute. You know? From Chapter 9? The thing that MySpace used to confirm the identity of celebrities?

Jesus Christ God Almighty, I'd been deleted for *being a Fake Jake.*

Me! Of all people!

I wrote angry letters, I screamed in protest, I even turned in people who were *actually* impersonating Jake (to no avail), but there was nothing I could do. In the end, I had to accept the inevitable.

Jake in '08 was gone.

Never before had failure been such a pervasive part of my life. Everything I did with Jake Watch seemed to fall apart. Everything. The blog felt like some twisted metaphor for my young adulthood; it didn't matter how much I worked, I never seemed to be able to move myself forward.

Before the month of August had ended, the Jake world learned that *Rendition* would be premiering at the Toronto International Film Festival in September, a full two months before its theatrical release in the United States. Jake was going to be there (it was confirmed this time) and I thought, *Fuck it. Fuck every stupid thing that's happened to me. I'm going to Toronto, and I'm going to meet Jake Gyllenhaal.*

I even had someone willing and ready to go with me. Marcia and I sat down at our computers, hundreds of miles apart, early on a Saturday morning, and waited for the magic moment when tickets for *Rendition* went on sale.

Marcia got stuck in a perpetual loop of waiting and refreshing, and by the time she got through, the film was sold out.

But for once in my life, luck was with me. I didn't have any problems at all.

"I GOT TWO TICKETS!!!!!!!!!!!!!!!" I reported back to her.

"OH MY GOD!!!!!!!!!!!!!" she wrote back.

We were going to Toronto.

The other day, some commenters were talking about the lack of, well, commenters lately and there seemed to be a consensus that interest in Jake is dwindling in these dry news days. [Regular reader] bmg had the last word, saying, "It's all Zac Efron these days. Or so I'm told."

Being the type to philosophize on the heavy issues, I took this statement to heart. Is Zac Efron really taking over as pop culture's It Boy? Or is the lack of post material so overwhelming that we are reduced to creating entire posts out of comments that even other commenters have ignored? It was time for a Jake Watch Investigation.

My first stop was the vital information provided by my set of "Heartthrobs of the Aughts" Jake Watch premiere trading cards:

From this, I was able to deduce what elementary visual analysis had already told me: Jake is taller.

This wasn't enough to go on, though. I was forced to sit down and draw up a comprehensive list of everything I knew about both individuals and then compare their attributes in a highly biased manner. My results:

Primary Audience:

Zac: People younger than Zac (and PG—tell no one!).

Jake: People older than Jake (and PG).

Winner: Jake. Age and wisdom go hand-in-hand, duh. Plus, the lack of shame.

Awards:
Zac: *Young Hollywood Award, Teen Choice Award.*
Jake: *Young Hollywood Award, BAFTA, Oscar nom, MTV Movie Award for Best Kiss, a bunch of other stuff.*
Winner: *Jake. For the Best Kiss thing, of course.*

Official Site:
Zac: *None. (Edit: Oops. Apparently he does have an official site but I can't look at it or else I'd have to change the winner.)*
Jake: *This mess. [Linked to official site.]*
Winner: *Jake, by default.*

Singing Credentials:
Zac: High School Musical 1 *& 2;* Hairspray
Jake: *One failed* Moulin Rouge *audition and an SNL skit in drag.*
Winner: *Jake, but only because I'm making Jake the winner in all the categories.*

Dancing Credentials:
Zac: *See above.*
Jake: *The Santa Dance [from* Jarhead*], the* Donnie Darko *Production Diary Dance [from the special edition DVD], and This Dance [a fan video of Jake backstage at a concert].*
Winner: *Jake, because nothing defeats the Santa Dance.*

Rumored G-fri:
Zac: High School Musical *co-star Vanessa Hudgens.*
Jake: Rendition *co-star Reese Witherspoon.*
Winner: *Jake, on account of being man enough to date someone more famous than he is.*

Internet Gayness Factor (numbers subject to change on a daily basis):
Zac: *996,000 hits on Google.*
Jake: *900,000 hits on Google.*
Winner: *Well, hot damn. Zac has more results than Jake? I'm forced to ruin the winning streak and give this one to Zac.*

Becky Heineke

Likelihood He'll Be Mistaken For a Girl:
Zac: 65%
Jake: 0%
Winner: Jake.

What's Next:
Zac: Footloose: The Remake
Jake: President
Winner: Hail to the chief!

Final Tally:
Zac: 1
Jake: 8
Draws: 1

In conclusion: Sorry World Consumers of Pop Culture, but you are wrong! Zac Efron is not as wonderful as Jake Gyllenhaal. My highly scientific method of comparing the two has shown that Jake is at least 7 times better. AND he's taller!

And as for my own question … turns out yeah. This was definitely all done because there's no news …

—"Examining the 'It' Factor of Two Male Popular Culture Icons In Accordance to the Arbitrary Standards of One Internet Community," Jake Watch, August 22, 2007

Toronto? Oh, Wow. Okay.

Hey Jake ...

...I mean, no pressure or anything, but I'm starting to get embarrassed at how well you're avoiding me. Give me a picture, let me introduce myself, say, "Jake Watch?" in a voice feigning familiarity (it doesn't have to be real ... you're an actor!) and I will be one happy camper.

—"Hey, Jake."
Jake Watch, August 29, 2007

Getting There and Day One

My boss's daughter lived in Toronto. My boss handed me her cell phone one day at work and excitedly told me her daughter was going to be in town the first night I was there and that the two of us should get together. Her daughter, four years younger than me, squealed into the phone, "Okay, I work until five, but this new person just started, and he's sort of, like, scared of me or something because I always boss him around, so I can basically just tell him, 'Hey, I'm leaving work,' and what's he going to do? I mean, I've been there longer than him, so it's not like he's going to fire me, even though he's, like, my boss. So when do you get in?"

I told her around noon.

"Okay, so I can totally take you around the city and stuff if you want, and then my roommates and I usually go out on Thursday nights, so we can go to a club or something afterward."

It all sounded great, aside from the fact that I was now faced with the task of having to explain to a relative stranger that, whatever our plans, I would be accompanied by a woman (Marcia) whom I had never met and whose age I did not know. It seemed rather foolhardy, though, to get into such details while I was using up my boss's international cell phone minutes. So instead I hung up, got online, and found her daughter's MySpace profile.

In January of that year, when Jake hosted *Saturday Night Live*, I left a party early to live blog the show for Jake Watch. I had cleared this in advance with the hostess, a very good friend of mine, in hopes of making a quiet exit, but as I made my way to the door, she called out to me, "Becky, if you're going to leave, why don't you explain to everyone where you're going?"

It was like a scene out of a bad movie. All conversation ceased, and everyone in the room turned to look at me.

"Um, I'm going home to watch *Saturday Night Live*?" I coughed out, feeling the full force of the lame-itude of that answer.

"Who's hosting?" someone yelled out.

"Jake Gyllenhaal," I said.

Clearly deeming Jake unworthy of my departure, someone else asked, "Well, who's the musical guest?"

"The Shins," I said.

"Are you a big Shins fan?" yet another unfamiliar voice asked.

"No!" my friend interjected. "If she's not going to tell you, then I will. There's this Jake Gyllenhaal fan club, and Becky's, like, the president …"

I know she didn't purposefully try to make me sound like a nine-year-old, but I would be lying if I said her interpretation of my Jake Watch duties wasn't mildly humiliating.

"Ugh! Thanks for making it sound so fourth grade!" I huffed as I flounced out the door, sounding suspiciously like a nine-year-old.

As it turned out, the party broke up early anyway. The hostess called me during the Weekend Update segment of SNL to apologize and to congratulate me on Jake's above-average hosting abilities ("Becky, he's doing *such* a good job!"). But the fact remained that discussing Jake Watch with people I didn't know made me nervous. Participation in most online ventures comes with a set of stigmas that those outside of friends and family aren't likely to overlook. Eight months after that party, I had yet to explain my involvement to someone new without cringing through my description.

Which is precisely why it took me a good twenty-four hours to think through my note to my boss's daughter (let's call her "My Boss's Daughter"). To my surprise, her reply came quickly. My Boss's Daughter assured me she had absolutely no problem with me stalking celebrities, and if Marcia was weird, we could just ditch her. (Easy for her to say. She wasn't sharing a hotel room with her. I was pretty sure I would be ditching clubbing before I ditched Marcia.)

I shot a relieved response back, confirming our plans, and set out on the much less daunting—though equally important—mission of explaining My Boss's Daughter to Marcia.

Again, my worries were unfounded. Marcia, it seemed, was thrilled with our prospective plans.

I flew into Toronto on Thursday and found myself in the customs line behind two elderly women, also in town for the film festival. They had been on my flight from Memphis and engaged me in conversation after twenty minutes passed and our position in line had not changed.

"Are you in town for the festival?" one of them asked me.

After responding affirmatively, I was questioned on which movies I would be seeing.

"I've only got a ticket for *Rendition*," I said, "but I'm hoping to see some other things while I'm here."

"Oh, I don't know which movie that is," the other woman said. "*We're* going to see the new Meryl Streep movie tomorrow night."

The new Meryl Streep movie was, in fact, *Rendition*.

"Yeah! That's the movie I'm going to!" I said. We then talked a bit about what it would be like to attend the screening.

"Do you think Meryl will be there?" the first woman asked breathlessly.

"Oooooh, wouldn't that be *something*!" the other said.

When the stars are in attendance at a screening at the Toronto International Film Festival, the event is referred to as a gala. I would not have been standing in the customs line in Toronto, Canada, that Thursday morning if the *Rendition* screening had not been listed as a gala. I told them as much.

"I just *adore* Meryl," the second woman reiterated. "Who else is in the movie?"

"Reese Witherspoon, Peter Sarsgaard, Jake Gyllenhaal ...," I listed off. "I'm pretty sure Jake will be at the gala."

"I don't know him," the first one said, looking to the second one for help and finding none.

The women, it turned out, thought that since we were on the same flight and were going to the same movie the next day, that I must be a fellow participant in their Smithsonian tour group. They offered to share a taxi with me to the hotel. But once it sunk in that I was there as a free agent, and that I really did only have one ticket to see one movie ("Just one? Really?"), we ran out of things to talk about. Eventually, the line started to move, and we politely agreed to look for each other the following evening.

It just so happened that the three of us had accidentally placed ourselves in the line for non-English speakers, and that accounted for our long wait. Close to an hour passed before I made my way out of customs and up to the baggage claim. For the sake of convenience, Marcia and I had timed our flights to arrive at roughly the same time. I fully expected her to be waiting for me, but with only one headshot to go by, I wasn't quite sure who I was looking for. After scanning several unfamiliar faces, I gave her a call and found that she was in a different terminal.

"Just start walking toward me," she instructed.

I was barely out of my own terminal when I noticed a woman in sunglasses frantically motioning me from a snack counter.

"Come here!" she hissed.

I looked around to see if she was talking to someone else. She smiled as I turned back to face her, so I jerkily made my way in her direction.

"Yes! You! Come here!"

She took two bottles of water off the counter, handed me one like we'd been friends for years, and off we went so she could smoke a cigarette. That was my introduction to Marcia.

Marcia seemed younger than I'd imagined her, but the cigarette caught me by surprise. I impolitely winced when I realized she was lighting up, a gesture I knew she caught because she started backing away from me. And that was Marcia's introduction to me.

After a perfunctory smoke, Marcia marched over to the cab line and snatched us a ride. We chitchatted for a few minutes, and then she whipped out her cell phone and called Shelley. I had no idea who Shelley was, but I pretended I did because I could tell from the phone conversation that Shelley was a Jake fan, and it seemed like a failure on my part not to be familiar with my constituents. Gazing out the window, I half listened as Marcia and Shelley talked a bit about Jake. And then some more about Jake. And then a lot more about Jake. And then we were at our hotel. I hoped like hell she hadn't booked us a smoking room.

She hadn't.

I took a long deep breath of hotel air-conditioned air as we entered our room and then dropped my bag on the bed nearest the window. "Do you care which bed?" I asked. Marcia mumbled she didn't, already distracted by her attempts to figure out the internet connection. Ten frustrating minutes later, she gave up, and the two of us chose instead to tackle the more immediate concern of finding something to eat.

It was around two when we found ourselves on a patio across the street, drinking cocktails and toasting the weekend ahead. Through another drink and our lunch, we talked about this and that: Whether we would meet up with Cindy (rumored to be making the trip to the festival herself). How I didn't have a Southern accent. How warm the weather was in Toronto …

We didn't talk much about Jake.

After polishing off my lunch, I announced that I was going to call my mom to check in. "Let her know you're all right," Marcia said knowingly. "Let her know I'm not some weirdo."

I smiled at her understanding, but was surprised when she took the opportunity to call her own mother, presumably to give her the same assurances. She talked to her mom longer than I talked to mine.

"I just called My Boss's Daughter," I told her once she'd hung up. "I left her a voice mail, but she said she'd take off work to give us a tour of the city, so I guess we can just wait until she calls back."

We ordered more drinks. Marcia smoked a couple of cigarettes while holding her arm at an unnatural angle so I wasn't in the line of smoke. I studied her, trying to figure out her age. I narrowed it down to somewhere between thirty-five and fifty-five and decided it didn't matter enough for me to ask. An hour passed, and My Boss's Daughter never called.

Sensing that our tour of the city might not materialize, we decided to walk down the street to pick up our tickets for *Rendition* and scope out the building where the gala was going to be held the following night. We had chosen our hotel based on its proximity to the theater where *Rendition* was going to be screened, and a conveniently short walk later, we found ourselves outside the theater and in front of a tent.

Inside the tent was a line for people with prepaid tickets. It was warm outside, but it was hot in the tent. Hot enough that Marcia opted to wait outside after we discovered the computer system was overloaded and the wait was going to be substantial. Thirty minutes later, feeling the weight of both the alcohol consumed at lunch and the oppressive heat from inside the tent, I stumbled back outside with our tickets in hand. Marcia was sitting in the shade beside a large schedule of the weekend's events. I silently sank down next to her.

"I kinda wanna see *The Assassination of Jesse James by the Coward Robert Ford*," I said five, maybe ten minutes later. "If we can get tickets, that is. But I've hardly heard of any of these ..." I flung my arm vaguely in the direction of the film schedule.

Marcia nodded, took a look at the schedule herself, and then we resumed our silent stupor. An indefinite amount of time passed and then ... then we were approached by a woman with a microphone.

"Can I ask you a few questions?" she asked. Marcia and I both looked up.

"Yes!" I yelped, my energy rushing back. I could sense the potential for plugging Jake Watch, and also I'd never before been interviewed by a woman with a microphone. The possibilities were quite electrifying. She was already getting her equipment in order, pressing a couple of buttons, thrusting out her microphone and ...

"Where are you from?" she asked.

"Memphis!" I said.

"Wow, you came all this way for the festival?" She was very close to me and flashing an unnaturally white set of teeth as she jerked her head up and down quickly, nodding her encouragement. Her proximity to me and the closeness of the microphone to my mouth made me feel self-conscious and, in my distraction, I started ending every one of my responses with "so, uh, yeah ..." and then trailing off.

"Yeah, I'm really excited. This is my first film festival, so, uh, yeah ..."

"What movies are you here to see?"

I began and ended my list by saying, "*Rendition.*"

She paused, perhaps expecting me to continue, still smiling and nodding all the while.

"Is that all?" she asked after a moment.

"Yeah, I'm really looking forward to it! So, uh, yeah ..." Her nodding was contagious. My head started to move up and down. Up and down.

"And who's in it?"

"Jake Gyllenhaal, Reese Witherspoon, Peter Sarsgaard ..." Up and down.

"So you like them?"

"Really, I'm just here for Jake. I'm a Jake Gyllenhaal fan! So, uh, yeah ..."

I really hope that the radio station in question has destroyed the tape in which I exuberantly chirped, "I'm a Jake Gyllenhaal fan!" because even as the words were leaving my mouth, I was thinking, *Why are you saying this? You sound like a goddamned idiot.*

It was a short interview.

"You did really well," Marcia said after the woman walked off. She was nice to lie to me. At least Marcia had had enough sense to ask the interviewer who she worked for and when the interview would be on the radio (the following morning between six and nine). I had just stood there, my stupor returning full force.

But seeing as how we were no longer sitting down, Marcia and I took the opportunity to walk the perimeter of the theater. We easily found the red carpet; it was already in the process of being set up. But as I surveyed the scene, my heart sank. Even in the early stages of preparation, I could tell that the red carpet would be across the street from the corral set up for fans. How strange that all those months ago in New York, I had assumed this type of setup was typical. Kara and I had been so nervous about being "allowed" to stand close to the carpet. And now? This was the only chance I was going to get, and I was going to spend it fenced off, quarantined with a thousand other people. Security was one thing. Security, I understood. But it was another thing altogether to confront the cold truth that as long as I was lumped into the category of "fan," nothing I had done, nothing I ever *could* do, would deem me worthy of standing on the other side of that fence.

It was fucking depressing.

But instead of wallowing in the inevitable, I suggested to Marcia that we go back to the hotel and wait for My Boss's Daughter to call. We got no farther than the ticket tent before we were stopped again. By the interview lady.

"Can I ask *you* some questions this time?" she asked Marcia, probably hoping Marcia was more socially adept at talking than I was.

"No," was the blunt reply.

Perhaps trying to soften her up a little, the interviewer asked Marcia when Jake's movie was going to premiere and I, not willing to let this second opportunity pass me by, jumped in with, "It premieres tomorrow, and I run a website for him!"

"For Jake?" she asked, a tad incredulously.

"Yes!" At my confirmation, her eyes lit up. Out came the microphone. Out came my bad interviewing skills.

"Yeah, I run a website for Jake Gyllenhaal, so, uh, yeah ..."

"So …" Even the interviewer didn't know where to go from there. Seizing the opening, I blurted out, "I'm trying to meet him! This is my fifth try, and I've never met him!"

I had not tried to meet Jake five times, of course. That was a lie. It was actually a lie I told on Jake Watch before arriving in Toronto, but that was Jake Watch. The whole point of Jake Watch was not to take me seriously. But on a national radio show people were probably going to take me seriously. And it wasn't even a good lie because it made me sound even more like a lunatic than I actually was. The interview wrapped up quickly after that, and the woman left.

I stood shell-shocked in the shadow of the ticket tent until Marcia finished her cigarette and again mentioned heading back to the hotel. She didn't bother with false flattery the second time around. We walked in silence, me replaying the interview in my head in horror until I realized that I hadn't given my name. Nor had I given the name of my website. Maybe no one would know it was me! I turned to Marcia.

"We need to get the internet up and running when we get back to the hotel," I said.

The internet situation involved a couple of calls to the front desk, but once I was able to check Jake Watch, I posted a comment asking our Canadian readers to listen the next morning for my interview. My theory (proven correct) was that no one outside of the Jake Watch community was reading Jake Watch comments. I hoped to avoid widespread mockery by alerting only the people who were least likely to make fun of me in the first place and trusting they would let me know what sort of damage control I was looking at.

But ultimately, it was all for naught. The only listeners I could account for were a couple of readers who streamed the program live from the internet and recorded it to their computers. A few hours of dedicated listening later, I was told my open confession to stalking Jake Gyllenhaal never hit the airwaves.

At least I hope it didn't …

More of Day One

At our hotel, the internet problems did not end with our initial connection. My laptop refused to work, which left us sharing Marcia's computer for the duration of our stay.

She patiently waited her turn while I dealt with the interview situation and then waited some more while I dealt with a second interview situation. Canadian *National Post* reporter Vanessa Farquharson had written an entry on her blog about the film festival and casually (and I do mean casually) mentioned that she would be interviewing Jake the next day, so if any fans had questions for him, she'd try to work them in.[1]

Poor Vanessa. There she was making a flippant aside, and next thing she knew, her comments section was infiltrated by crazy Jake fans. In every inbox I had, there was at least one e-mail frantically alerting me to her offer.

Much to my personal pride, a few of the inquiries left on her blog were about the Jake in '08 MySpace profile. So I wrote her an e-mail, explaining who I was and how much deep personal gratitude I would owe her if she chose to slip a Jake in '08 question to Jake. Then, satisfied with my dealings with the press for the day, I handed the computer back to Marcia.

I'd barely made it across the room to grab the television remote when she waved me back over to her screen.

"Do you want to see Jake's house?" she asked.

"Er, okay," I said halfheartedly. I didn't want our Jake-related vacation ruined by too much Jake talk. But I also wanted Marcia and me to get along. I supposed I could humor her on this one topic.

She pulled up a series of Google Earth images in various stages of magnification. I could tell immediately that we were looking at Los Angeles and was a little disgusted at myself for it.

"There it is, right there. And here it is a little closer. And there's his pool," she pointed out, putting her hand over her heart. "And that's where his parents live, over there. And see here," she pulled up a wide shot, "is where Heath lives."

I was relieved of my obligation to respond by the ring of my cell phone. My Boss's Daughter. At last. "She must have finally gotten off work," I said to Marcia (who was still enthralled by the aerial view of Jake's house) as I answered the phone.

"Well, I sort of slipped at a bar last night and hurt my leg, so I didn't go into work today," My Boss's Daughter drawled. "But we're still going out tonight if you guys want to meet up with us."

I explained that Marcia and I had talked it over at lunch (which we had), and we were not only tired from the trip, but would probably be

---

1 http://greenasathistle.com/2007/09/06/jake-gyllenhaal-gets-two-pages-max-day-190/.

getting up early the next morning. "Why don't you meet us somewhere for dinner? There are a lot of restaurants over by our hotel," I suggested.

Long pause.

"I gotta talk this over with my roommates. I'll call you back."

Click.

I snapped my phone shut and sat for a moment, analyzing her weird tone at the end of the conversation. I looked over at Marcia, giddily squinting at the screen as she zoomed in on Jake's house, and it suddenly became very real to me that I was never, *ever* going to go on another one of these trips again.

It would be over a year before I spoke to My Boss's Daughter again, but not knowing, at that juncture, that she wasn't going to call me back, I sat on the bed watching TV for two hours while Marcia looked at pictures of Jake on her computer. She murmured things like "Hi there, baby" and "You are so handsome" while stroking her monitor, clearly not caring that I was watching her. (What's a little laptop groping between friends?) I tried to focus on the TV as Marcia continued to chatter away. I was only half listening.

" … when this really good friend of mine had sex with [male cast member of *Buffy the Vampire Slayer*]."

"What?!" I shouted, shifting my focus from the TV back to her.

"Oh, yeah," she said. "She had sex with [male cast member of *Buffy the Vampire Slayer*]."

"She had *sex* with [male cast member of *Buffy the Vampire Slayer*]!?"

Marcia nodded rapidly, a smug smile on her face.

"*Sex!?*" The volume of my voice had risen to an alarming level.

"Mmm hmm," Marcia said, still nodding. "Twice."

"*Twice!*" I yelped. "You mean, like, in the same night!?" (As if it mattered.)

"No," she said. "On two different occasions." (Well, maybe it did matter.)

"She had *sex* with [male cast member of *Buffy the Vampire Slayer*] on *two separate occasions!?*"

"Yup." More nodding.

"*Oh. My. God.* Start at the beginning and tell me everything." I sat rooted to the bed. Not that there was another option. I couldn't have moved if I'd wanted to. When someone tells you that her dear friend had sex with [male cast member of *Buffy the Vampire Slayer*] it is physically impossible to do anything other than sit still and hear that story out.

And hear it out I did. Mistaking my speechlessness for admiration, Marcia explained how she and her friend had met [male cast member of *Buffy the Vampire Slayer*] at a *Buffy* fan convention and through a series of circumstances that were not wholly remarkable, this led to sex, and then more of it at a second fan convention. She sat back triumphantly. Story over. My mind was immediately filled with memorable scenes from *Buffy the Vampire Slayer* featuring said cast member. And oh God. They were totally weird for me now. They were going to be weird for me from now until forever. And Marcia was still talking.

"So if you run into Jake, you *don't* want to play the fan card. [Male cast member of *Buffy the Vampire Slayer*] didn't even know she was a fan. You gotta act like you're not nervous or anything."

Aha. So *that's* why she told me the story. To give me advice on picking up Jake in case we happened across him in a scenario conducive to a one-night stand. Had hell frozen over and no one told me? I closed my eyes and mentally envisioned my goals for the weekend and … nope, they were still just to say the words "Jake Watch" to him and maybe get a picture. I was all about aiming low.

"Hey," I said. "I don't think My Boss's Daughter is going to call me back. So, how about dinner?"

Yet More of Day One

Over dinner there were more drinks and some preliminary plotting for tackling the next day, Friday, which would likely be our only chance to meet this Jake guy we'd all heard so much about. Marcia didn't seem particularly anxious, and I wasn't used to drinking quite so much alcohol over the course of an afternoon and evening, so I wasn't anxious either. Actually, considering my past excursions, I had already accepted failure as a near certainty. I'd seen the red carpet setup. I knew our chances weren't great even without my perennial bad luck weighing us down.

As we ate, Marcia asked me about the other trips I'd been on, and I groaned when I recounted my excursion to Jake's high school a year and a half earlier.

"God, I would *never* do that now!"

"Why not?" she asked, obviously surprised.

"Because it's creepy and weird, and I'm totally embarrassed that I ever did something like that," I said.

"Why? You shouldn't be," she said. "There was nothing wrong with that! I remember reading your story, and it sounded like you had fun."

I had had fun. But it wasn't that cut and dry. Sometime between my defense of Sex and the City Girl in New York and my dinner with Marcia in Toronto, I'd made a 180-degree turn. The longer I was exposed to other people's strange behavior, the more paranoid I had become that my own behavior was strange. Going to that school seemed weird in hindsight. Then again, in the very early days, I wouldn't have been embarrassed to announce to a roomful of people that I was going home to watch SNL, and I wouldn't have freaked out at a restaurant when someone used the word "obsessed."

But now I knew, intimately, the ins and outs of the fanbase. And with that knowledge came an ever-increasing desire to distinguish myself as different from the people I wrote for. It didn't matter that the outside world had no idea what it was like inside the Jake one. *I* knew. The more time that passed, the more careful I'd become about what I said, what I did, and whom I told. I didn't want *anyone* to lump me into the generic category of "Jake fan," because I knew those people, and those people were fucking weird.

But I wasn't about to get into it that deeply with Marcia.

"I don't know," I said. "I guess I just wouldn't care enough to go to his high school at this stage of the game."

And that was true too. Thankfully, the conversation moved on.

Back in our hotel room, I was prepared to go to sleep, but Marcia made a beeline for the computer. A substantial period of time later, she asked if I wanted to check anything. I almost told her just to turn it off, but then thought better of it.

"Have you checked Cindy's blog lately?" I asked. She hadn't. I figured if Jake had made it to the city of Toronto, Cindy was the most likely person on the internet to know about it. And it was pretty much a statistical certainty that her response to finding out such information would be to blog about it.

Yawning, I propped my head up and opened up the browser … clicked … typed … and holy shit. "Son of a *bitch!*" I said, loud enough to catch Marcia's attention in the bathroom.

Jake was in the city, all right. And so was Cindy. In fact, Cindy knew that Jake was in the city because Cindy had seen him. Personally. Walking out of his hotel. She'd been in the city less than a day, and she'd managed to find out where he was staying, stake him out, see him, and then write a blog about it.

First point to Cindy.

Marcia shook her head in disbelief as she looked at the screen over my shoulder. "Where is that picture from?" she asked.

"It's the view out of her hotel window. I guess she didn't get a picture of Jake, but I can't *believe* this!" I said. "She *knows* I'm here, and she didn't bother to e-mail me or anything?"

I left Cindy a comment on her blog. And then I left her a voice mail message. And then I wrote her an e-mail. It was probably the most stalker-like conduct I exhibited during my time with Jake Watch.

I reflected out loud that I hadn't been in contact with Cindy much lately. Marcia conspiratorially theorized that she was avoiding us because she wanted Jake all to herself. "She's probably going to try to get an interview with him. I'll bet you anything," she said.

Having the experience that I did in trying to arrange such a thing, I knew that was about as likely to happen as me having a one-night stand with him at some point during the weekend.

"Is she really thirty-five?"

"Huh?" I stopped scowling at the monitor long enough to look over at Marcia.

"Cindy—is she really thirty-five?"

Cindy? Thirty-five?

"Cindy? Thirty-five?" I asked. And then I started laughing because I thought she was joking. But she wasn't laughing with me.

"She's ... not ... that," I said, no longer smiling. "I guess there was a *time* when she was thirty-five ..."

"I wasn't sure," Marcia said. "She's been telling everyone that she's thirty-five, and Shelley and I didn't really believe her." She walked back to the bathroom, still talking. Thirty-five!?

"Hold on!" I heard from the bathroom. "Let me see that picture again!" Marcia was suddenly back at the computer, pulling up websites and working Google Earth.

"I'll be damned," she muttered.

"What?" I asked.

"She's staying at the hotel where the press conference is going to be tomorrow," she said.

"What press conference? There's a press conference?"

Marcia swung around to give me an exasperated look. "Yes, there's a press conference! They do press conferences for the movies before they premiere. The one for *Rendition* is going to be at the hotel she's staying at."

How did she know? How did Cindy know? Why did I *not* know? And how the hell had Marcia figured all that out from one picture out of a hotel room window?

"When's this press conference?" I asked.

"I don't know," came the mumbled response. "Sometime tomorrow."

"Then we'll be at that hotel first thing tomorrow morning," I said with certainty. Hot damn. If there was a press conference, maybe we would see Jake *there*. That sounded much more promising than that idiotic red carpet setup.

"I'm turning this light off, all right?" I said.

"Yeah, I'm just going to check a few more things," she said.

I crawled under the covers, and a few minutes later threw a pillow over my head. Still mumbling, clicking, and typing, Marcia didn't leave her computer for a long time.

Day Two

The alarm went off at six thirty. *The Assassination of Jesse James by the Coward Robert Ford* was premiering the following night, Saturday, and I had been advised at the ticket tent the day before to come back the morning of the showing to see if any seats were available. Marcia had somehow misinterpreted this to mean that we should be at the ticket tent the day *before* the showing, and I did not correct her. I had known Marcia less than twenty-four hours and had already guessed that it was going to take her a very long time to get ready in the morning. I went along with the *Jesse James* misunderstanding in hopes of getting her out of the hotel before noon.

What I didn't anticipate was her need to check the internet the second she rolled out of bed, which prolonged the getting-ready process. That morning, not only were there new paparazzi pictures of Jake arriving in Toronto, but in those pictures he was wearing wings.

"*Oh my God!*" Marcia yelled. "That is the most adorable thing I have ever seen! Oh, baby, you are so *cute!*"

I peeked over her shoulder and, sure enough, stuck on Jake's shirt was an Air Canada pin. You know, like the wings they give kids when they visit the cockpit? Dammit, even I had to admit that was cute. Sort of. Marcia was touching the screen again, so I moved away to give her some privacy.

I got dressed, sorted through my luggage, fired up my own laptop, determined I still did not have internet access, and all the while Marcia was still stroking her monitor.

"Do you think they took him up to the cockpit?" she said. "Or maybe he got them from one of the flight attendants?" I mentioned something about maybe getting ready to go, and she answered, "Yeah, yeah, yeah. In a minute."

We later learned that one of the flight attendants on Jake's plane was none other than the boyfriend of a very prominent member of a well-known *Brokeback Mountain* fan community, so there was a lot of detail floating around the internet about Jake's flight. I cannot confirm that the boyfriend was the one who gave Jake the wings. I can confirm that the boyfriend procured a personalized autograph, which in and of itself is a rare and treasured thing for a Jake fan.

People talked about that flight for weeks.

When Marcia finally vacated the desk, I darted over to quickly check my e-mail. To my annoyance, Cindy had not e-mailed me back. To my delight, Vanessa from the *National Post* had. She warned she wouldn't have a lot of time with Jake, but she'd try to ask him as many fan-written questions as possible ... and Jake in '08 was at the top of her list.

"No way!" I screamed, prolonging our departure a little longer by luring Marcia out of the bathroom.

"Vanessa wrote me back! And she was nice to me! And she said she'd ask about Jake in '08!" I reported to an impressed-looking Marcia. "That's the first time anyone I've written hasn't ignored me or totally blown me off!" Marcia congratulated me on my victory and went back to getting ready.

While I waited for her, I flipped through the free magazine sitting on the desk ("Where: Timely Information for Travellers," Toronto edition) and ran across a two-page article/advertisement for *Rendition*.

I hadn't brought anything with me for Jake to sign. The last time I'd thought about autograph possibilities was before my second trip to Los Angeles. Prior to the *Zodiac* premiere falling through, Susie and I had come up with a formidable list of potential autograph items (packages of socks, *Bubble Boy* memorabilia, that sort of thing). She'd almost talked me into having a full-sized *Day After Tomorrow Never Dies* movie poster printed up when the news broke that Jake wasn't going to be there ...

This time around, I hadn't given it any thought whatsoever. I dug around in my purse and found the unused Sharpie I had bought for Robert Downey Jr. I threw it back in my purse and stuck the magazine with it.

Good enough.

Thirty minutes after we should have been at the ticket tent, we left the hotel. "Oh, no one's going to be out there this early!" Marcia said. If I'd actually thought we might get tickets and/or hadn't just been told Jake in '08 would be in a Canadian newspaper, I might have argued that point. As it stood, I dismissed the comment and pushed through the lobby door, out into the cool Toronto morning.

We'd gone less than a block when my phone rang. It was Cindy, at last acknowledging the garish number of messages I had left her. I turned to confer with Marcia, and the three of us agreed to meet at Cindy's hotel for breakfast. Having completely forgotten the pretenses under which I had dragged Marcia out of bed, I made a motion to go back toward the hotel to get a cab.

"Aren't we going to get tickets?" Marcia asked, confused. Right. I dutifully led the way to the ticket tent, asked a vendor about availability, and got the response I already knew I would, that we should come back the next day.

I had no sooner walked out of the tent when my phone rang a second time. This time it was a Canadian Jake Watch reader by the name of Alice.

Alice was a longtime supporter of our site but somewhat of a mystery to me. She once sent me an e-mail regarding my use of the term "America" in reference to the United States. "Do you have any idea what that does to a Canadian???" she wrote. "I must tell you that America is two Continents, there is South America, and then there is North America." I preferred to think that she was being at least semi-facetious in her e-mail, but one can never be completely sure about these things.

Because Alice and I had been in e-mail contact for the past few days, I knew that she hadn't been able to get a *Rendition* ticket in advance. Her plan was to call the ticket office that morning. If she managed to secure a seat for the premiere, she would drive in to meet us later. As it turned out, she was successful, snatching a ticket around the same time Marcia was massaging the Air Canada pin on Jake's chest. Her phone call was to give me the news, and it was the first time we'd spoken in person.

"Hi, is this Alice?" I asked as I answered the phone.

"PG?" Alice said. PG. She wanted Prophecy Girl.

"Yeah! Hey! How are you?" I said.

Alice paused before saying, "You don't have a Southern accent."

"No, not really," I said slowly, noting that now she and Marcia both had brought this up. Remembering Cantara's strange questions in New York about fashion and Halloween, I was beginning to notice a pattern of clichéd expectations of me from those living north of the Mason-Dixon line.

"Why not?" she demanded. "I'm disappointed because I thought you'd have one." I silently gave her credit for openly admitting her disappointment. And for addressing the issue so early in our conversation. I looked around for Marcia, but she'd wandered off to smoke a cigarette.

Alice then asked about the plan for the day, at which point any lingering assumptions she may have had about me went out the window. I was so good at being Prophecy Girl when there was a computer in front of me. But two minutes into a phone conversation with another fan, and it all fell apart. I admitted I had no idea what we were doing or where we were going, and that I was just following along behind people more competent than I was.

"There's a press conference, I guess. Or something. And then the premiere is afterward, maybe? I have no idea what the hell is going on," I told her. As expected, my lack of knowledge took her by surprise, and there was a heavy silence. When she didn't say anything, I asked if I could call her later in the day, when I knew more.

"Oh, wait! I don't think I can!" I corrected myself. I'd had to use an old international calling card to call Cindy, and I was nearly out of minutes. "I don't think my phone plan covers international calls. Uh, can you call me?" She said she would. I then apologized for being entirely unhelpful when it came to everything ever.

Day Two, Continued

Marcia hailed us a cab, confidently telling the driver where we were going. As in Los Angeles, Cindy had given me her room number, so when we arrived at her hotel, we dodged the press gathering in the lobby (*Rendition* was but one of many movies hosting a press conference there that day) and made our way up to her room. I knocked a few times before Cindy peered out cautiously and then broke into a wide grin when she saw who was at her door. We exchanged good-to-see-yous and hugs, and we moved inside.

Before the door even shut, I could see that I had made a grievous and irretrievable error in bringing Cindy and Marcia together. Because we hadn't been in the room more than five seconds and Marcia (who had never met Cindy) was asking, "Did you see *the pictures?!*"

And Cindy (who recognized a kindred spirit when she saw one) laughed. "Yes! And he's wearing *wings!!*"

As simple as that, the entire weekend shifted. I was powerless against it. From here until the end of this overly long chapter, my behavior will be that of a petulant third wheel, for that is exactly what I was.

Cindy was already on her laptop, pulling up the photos, and Marcia was standing behind her, giggling appreciatively, and I, watching the alliance form between them, yelped, "Do we know when the press conference is?"

Neither of them even looked up. "It won't be until later," Marcia confidently assured me.

I looked at the clock. It was well past nine already.

"But what if it isn't?" I said. "I mean, what if it's going on *right now* ..." I left the sentence unfinished. What if I missed my opportunity to meet Jake because we were sitting in a hotel room looking at pictures of him on the internet?

Marcia was the first to look up when the silence turned uncomfortable. "We'll go and check it out," she said. She pried herself away from the photos, and Cindy followed suit a few seconds later.

I was wearing flip-flops, but planned to wear something a little nicer to the premiere later that evening. "Do you mind if I just leave these here, so I don't have to carry them around all day?" I asked Cindy, dropping a pair of sandals on the floor.

"Oh, that's fine," she said. "I'm sure we'll be back here before the premiere."

And out the door we went.

We found the press area with no trouble. The atmosphere was busy but unhurried, and the doors to the interview room were still open. It appeared that the interviews hadn't started yet, though judging by the suffocating number of photographers and reporters, they would soon.

"We need a schedule," I declared, looking around for someone to ask. Marcia shot me a look rife with skepticism. Cindy was already backing out toward the lobby. "We'll come back later," Marcia said, and she started pushing her way through the crowd in the direction Cindy had gone.

The next thing I knew, the three of us were outside, standing on the sidewalk.

"Do you want to go to breakfast?" Cindy asked.

I looked back and forth between the two of them and wondered what had just happened. Weren't we here to see Jake? And why were those two dictating all the rules here?

I spun around and sprinted back toward the door. "The worst they can say is no! I'm asking!" Cindy reluctantly (and at a slower speed) followed me. Marcia took a smoke break.

I found the woman with the schedules quite easily. "I'm sorry, who are you with?" she asked. Damn her.

"Well, I'm not an official member of the press, but I'm covering the premiere of *Rendition* for a blog," I said. Cindy walked up beside me and said, "Me too."

"Thousands of people are waiting on our reports," I added.

The woman smiled the tight smile of a person who is not paid enough to deal with inquiries from bloggers and informed us that if we wanted a movie schedule, we could go down to the gift shop.

"Well, thank you, but what we're looking for is an *interview* schedule," I said.

"You can buy a *movie* schedule in the gift shop," she said. Tight smile.

Taking our cue, we turned and walked toward the door. "I didn't think …," Cindy started, but just then we were approached by a hulking Australian with a camera around his neck.

"I couldn't help but overhearing. Who is it that you want to see?" he asked.

"We want to know when the *Rendition* press conference is," I said, and I thanked him prematurely for his help. He shrugged off my gratitude and flipped out a small notebook. He started paging through it.

"Who's in that?"

"Jake Gyllenhaal," I answered.

"Don't know him. Oh, here we go. Two thirty. I don't know why they're so secretive. They're such jerks to the fans here. What do they think you're going to do?"

"I know, right? Like, who else is going to see these movies?" I said. I thanked him again, and we were back outside before Marcia finished her cigarette.

"Two thirty," I told her. "We have plenty of time. *Now* we can go to breakfast."

We ate at Jake's hotel. Cindy showed us where she'd seen him the night before, pointing out the doorway he'd swept through twelve hours earlier.

"How did you know where he was staying?" I asked, watching her carefully.

"Just luck," she sighed. "Really good luck."

I didn't find that to be a particularly satisfying answer.

The hotel's café had an outside patio strategically located by the door, so that's where we sat. I ordered the cheapest thing on the menu, a plate of three muffins that were no bigger than a quarter in circumference and came on an enormous plate that seemed to be mocking me with its expanse of empty space.

"Oh, God! I'll die of hunger before lunch!" I whined when I saw what I'd wound up with. Marcia told me I could have her waffles.

"No ...," I said.

"I'm not hungry," she insisted.

During our meal, no one of interest walked out of the hotel, or by the hotel, except the two elderly women from the non-English-speaking customs line the day before.

"Hey! I know those women!" I told Cindy and Marcia. I waved as they walked by. They didn't see me.

"Well, we were on the same flight," I said as we watched them walk across the street. "They thought I was part of their Smithsonian tour group." That assumption seemed even more ridiculous now that it was apparent I couldn't even afford to buy breakfast.

After we ate, Cindy led us back to her hotel, though not, as I had expected, back to the press area. Instead, she took us to an adjacent street. Photographers swarmed a side entrance to the building, and a short red carpet led from the curb to the doorway. I asked Cindy if this was where the celebrities entered the hotel.

"Yeah," she said. She looked over to where a fan was standing on the sidewalk. It was Carol. I knew this because Cindy pointed at her and said, "And there's Carol!" Whoever the hell Carol was.

Carol's daughter Jan was there too, and I was introduced to them as if I should have known in advance that other people would be joining our party. We stood across the street, parallel to the excitement on the other side, and Jan, who was around my age, asked me, "Are you here for Jake too?"

I nodded, "Yeah."

"Yeah, my mom is too. I don't get her thing with him *at all*."

"Really? Then who are you here for?" I asked.

"Today? Whoever I can see. But I'll go home happy if I see George Clooney this weekend." And then she walked off before I had a chance to respond.

Carol hit me next. She cracked a joke about the security team by the rope line being run by Jake Watch. She must have been a reader then.

It was nothing against her personally, because she seemed very nice, but I effectively shut down the second she mentioned Jake's name. I couldn't do it. I couldn't be Prophecy Girl for her. It was too much. All of this was too much. All I wanted was the same stupid, impersonal fan experience that Jake gave everyone.

I was so goddamned close to getting it too. If he would just show up already … I could put all of this behind me. I could walk away from Jake Watch proud because, at long last, I would be able to say that I *hadn't failed*. All I needed was for him to get here. And then I would never have to do this again. I would never have go out in the world and pretend for other fans.

Ally had quit IHJ not long before this trip, leaving her site in the hands of a more than capable replacement. In the hotel the night before, Marcia had shaken her head and told me, "She's young. Her interests are going to change."

Or maybe, I thought, maybe she just got tired of putting up with everyone else's shit. Maybe she was tired of doing a thankless job. And maybe I knew more about Ally's decision than Marcia did. Because for all intents and purposes, I was young too, and my reasons for frustration were a lot more complicated than just growing out of an interest.

I'd had my fill of opinions, and I really wasn't interested in entertaining yet another person's ideal vision of Jake. So after a short conversation with Carol, I decided it was probably for the best if I stood away from the group for a while.

Day Two Finally Gets Interesting

They all left me alone to glower in peace.

I watched as a line of black SUVs circled the block. It was several minutes before we solved the mystery of who they were waiting for. Jodie Foster and Terrence Howard, leaving a press conference for *The Brave One*, stepped out of the hotel and spent a couple of minutes signing autographs for the people on their side of the street. Not thinking, I stepped into the road with my camera to try to get a picture. And for the second time in my life, I was bellowed at by a security guard to get back on the sidewalk.

The celebrities left, and I continued to stand away from the group, watching a new set of SUVs (or were they the same ones?) make perpetual loops around the building.

Alice called to ask where we were. And not long after she called, she arrived, ambling up the sidewalk and (God bless her) wearing a Jake Watch T-shirt.

She made the rounds, introducing herself to everybody. Alice was the right age and seemed to be integrating into the group well enough, so I left her to it. Even Jan didn't look sick of the Jake talk just yet. Only me.

I remained antisocial.

We waited. And waited. SUVs pulled up to drop off passengers, but no one we recognized. Photographers strolled back from wherever they'd gone. Cindy pulled me aside and very seriously said that Jake would probably be arriving soon, and we needed to put aside any competition between our blogs. I pulled my magazine and Sharpie out of my purse.

"Will you share pictures with me?" Cindy asked. "I'll share with you. This isn't about competition. This is about getting the best experience with Jake." The wind was howling, blowing my hair everywhere and crinkling the pages of my opened-to-the-middle magazine. I twisted my hair up into a bun while I scanned the streets and said, "Yeah, sure. This isn't a competition."

Then Jake arrived.

We were still on the wrong side of the street, but his SUV pulled up to a door just past the red carpet, one that didn't require him to walk past the group of paparazzi. He bolted from his car to the door, stopping for a fraction of a second to wave at the screams directed toward him from the bystanders. I snapped a quick picture from my position many yards away and started muttering expletives as the door slammed shut.

Another miss.

The rest of my convoy was hysterical. While I had been busy watching the all-too-familiar back of Jake's head through my viewfinder, I had missed the exit of a second person from his SUV. A blonde. Marcia was the first person to address me.

"*Reese* got out of the car with him! They were in *the same car*!" She was shaking her head in astonishment. Judging by the chatter surrounding me, she was not the only one to consider this a development of staggering importance.

Which, Jesus. Okay.

Might As Well Get the Gyllenspoon Talk Out of the Way

Jake Gyllenhaal and Reese Witherspoon, costars of *Rendition,* had been dating for God knows how long but had gone to military-level lengths to cover up their relationship. Everyone knew they were together (*we've* known since page 164); the couple had made the cover of *People* magazine a full five months prior to the events described here.[2] And it wasn't just the gossip world that was talking. Stephen Colbert brought them up on *The Colbert Report,* dubbing them "Jeese."[3] Fansites had been created in their name. New MySpace profiles devoted to celebrating their Hollywood-couple-ness had cropped up and were collecting new friends with wild abandon.

And yet Jake and Reese never formally acknowledged they were a couple. They avoided being photographed together, they avoided talking about each other, and it was reported that during an interview during that very Toronto International Film Festival, Reese's publicist *crawled across the floor in the middle of an interview* to tell a reporter not to ask any questions about Reese's personal life.[4]

Obviously, the thought of Jake dating a woman was a blow to the convictions of the Jake-is-gay! crowd. They weighed in with the argument

---

2   The April 23, 2007, edition of *People* magazine offered the scintillating teaser "Reese's Romance: Why she fell for Jake" just to the right of Marcia Cross's twins and directly above the picture of "Knut: Cutest animal alive!" (http://www.people.com/people/article/0,,20034622,00.html).

3   April 16, 2007; via my own transcript, in the comments section of Jake Watch: "What about Jake Gyllenhaal and Reese Witherspoon? How about 'Jeese?' Anytime they show up, you can just go *disdainfully* "Jeeese ..." (http://jakegyllenhaalwatch.blogspot.com/2007/04/boos-mysterious-disappearance-solved.html).

4   "Although I stress that I am not trying to pry into her private life—and I wasn't—as I finish my question, I am startled to see her publicist suddenly come crawling into the room on her hands and knees from the hallway, where she has evidently been hiding. Without getting up, she admonishes me not to ask personal questions." (http://entertainment.timesonline.co.uk/tol/arts_and_entertainment/film/article2582742.ece).

that Reese was just a cover to bolster Jake's career and that Jake actually led a double life, a public one with Reese and a private one with his boyfriend with whom he was fathering a baby with a surrogate mother. *Wars* were fought on message boards and gossip blogs. It was a very dramatic time in the online world of Jake.

For our part, Jake Watch ran an exclusive story unveiling a secret romance between Jake and ALF.[5]

Arriving in the same car together, though, would have been as good as Jake and Reese publicly admitting they were a couple, and a high percentage of the people I was standing with were on pins and needles waiting for the opportunity to voyeuristically watch Jake date again. Everyone was *very excited.*

And then it turned out that it wasn't Reese. A fellow bystander, who had actually seen Reese enter the building at another entrance, confirmed that the blonde who had gotten out of Jake's car was *not* Reese, but instead one of Jake's personal assistants, a short, blonde woman dubbed by Jake fans as (I'm not making this up) "The Reese Look-Alike." Marcia was expert enough in Jake's entourage that she could name, by sight, all of his assistants, his bodyguard(s?), and everyone involved in his management. Yet even she had been fooled by the nefarious Reese Look-Alike. She was quite sad when her visual identification proved incorrect. But in the meantime, she and Carol would spend many very long minutes discussing how cute it was for two people to ride in a car together.

Meanwhile, Back in Real Time …

Cindy grabbed my arm. She was shaking. "Did you see him?! Did you *see him?!?*" she asked with mounting hysteria. "Oooaaahhh!" Cindy was making some noise, I can only assume in bliss, and clenching my arm with a strength I didn't know she had.

"We're so lucky!" she shrieked. "We saw him! Do you know how few people get to see him? And we saw him! We are so lucky!"

Lucky? I looked at her incredulously. Lucky was not the word I would have used to describe the experience we just had. I was ready to leave.

Cindy was all but oblivious to my presence, eyes glued to the spot across the street where, for all of two seconds, the man himself had just stood.

"I got a picture. Did you get a picture? Oh, I'm shaking!" Cindy moaned.

---

5   http://jakegyllenhaalwatch.blogspot.com/2007/06/hot-of-press.html.

Shaking she was. Shaking so hard she couldn't hold her camera still to view the picture she'd taken. Finally she pulled it up and a single blurry shot, obviously taken from a distance with a trembling hand, popped onto her screen.

"I got a picture!" She ran over to the others and showed them before walking back over to where I was looking at a non-blurry version of the same picture on my camera.

"We're so lucky! We saw him!" she whispered as her camera vibrated in her hand.

"Yeah, if I zoom this in enough, it might be an okay shot," I said with pointed indifference, looking at my own screen.

Then I looked over at Alice, seemingly the only other person in attendance who wasn't completely exhilarated by Jake's arrival. "Which one do you think I should get signed?" she asked, holding up a *Brokeback Mountain* calendar. I took it from her and found a picture of Jack Twist looking Jack Twist-y.

"How about this one?" I said. She nodded her head in approval. I looked at her. She seemed pretty confident she was still going to get an autograph.

"I wonder how long he'll be in there," she said.

It was then that I realized (duh) that Jake would have to *leave* the building at some point.

I figured I'd stick around a little longer then, in that case.

Then Peter Sarsgaard pulled up. His SUV parked in the same place Jake's had just vacated, but he walked past the doors Jake had gone into and made his way toward the photographers. I jumped up and waved my hands over my head shouting, "Peter!!" He looked over with a smile and waved back. And then he was gone. And Cindy was still shaking.

"Do you mind if I run up and get my shoes?" I asked, thinking that now, while we were doing nothing but standing around waiting for Jake to come out of the building, would be a good time. Still dazed, Cindy gave me an affirmative nod and, struck by inspiration, grabbed me again and said, "Yeah, let's go up, and I can post this picture of Jake on my blog!" Great. She was going to scoop me. So much for this not being a competition between blogs.

In agony, I waited in Cindy's hotel room while she got her post together ("Oooh, the image-upload isn't working!"). She finally got the picture posted, but the typing of the extremely brief explanation took longer than expected owing to the fact that she was still shaking ("I can't type!

I'm shaking so bad! We're so lucky!"). Beyond impatient by the time she finally got the post up, I asked if she wanted to stop by the floor where the press conference was being held. I was concerned we wouldn't make it back outside before Jake left. She agreed, but the interview door was still closed when we got there, so we sprinted back to our station behind the building.

Everyone was standing right where we'd left them. Except for Alice.

She was across the street, right on the rope line beside the red carpet. And she was alone, not a photographer in sight. "Come here!" she motioned to me. I looked at her skeptically. "Are we allowed?" I yelled back to her, wary on account of my past history of being reprimanded by security guards.

She nodded. "They said I could," she said, pointing to a couple of policemen standing in the street.

"Give those here," Marcia said. She took my extra pair of shoes from me and put them in her purse.

"Go on!" she shooed, so I walked over and joined Alice. During the course of our short exchange, a couple of other people had appeared to take their place behind the crowd barrier. Alice told me to stand in front of her, right up on the rope because, she said, "This means more to you than it does to me."

I don't know if that was true or not, but I appreciated it all the same. I stood there for a couple of minutes talking to her about her calendar, and then I looked over ...

... and there he was.

He was standing in the doorway, looking at his phone. It was eerily calm, and I realized that of the twenty or so people now standing around me, I was the only one who'd noticed him.

People always said he was more good-looking in person. They talked about not being able to breathe once they saw him, not being able to wrap their heads around the fact that this movie star was *actually* right in front of them. I hadn't felt that way in New York, but that seemed so long ago. And I'd mostly seen him from the back. As he lingered in the doorway, still looking at his phone, I waited for something. Some nervousness. Some tension. Some *anything*. Because this was it. After all this time. There he was.

But he just looked so normal.

He pocketed his phone, stepped out of the doorway onto the sidewalk, and ... pandemonium.

My hands were on the ground, planted on the wrong side of the rope line. I'd been shoved forward by the crowd and lost my balance. I grasped at the concrete, trying to hold onto my Sharpie and my magazine as I pushed myself back to a standing position. Straightening up, I thrust my autograph material in Jake's direction before he'd finished his first signature. I even managed an extra-friendly smile as I asked, "Jake, can you sign this?"

To which Jake said, "Sure."

To which I said, "I run a website for you."

"Oh, yeah?"

"Yeah! Jake Watch!"

"Oh, wow. Okay."

And then there was a very brief awkward pause while I searched his face, smiling and nodding encouragingly, looking for any sign of recognition. But he had on a pair of shiny aviator sunglasses, and all I could see was my own reflection. Was that all he was going to say? He was already moving on to the next autograph ...

"I'm taking some pictures of you. I hope that's okay."

"Sure, that's fine," Jake said, looking up again for half a second and smiling.

"Thank you!" At that, I exhausted my reservoir of things to say.

Alice, having just gotten an autograph herself, leaned toward me, "Talk to him more! He's getting away!"

"I don't know what to say!" I said. In fact, he was already in his car. No more than thirty seconds had passed since I'd spotted him in the doorway. Right before his door shut, I yelled out, "See you tonight!" meaning at the premiere of *Rendition* in a few hours. But the words sounded creepy even to my own ears. Not that he heard me; he was back on his phone the second he climbed into his seat.

I didn't even get my picture taken with him.

"Did you get an autograph?" Alice was asking me.

Before I could answer, Peter Sarsgaard appeared at the same door Jake had emerged from. I'd forgotten about the possibility of getting his autograph, so his arrival got a much more enthusiastic response from me than Jake's did.

"Ooh!" I yelled. "Peter, can you sign this?" I thrust my same opened-to-the-middle, free-from-the-hotel, cheap-ass travel magazine that Jake had signed in Peter's general direction.

"Sure!" Peter said. I glanced down and noted that the page I was asking him to sign featured a tiny picture of Meryl Streep, a picture of Reese Witherspoon (over which Jake had scribbled something resembling a signature), and a large picture of Jake. Jake was really Peter's only option for signing.

"Er, sorry it's a picture of Jake," I added.

Cindy was even worse off, offering a magazine with Jake's face on the cover. I didn't even realize that she was standing next to me until she started apologizing as well. Peter good-naturedly laughed at us.

"It's fine," he said.

"Can I take some pictures?" I asked.

"Sure!"

I snapped a couple and then desperately searched my mind for a quick and effective way to convey that the fansite I co-ran for his brother-in-law had adopted a red panda at the Chester Zoo in his daughter's name. If only I had some confirmation that Stephen had given Maggie and Peter the congratulatory card that I had handed to him almost a year ago ... but I was sure he hadn't ... and Peter had stolen my Sharpie ...

"Whose Sharpie is this?" he called out seconds later as the autograph session wrapped up. "Was it yours?" he asked, turning to me. A photographer standing opposite of us snapped a picture of Peter returning my pen to me, an image that later wound up on WireImage.[6] Peter climbed into his car and was gone.

"Is Reese coming out?" a guy standing next to me wondered out loud. He sounded tense. No one answered him. I turned around to see how Alice and Cindy were holding up and accidentally bumped into him.

"Watch it!" he snapped. I quickly apologized, but he continued to glare at me.

"It really was an accident. I'm sorry," I said. He had a *Legally Blonde* DVD in one hand. "Nothing was hurt, was it?" I asked, indicating his autograph material.

"No, but I've been waiting here a long time. I'm not moving."

"I wasn't trying to take your spot, I promise," I said. He half-smiled, but I could tell he didn't believe me. He couldn't have been there much longer than I had been because Alice was alone when she'd first waved me over. He was so angry. I wondered what his story was, but I wasn't about to ask.

---

6   The picture is mainly of Peter's back, following in the long tradition of my association with photographs of the backs of celebrities.

Reese never came out.

Not long after Peter left, the photographers started to move away, and the security guards indicated another group of stars, for another movie, would be arriving soon. Alice had gotten an autograph from both Jake and Peter. So had Cindy. Marcia was standing off to the side, and Carol was standing on the street (showing up in one of my pictures of Jake with her hands clasped on her head, a look of rapture on her face). As we moved away from the red carpet, everyone was talking to me at once.

"How was it?"

"You did it!!"

"What did he say to you?!"

"Um, I need to call my parents," I responded.

My mom answered on the second ring. "Well," I said in an emotionless voice, "I met Jake." My mom sounded happier than I was.

The group of us maneuvered our way to the front of the hotel. Marcia delightedly noted that Omar Metwally, *Rendition* cast member (and person whose name I did not know at the time), was standing just outside the door. Marcia lit a cigarette and gestured emphatically at me to go over to him. "*Omar*," she whispered. "Get over there! Go talk to him!" Omar was on the phone. I turned my back to him and called Megan, Marcia groaning at me all the while. Megan's excitement level topped my mom's.

"Yeah, I'll tell you more later, but can you do me a huge favor?" I asked.

"Anything!" she said.

"Are you by a computer?"

"No, but I will be soon. Hold on, let me get a piece of paper!"

It sounded like she was driving. Months later I would climb into her car and find the note she'd written to herself while on the phone with me.

"Go to Jake Watch," I instructed, "and can you post a comment on the latest post that just says that I met him? I don't know if Susie's putting up posts while I'm gone or not, but just comment on the newest thing that's up. I know there are a lot of people who are waiting to hear back, and we're headed to the theater now, so it'll be hours before I can get online. I'll write something big later and make it sound good, but I know people will want to know."

I hung up. I felt numb.

Marcia, Cindy, and I climbed into a cab. Alice was driving to the premiere separately, in her own car. Carol's daughter was off to find George

Clooney, and Carol promised to meet up with us later. We still had several hours before the movie, but everyone agreed we should move in the direction of the theater.

On the ride over, Cindy and I compared pictures on our cameras, and then she and Marcia started going over what had happened. I should have jumped in, but I just … couldn't. I couldn't deal with them right now. I pulled my phone back out and started at the top of my contacts list and worked my way down. Anyone I thought might care got a call. Every time I told the story, it sounded less exciting to my ears. Yet friend after friend after friend sounded so incredibly happy for me.

The cab dropped us off at a restaurant across the street from the theater. Taking advantage of our location, we grabbed a table on the patio. In a gap between calls, Alice called me to say she was going to stand outside the theater to see if she could have another encounter with Jake. After I hung up, Marcia, Cindy, and I agreed as a group to forego a second autograph attempt and try instead to get in line early for our seats. Our tickets were general admission. In the balcony. The closer we were to the front of the line for ticket holders, the better.

"*Nothing's* going to top the experience we just had," Cindy said. "We'll be better off trying for good seats."

We all ordered beers and food, and I continued to make phone calls. Cindy and Marcia were deep in discussion but looked up expectantly every time I hung up. And every time I looked back down at my phone and came up with someone else to call. (I almost threw up when my phone bill came later that month.)

"I should call Susie," I announced to the table. "Susie should know about this." I took out my international calling card with just a few minutes left on it. I didn't have Susie's number, though, so I called my brother. He was in line for a call anyway.

"Okay, I just met Jake and I need to call Susie, but the only place I have her number is in a message in my MySpace inbox. So I need you to log in as me and find it for me."

A few minutes later, he was sifting through my inbox.

"So what happened?" he asked.

"What do you mean, what happened? Someone sent me her phone number in a message, and I didn't delete it. It's there somewhere."

"No," he said, a little exasperated, "I mean what happened *with Jake?*"

"Oh. Right. It wasn't really that exciting." I filled him in quickly.

"That was it?" he said.

"Yeah," I said. "But I knew how it was going to happen before I came here. Every fan encounter is the same."

"Okay, well, whatever. I have her phone number here." I could always count on my brother to show the appropriate level of enthusiasm.

As soon as I hung up, Alice called again.

"Can you call me back?" I asked. "I'm trying to dial out of the country." She sounded confused but agreed to call later. I snapped the phone shut.

"Oh, crap!" Cindy and Marcia looked up, surprised. I hadn't meant to say that loud enough for them to hear. "It's fine. I just told Alice I was making an international call after I told her before that I couldn't call her phone because I couldn't make international calls. I'm pretty sure she thinks I'm lying to her now." I waved the calling card.

"This only has a few minutes on it ...," I clarified. I started punching in numbers before either could answer me.

My phone call to Susie was hindered by a poor connection, and the couple at the table behind us turned around to watch as I bent over, hunched almost completely under the table trying to get better reception, and yelled, "I met Jake. What? No, this is *Becky*. Yeah. I'm in Toronto now. I just met *Jake!* What? No, Jake *Gyllenhaal!*" I relayed the details as well as I could, but most of it had to wait until I could e-mail her. ("Nothing special," I wrote. "I'm slightly relieved the meeting didn't boost your enthusiasm because I don't think I could have coped!" she wrote back.)

Cindy and Marcia were, by this point, on their second beers, but our food had not yet arrived. I made it to the end of my contact list and then scrolled through my phone one more time to see if I had missed anyone. And I had. Greta.

The squeal Greta let out when I told her my news was so sincere and so glee-filled that something inside of me broke. I started crying, and once I started, I couldn't stop.

I finished the call just as our food arrived. Marcia and Cindy looked on sympathetically as I put my phone away.

"I don't know why she was so happy for me," I sniffed.

"Meeting Jake is a really emotional experience," Cindy said.

"Yeah, just let it out," Marcia added. "You've been wanting this for so long."

But that was just it. Meeting Jake *wasn't* emotional. It was meaningless. I wasn't crying because I was happy that I'd met him. I was crying because

I *couldn't* be happy that I'd met him. I was tapped out. Empty. Nothing
left.

I ached to feel the happiness everyone was feeling on my behalf. But
there was nothing there. It was horrifying to realize how little I cared. I
didn't even care about the stupid movie we were about to see. *Rendition*
was a film about torture. It was something I wouldn't have even considered
seeing if the circumstances hadn't been what they were.

But here I was. About to go see it and crossing off "talk to Jake" from
my list of things to do before I quit Jake Watch. Mission accomplished,
right? Fifteen months of my life reduced to "Oh, wow. Okay."

He hadn't been the answer to anything.

I picked at my chicken fingers and listened as Cindy talked. And
talked. And talked.

"Aren't we so lucky?" she said, head in hands, barely touching her food
("Oh, God, I can't eat just now!"). "Just ... just so very few people get to
see him, you know? Just think of all the people out there who *never get to
see him.*"

Marcia got up to go to the restroom, and I was left with Cindy. She
continued to talk. And talk.

"I'm quitting soon," I interrupted her. "I'm not telling anyone when
it's going to be over, but there's been an end date for Jake Watch for a long
time now."

Cindy looked at me, obviously taken aback. "Oh, Becky," she said after
a moment. "Will you keep traveling to see him?"

Wait. *That* was her follow-up question?

"No," I frowned. "This is my last trip. It was always going to be my
last trip."

"Well, you'll really be missed." Cindy looked at me intensely. "Nothing
will be the same without Jake Watch."

For just that moment, all of my exasperation with her vanished. It was
such a relief to know that someone felt that way; that *she* felt that way,
when she had left us the way she had. I knew we'd be taking a unique
perspective away from the fan world when we went, but neither Susie nor
I had been feeling very appreciated lately. There was comfort in knowing
we'd be missed.

"But I can understand," Cindy continued. "It's a lot of work running
a blog. I never had any idea until I started mine."

I nodded. "It really is like a second job." It was. There were weeks I
easily put in forty hours.

"Yeah, but he's so amazing, isn't he?" Cindy said. "I couldn't do it for anyone else. God, I just still can't believe we *saw him*."

Moment over.

STILL Day Two

When Marcia returned, we paid our bill and headed over to the theater. The sun was starting to dip lower in the sky. From our position in line, we had a nice view of the area roped off for fans. The red carpet was directly ahead of us, but it was difficult to see through the line of people.

The couple in front of us was friendly.

"I can't honestly say I'm looking forward to this movie," I told them. Marcia and Cindy were standing behind me, though I wasn't sure if they were listening. "I had to stop watching *ER* after Dr. Romano had his arm chopped off by a helicopter. Too traumatic. I'm not sure this torture thing is going to go over well with me."

"So why are you here?" the woman asked.

"Oh. Well. I run a website for Jake Gyllenhaal," I said. "I'm covering this event for a lot of fans. Or at least that's what I'm telling myself."

"We're *all* big Jake fans!" Cindy's voice came from behind me. I guess she was listening. "We met him today!"

After Cindy treated the couple to a full recap, I leaned over toward the woman. "I'm not into this the way they are," I said, silently pleading with her to understand. I'm not sure why I said it, except she just happened to be there and after hearing Cindy tell the story, I felt an insistent need to distance myself from her obvious elation.

"Okay," the woman said, puzzled by the intensity of my declaration.

It was several minutes before she addressed me again, asking what other celebrities I'd seen. I told her about seeing Jodie Foster and Terrence Howard, as well as Peter Sarsgaard.

"Isn't it weird that they're just walking around?" she said. "Like, they're just staying in these hotels where tourists are staying. That's so weird. I always wonder if they're just complete jerks in real life. Like, [female cast member of *Buffy the Vampire Slayer*] was *such* a bitch when I met her."

"What!?" I said. *Another* Buffy story? "When did you meet [female cast member of *Buffy the Vampire Slayer*]!? *Buffy's* my favorite TV show of all time! Seriously, my blogger name for the Jake site is 'Prophecy Girl.'"

She nodded in approval, as if by telling her this I had adequately convinced her that I was a true *Buffy* fan. "We met her at this fan convention," she said, pointing to her male companion, who had been silently nodding behind her since the start of the conversation. I realized that if the two of them were frequenting *Buffy* fan conventions, they were unlikely to find anything odd about the behavior of my group. She then told me her story of meeting [female cast member of *Buffy the Vampire Slayer*]. She'd had to pay for an autograph, and extra for a photo, and then [female cast member of *Buffy the Vampire Slayer*] was rude to her, and most everyone else there. "It was like she didn't even want to be there," she told me, arching one incredulous eyebrow.

I thought she was trying to tell me something through her story. Or maybe the universe was. Maybe there were certain life lessons I could only learn by hearing tales of *Buffy* fan conventions.

"That's horrible!" I said. "Although oddly not as surprising as some other stories I've heard about fan conventions. I guess I should be happy I didn't have to hand Jake money before he signed my magazine?" I guessed.

Judging by the look she gave me, that was not the response she'd been aiming for. Perhaps that story had just been a story, and not a life lesson. We didn't talk much after that.

Carol reappeared just before the line started moving. It was at the precise moment that my feet began shuffling forward that Jake showed up. I couldn't see him, but I could tell where he was by following the flashbulbs in the crowd. Security waved us inside. "Keep moving!" they shouted. I walked with the line, missing it as Jake signed autographs for a few minutes outside and then turned away from the crowd after one last signature to the person standing next to Alice. Out of luck, she came over to the line for ticket holders, which was now inordinately long and already moving into the building, and we lost her for the rest of the night.

Once inside, I was ready to rush up to the balcony to grab the best available seats, but the red carpet wound its way from the sidewalk and through the lobby of the theater. It ended at an elevator that took important non-balcony-seating people to their seats down below. Our group thought it a better move to stand by the red carpet than to find our seats just then.

A man who was obviously very sick walked up behind me. "That's Gene Siskel!" Carol whispered from my left. "*That is Gene Siskel!*" But it wasn't Gene Siskel because Gene Siskel had been dead for close to a decade.

It was Roger Ebert. No one recognized him or bothered him or even said anything to him. He stood next to me, patiently, until a woman escorted him into the elevator.

And then there was Jake again. He walked by without looking at any of us. Peter, who filed in after him, smiled when I screeched his name for the third time that day. The lights started to dim, and the crowd scattered, running to get to their seats. On the way to the stairs, I caught a glimpse of the top of Reese Witherspoon's head as she, too, made her way to the elevator.

We were almost late, as by the time we started climbing the stairs all of the lower balcony seats had been taken. Flight after flight we went up. I wound up sandwiched between Cindy and Carol, Marcia on the other side of Cindy, in the topmost level, all of us sitting down just as the action started below. We were way off to the left, and the screen was a story or so below us.

When attending a gala screening at a venue such as the Toronto International Film Festival, one is treated to some preshow entertainment, courtesy of the people involved in the film's creation. A couple of people give speeches; the actors march across the stage; everyone in the audience applauds even though no one's seen the movie yet ...

Four sets of eyes high above the stage were glued to Gavin Hood, director of *Rendition*, as he began introducing the key players in his movie. Carol clutched my arm when Jake walked onto the stage. Reese was introduced and walked out after him. Peter came next, but suddenly I couldn't hear what was going on down below. Carol had launched into a running commentary of what she thought was happening between Jake and Reese as they stood next to each other.

"Oh, here comes Jake now, and look! Reese is right behind him! See that? Okay, they're stopping. *Oh,* see how far apart they're standing?" she asked me happily. I didn't think they were necessarily standing any farther apart from each other than anyone else, but I chose not to voice this opinion. Jake put his hands in his pockets, and Reese followed suit. To Carol, this was roughly equivalent to them groping each other on stage.

"They want to touch each other! They're trying to *keep from touching each other!*" she cried, uncomfortably loudly. She reached across me to tag the others.

"Are you *seeing* this?! They've both got their hands in their pockets!" She got an animated response from those on my left, and I continued not to hear what was being said below.

"They're so *cute!*" Carol moaned. "Do you see that? Are you watching them?"

"Yeah," I said, motioning down toward the stage to indicate that I was trying to listen.

"They want to touch each other! Are you seeing this?!" She shook my arm for emphasis.

Finally the people on stage filed off, and the lights dimmed and the movie started.

Regarding *Rendition*

Anyone who has seen *Rendition* (and let's be honest, there aren't many of you) will know that in Jake's first appearance in the film, he is in bed and shirtless. He climbs from his bed, walks into the bathroom, and, still shirtless, proceeds to make out with some random chick who flits in and out of the movie without a lot of character development.

I have never, neither before nor since, held witness to such a strong female reaction to a male body as that which occurred on either side of me as Jake's image flooded the screen. It was now Cindy's hand clutching my arm as she whimpered in apparent agony. Carol was fanning herself and breathing heavily. I couldn't see Marcia in the dark, but that was probably for the best. Cindy sucked in a lungful of air and held her breath. Carol started making an odd laughing noise, and Cindy's eyes started to glisten.

I tried to pay close attention to the action on screen, as the scene just mentioned was one much anticipated by the audience I was writing for. I had already promised to describe it in detail on Jake Watch. Later, people would tell me they were disappointed when they finally saw the scene for themselves. I certainly didn't memorize the make-out in photographic detail, but I did remember the orgasmic reaction that was flanking me and thus perhaps described it as slightly more exciting than it actually was.

Less than a week later, when I wrote my "official" review of *Rendition* for Jake Watch, I started by saying that the best thing about seeing the film at the Toronto International Film Festival was that I would never have to see it again. I also wrote that the best line of the movie was Jake's delivery of "This is my first torture." He would later repeatedly state that that one line was the reason he did the movie. One line. Five words that landed me in a theater in Canada with three women old enough to be my mother. Sometimes I wonder how different my Jake

Watch experience would have been had those five words not made it into the script.

My assessment of the movie, however, was not one shared by the women I was with. They loved it. So did Roger Ebert.[7]

Man, Freaking Day Two Never Ends

When we exited the theater, we passed through the crowd lining up to see George Clooney and/or his movie, *Michael Clayton*. There were a lot more people around than there had been when we were standing in line. But we didn't stick around to people watch. We hailed a cab. Carol, Cindy, and Marcia climbed into the backseat, loudly rehashing *Rendition* in extraordinary detail. Up front, the driver and I talked about Hilary Duff.

"She is giving a concert tonight in town!" the driver exclaimed through a thick accent.

"That's awesome! I love her *Metamorphosis* CD," I said, overjoyed at the opportunity to talk about something other than Jake. "I'm not just saying that, either. I, like, know all of the words."

"Yes, so many people are in the city right now," he said, glancing over at me.

We stopped at a red light, and he shifted toward me.

"So ...," he said, smiling happily, "you are one of the celebrities, yes?"

If I was a celebrity, I would have had the strangest entourage ever. Right now they were behind us talking about Jake's shirtless scene again.

"Ah, I'm sorry, no," I said. "I'm just a tourist. I came in for the festival."

"Oh, oh," he said, not nearly as enthusiastic as he had been moments before. "Well, who have you seen that is famous?"

"Uh, well, we saw Jake Gyllenhaal today."

He gave me a blank look. "Who?"

He dropped us off just down the street from our destination. Where else, but Jake's hotel. There were swarms of civilians lining the sidewalk. I had no sooner stepped out of the cab than a black SUV pulled up to the curb, and a man in a suit leaned out the window and asked me if I was

---

7   http://rogerebert.suntimes.com/apps/pbcs.dll/article?AID=/20071018/
REVIEWS/710180307/1023.

waiting for a ride. For the second time in ten minutes, I apologized for not being famous.

"Come on, we're going to the bar," Marcia said, grabbing my arm.

Carol's daughter had been holding vigil at the bar at Jake's hotel since late that afternoon, hoping that George Clooney might come in for a drink before going to his screening of *Michael Clayton*. There were only a few hotels in town where the celebrities were staying (such hotels were immediately identifiable by the persistent swelling crowds blocking the sidewalks outside), and I don't recall if she had reason to suspect George was staying at Jake's hotel or if she was just hoping to get lucky.

She did not get lucky, and it seemed as if we hadn't been the only people with the idea that the bar might be the place to be that evening. It appeared the whole city of Toronto, sans any celebrities, had crammed themselves into the small room.

We stayed an hour, and then hunger set in, at which point we headed to a restaurant directly across the street. Once seated, the conversation turned to, of all things, Jake.

Jake was so wonderful.

Jake had been so nice to us.

Jake had done such a good job in *Rendition*.

Jake. Jake. Jake. Jake. Jake.

I didn't speak. I barely lifted my eyes from the table. I was hungry and I was tired and now that we were robbed of all other distractions, now that I was entombed within this bubble of Jake hysteria with no escape in sight, I was starting to think that if I heard the name "Jake" one more time, I might scream.

But I didn't. I took the much less healthy approach of sitting in stony silence and slowly growing more and more irritated with everyone sitting at the table with me. Even Carol's daughter seemed to be handling the one-topic conversation better than I was. Much better. The only words I remember saying at dinner were, "I didn't like the movie all that much." I said them to Jan while the rest of the table talked plot points, and Jan looked at me as if she didn't believe me and said, "Really?" before turning to her mom.

As the meal wore on, Cindy began fidgeting, gradually becoming more restless until she finally blurted out, "My intuition is telling me I should leave!"

Cindy relied on her "intuition" to keep her in tune with Jake's movements. Apparently it was her intuition that led her to Jake her first day in the city, and not listening to her intuition had led to the disastrous *Zodiac* trip in March. At the moment, Cindy's intuition was telling her that Jake had gone out to dinner after his big premiere and was heading back to his hotel ... right *now*.

Almost immediately after making her declaration, Cindy stood up, throwing far more than her meal's worth of money on the table, and darted out as the rest of us waited for the bill. When we met her outside a few minutes later, she informed us that Jake had not been seen, and therefore he must not yet be back at his hotel, and therefore we must all stand around and wait for him to show up.

The crowd on the sidewalk had diminished somewhat in the hours that had passed since the cab dropped us off. But there were still close to a hundred people standing around. Several long minutes of restless waiting passed. No one came out of the hotel, and no one went in. I jumped in surprise when I heard Marcia's hushed voice behind me.

"Did you see Peter?" she asked. Peter Sarsgaard had just walked out of the hotel and down the street. Marcia had followed him long enough to see him duck into a steakhouse not a hundred feet from the restaurant where we'd just eaten. That bit of information directly begat further long minutes of restless waiting standing across the street from the steakhouse.

People were *everywhere*. No one knew who they were waiting for or when something was going to happen; they just *waited*. And sometimes their patience paid off with a glimpse of someone rushing into a car. But more often than not, no one saw anything. People just stood, for hours, and walked away disappointed, only to come back later and wait for more hours. Every time we crossed paths with a crowd, I would ask, "Who are you waiting for?" And every time the answer was, "I don't know." No one ever knew. They just *waited*.

The crowd we were with that night had largely missed Peter's departure in the dark. All that waiting, and they'd missed what they had been waiting for.

The five of us were alone, though, watching the steakhouse.

"Do you think they're in there having a romantic dinner?" Carol marveled aloud of Reese and Jake as we stood on a stretch of sidewalk down the street from the hotel. Not that we knew that Reese and Jake were inside. We only knew that Peter had gone inside. He could have met up with anybody. Or nobody.

"They *have* to be in there," Carol decided.

Jan, who had been so patient throughout the afternoon and even through dinner, rather abruptly lost it. I was never sure what it was exactly that set her off, but I was secretly glad I hadn't been the first to snap.

"Mom," she snarled. "*When* are we leaving? I *need* to sleep!"

"Just a few more minutes!" Carol said. They argued back and forth until Jan got her way.

"Call me!" Carol shouted back to us as they walked off to find a cab. "If you see anyone, I want to know!"

She rounded a corner, and that was the last I saw of her.

"You know, we could just go into the restaurant. I know we just ate, but we could get dessert or something," I suggested when it was just the three of us again.

Neither Cindy nor Marcia was up for trying.

"Or we could just go back to the hotel," I said hopefully. Marcia was starting to get tired herself, and she agreed. Cindy stayed.

Marcia and I were walking into our hotel room when my phone rang. Waiting having paid off, Cindy had seen not Jake, but a close friend of Jake's (who, not being famous, was not recognized by anyone but Cindy) leave the steakhouse. She watched him go back to Jake's hotel and then saw him turn on the light in his room, which happened to be facing the street. She breathlessly described the sensation of witnessing him look out his window at the crowd below.

I relayed as much as I could to Marcia without vomiting, and then I sat down at her laptop because I still needed to write a post for Jake Watch about meeting Jake.[8] As tired as I was, it took me a long time to type out even the most basic description, but Marcia waited patiently for her turn at the computer. After promising everyone I would write about *Rendition* when I was back home, I left Marcia to it and locked myself in the bathroom to take a long shower and wash the day away.

Marcia was still online when I came out. There was a club just across the way, and the bass thudded until three in the morning. Marcia stayed on the computer, not breaking away until the club shut down. She apologized for keeping me up, but I told her, truthfully, that I couldn't have slept with the music in the background anyway.

I knew, long before I finally fell asleep, that I wouldn't be making it back to the ticket tent the next morning early enough to snatch tickets to *The Assassination of Jesse James.*

---

8   http://jakegyllenhaalwatch.blogspot.com/2007/09/jake-and-pgs-excellent-conversation.html.

My movie viewing for my first international film festival was already over.

Days Three and Four

I woke up midmorning. By the time I'd brushed my teeth, Marcia was already at the computer, squinting at her screen in the dark, curtains still shut tight. I did her the favor of allowing natural light into the room, then went through the same routine as the day before, slowly getting myself ready before running out of things to do and settling for watching the weather on TV for half an hour. Still Marcia was on the computer.

All of the paparazzi pictures from Jake's public appearances the day before had shown up overnight, and each and every one had to be inspected with care. Furthermore, a paparazzi video of Jake opening the curtains of his hotel room window had shown up on a gossip blog. Overjoyed by this seconds-long voyeuristic treasure, Marcia felt it necessitated several hundred viewings, all while she prattled about how handsome and wonderful Jake looked as he opened his blinds. I pointedly opted not to look. Even by paparazzi video standards, it was a pretty intrusive offering.

Making it all the more interesting was the fact that with Cindy's description of where Jake's friend had been staying, Marcia quickly deduced that Jake was staying one floor above him.

"Isn't that *sweet?!*" she said. "He's staying right under Jake! Awwww."

I wondered if she even noticed I wasn't answering her. Maybe she always talked like this while browsing the internet. This revelation, however, that Jake and his friend had rooms vertical to each other, would become a hot source of conversation between Cindy and Marcia for the rest of the day. For when we did meet up with Cindy later in the morning, she too was ecstatic about the video and what it revealed about room placement.

When the fun of repeatedly watching Jake open his curtains had been exhausted, Marcia got up to get ready for the day. It was my turn at the computer and, as predicted, my inbox was full of e-mails from readers anxious for details of what had transpired the day before. The comments on Jake Watch were similarly congratulatory ("PG & JG met? They interacted? :-O This is the end of the world as we know it!"). I don't know if it was a fluke or a tacit acknowledgment that it was Becky in Toronto and not Prophecy Girl, but a surprisingly large number of the comments on the blog were addressed to Becky. They were even talking about me on IHJ. "Looks like Becky (Prophecy Girl at Jake Watch) got her wish. She met Jake and spoke to him too! Lucky ~~bitch~~ girl! Aww this is exciting," someone wrote. "Yes. Just read it at Jake Watch—she so deserved it …" another poster replied.

Feeling the weight of the unexciting encounter blown so out of proportion, I calmly tried to explain that it really wasn't that big of a deal.

"I just really wanted to look him in the eye after all this time and I did," I wrote in a comment.

"Sounds like the end of *Zodiac* to me …" a Jake Watch reader replied. Jake had played author Robert Graysmith in the film, and the commenter was referring to a scene near the end where, for his own personal satisfaction, Jake's character tracked down the killer and looked him in the eye. Someone else noticed my unintentional parallel too: "It does indeed seem that PG has finally looked the Zodiac in the eye."

Just what every celebrity wants: to have his fans equate him to a serial killer.

"Did he seem to know what JW was?!" someone else wrote.

It was by far the most difficult question anyone asked; it was also, as the days wore on, one of the most frequent. I thought long and hard about Jake's reaction, his inflection of "Oh, wow. Okay."

I told everyone who asked that I didn't know. "I honestly have no idea. I couldn't tell," I wrote.

It was easier to say that than to say "no." "I couldn't tell" had such a soft ring to it. After all, wasn't that what one did after such encounters? Spin the story a little so the myth didn't die for everyone else? I wasn't even sure I was doing it for anyone else. Maybe it was easier for *me* to be uncertain, rather than to acknowledge the truth. Who benefited if I admitted he hadn't known us? No one.

So ambiguity it was.

For all the discussing and recapping that was done during and following my trip to Toronto, the most precise summation of the encounter came weeks later, for Jake Watch's final post. I boiled the whole trip down to two short sentences: "At last they meet! Both are underwhelmed."

Marcia was finally ready. And much to my dismay, she was back at her computer. "You gotta see this," she said. She pulled up a video of a ten-year-old Jake at the premiere of *City Slickers*, talking about riding a horse. Marcia spoke the words along with little-boy-Jake as the video played.

"Wasn't he such a cute kid?" Marcia laughed. She tweaked ten-year-old Jake's nose.

I mentioned breakfast. No response. She was on to Jake's SNL appearance. I thought she would turn it off after his opening monologue, but the video kept playing, and it seemed she was settling in to watch the entire episode. I really wanted to go to breakfast. And this guy was in the same goddamned city as we were. The time for watching his SNL appearance on a laptop was decidedly not now.

"Okay, let's order room service," Marcia suggested when I brought up breakfast yet again. I couldn't keep the hysteria out of my voice as I screeched, "Room service!? I really think we should get out of the hotel!"

She turned around, looking a bit stunned by my outburst. "Of course we'll go out. Of course," she said.

Cindy met up with us after breakfast, at which point we made an obligatory stop by Jake's hotel so that Cindy could point out to us, in person, which room she had seen Jake's friend in, and we could all see, in person, the room from which Jake had been filmed opening his curtains. There was some movement in Jake's room, and for a moment we all three froze. But it was only the maid. Her appearance opened up a burning debate over whether Jake was just out and about in Toronto or if he had left the city. Cindy and Marcia, with nothing to go on but "intuition," came to the joint conclusion that he had grabbed an early morning flight out of the city and was gone. A certain sense of gloom hung over the two of them once the conclusion was reached, for Cindy especially. In the first of several thousand times she would say it that day, she pined, "Where do you think he's gone?"

Having no movies to attend, the three of us wandered aimlessly around Toronto. We wound up in a park. I sat in controlled silence and listened to a ten-minute conversation about the shape of Jake's upper lip.

"The first time I saw him, I immediately took note of the shape, and it was one of the things that attracted me to him," Cindy stated.

Marcia agreed that as far as upper lips went, Jake's was just about "perfect."

Jake. Jake. Jake. Jake. Jake.

The minutes … dragged … by …

Finally it was time for lunch.

He was the topic as we walked to the restaurant, while we were being seated at the restaurant, while we drank our drinks at the restaurant, while we ate our meal at the restaurant, and while we sat listlessly in the restaurant long after we had finished our food. (Actually, it was just me who was listless.)

Hours passed. The sun's position in the sky changed, but our topic of conversation did not. Not as we sat through another drink. Not as we got up to finally leave. Not as we walked down the street. Not as we sat down in yet another bar and ordered yet more drinks, at which time the discussion turned yet again to the events of the day before.

"You know, I'm just so happy," Cindy said, as she'd been saying over and over and over for the past thirty-six hours. "It was the perfect day, wasn't it? I'm going to remember yesterday for the rest of my life. It was just so great to go through the whole experience of the day and then end it with the movie. It was brilliant. Just absolutely *brilliant*. We shared the whole day with him. We were there everywhere he went. I mean, do you know how lucky we are? We got to do something that most people will *never get to do*. We shared the whole day. And I saw him the night before, so it was really like twenty-four hours for me. I'll just remember it for the rest of my life. It was a perfect day. Just absolutely *perfect*."

I was fairly certain that I, personally, had not spent the entire day with Jake Gyllenhaal the day before. Nor was I convinced that Cindy had spent an entire twenty-four hours with him. Marcia nodded her head as Cindy droned on, but my mouth hadn't opened in hours. And hours. And hours.

Marcia's phone rang. It was her friend Shelley, reporting on Vanessa's interview with Jake for the Canadian *National Post*, which had just gone up online.

Which I had temporarily forgotten about.

"Oh! Oh! Ask her what he said about Jake in '08!" I said. No one seemed to notice that my energy level had ricocheted up a hundredfold at the word "interview." Marcia shushed me and listened. Even Cindy was silent, in rapt attention, as she watched Marcia talk on the phone.

"Uh huh. Uh huh. Oh, really? Uh huh. Oh, he *did*?" She laughed, and the minutes ticked away as Shelley read her the entire interview over the phone. Cindy stared intensely from the other side of the table and then leaned across it, whispering almost mantra-like, "Did he say anything about new projects coming up? Ask her if he has any new projects. Please. Did he say *anything* about new projects?"

"Oh, yeah. Okay. Jake in '08. Wow, no, I don't." Marcia looked over at me and put her hand over the mouthpiece. "He didn't know anything about it."

"Is that it?" I asked. "What did he *say?*" I didn't realize at the time that the last four words Marcia had spoken were Jake's verbatim response to being asked about Jake in '08. "Wow, no, I don't." Which was not all that unlike, "Oh, wow. Okay."

It was a weekend of wows for Jake Watch.

Cindy started talking a little louder. "New projects! Ask her if he said anything about *new projects!*" Marcia waved her off and continued to laugh at whatever Shelley was saying. "New projects!" Cindy hissed, near hysterical. Marcia again put her hand over the mouthpiece. "He didn't say anything about any new movies." Cindy slumped back in her chair. She looked at me. "I'm really worried. Why hasn't he signed on for any films?"

I shrugged.

In the end, Vanessa had been able to sneak in four questions from fans:[9]

Q: Many of your fans are wondering if you still have Boo, your puggle? We haven't seen him in a while.

A: (After a pause and a sigh of what sounded like lament, looks to the floor and responds) I don't have my puggle … I don't have my puggle.

Q: Do you ever read anything about yourself on the Internet?

A: (Another pause) Sometimes people send me funny things … I'll leave it at that.

Q: Do you know about the Jake in '08 presidential campaign? It was a MySpace page but then it got taken down.

A: Wow, no, I don't.

Q: We know you're really into food—how do you feel about cilantro? Some people love it but other people think it tastes like soap.

A: Oh, I really don't like cilantro! It's like the only herb that I don't like.

Q: It's a very divisive herb.

A: It is.

Three of those questions came from a single devoted Jake Watch reader; the fourth came from Alice. Vanessa credited all of them, and the Jake in '08 campaign, to IHJ.

The interview ran twice, once during the festival and once the weekend *Rendition* hit theaters. The second time, I wrote her to explain that Jake Watch, not IHJ, had been responsible for the questions and for the presidential campaign. She was nice enough to apologize and even offered

---

9   http://greenasathistle.com/2007/09/08/an-update-for-the-gyllenhaalics/.

to correct the error if she ever interviewed Jake again. Vanessa remained the friendliest and most helpful professional I talked to outside of the Jake Watch community, and all she did was give us two minutes at the end of an interview. She asked four simple questions from the only group of people who really cared about Jake's answers anyway: fans.

As for the "funny things" comment, many of our readers painfully clung to the hope that it was Jake's admission to reading Jake Watch. ("It *has to be Jake Watch*, what else could it be?? Jake Watch is the SNL of his online fanbase!")

But I never believed that. I thought it was much more likely he was referring to those rumors about the baby by a surrogate mother.

I'm Stalking Brad Pitt!

I wanted to see Brad Pitt. Not that I'm, like, some huge Brad Pitt fan, but it seemed like if one had the opportunity to see him, one should take advantage. And since this one had lost her opportunity to see Brad's movie (*The Assassination of Jesse James*), she wasn't above using guilt tactics to convince her party that the remainder of the evening should be spent trying to see him in person.

"I would *really* love to try to see Brad," I stressed. We were still at the bar, and Marcia had just hung up with Shelley. She and Cindy couldn't have possibly looked less interested. But Marcia finally relented, and Cindy found herself outnumbered. They were both half drunk.

It wound up being quite a walk to the theater where *The Assassination of Jesse James by the Coward Robert Ford* was premiering. It was the same theater, incidentally, where *Brokeback Mountain* had premiered two years earlier.

Unlike outside the *Rendition* premiere, the crowd hysteria for *The Assassination of Jesse James* was palpable from a distance. *Thousands* of people lined both sides of the street. Cindy and Marcia, being shorter than me, stuck to the sidewalk. They couldn't see anything from their vantage point. I worked my way as far into the crowd as I could (not far), and on the very tips of my toes, I could occasionally catch a glimpse of the theater and red carpet ahead of me.

A flamboyantly dressed woman with a camera crew sashayed through the crowd and interviewed a couple standing next to me. They'd been waiting for two hours and were in no better position to see than me, and I'd just arrived. The woman worked for MTV and was working the crowds because she hadn't been able to get clearance to stand across the street with the rest of the press. Security was tight.

Eric Bana arrived first (was he even in that movie?). His welcome was lackluster, as everyone was waiting for the main event. Surprisingly quickly, a limo pulled up, and the screams reached deafening levels. A guy standing in front of me turned around and shouted, "Give me your camera! Give me your camera!" I gave it to him, and he held it high above his head, snapping as many pictures as he could. Through the crowd, I caught a fleeting glimpse of Brad walking down the street with Angelina Jolie on his arm. They crossed to the opposite side of the street, screams following them and the crowds pushing forward to get a better look. I could only tell where they were by the peeks of their security entourage that I briefly caught when the crowds parted the right way. Most of the time I could see nothing but the mob in front of me. The guy with my camera never put his arms down; he held my camera up and continued to take picture after picture. He was half a foot taller than I am, and he couldn't see anything either. He just pointed where he thought Brad and Angelina might be and snapped away. I could hear the screams moving back toward the theater and, assuming the couple was done walking the crowds, everyone in my surrounding area groaned in disappointment. I took my camera back, and my picture taker sadly reported that he wasn't sure he got anything. I thanked him for trying and went back to Marcia and Cindy.

Just as I was telling them that we could leave if they wanted, I heard the crowd again scream, and the guy who had taken my pictures frantically turned around to look for me. Brad Pitt had walked right over to the crowd, within five feet of where I had been standing. I fought my way back through the mob, but by the time I got there, he was long gone. Crestfallen, I walked back to the sidewalk.

"I can't believe that just happened. I have the worst luck of anyone I've ever known," I said.

Marcia gave me a sympathetic smile. Cindy just looked out over the throngs of people and said, "Well, I hope Jake never gets that famous!"

I was somewhat distressed to realize there was still a meal left to eat that day. We ate at a restaurant close to the *Jesse James* premiere, nowhere near our hotel. It was a long meal, and after we left, Marcia ducked into a coffee shop to buy something dismayingly large and caffeinated. Cindy left us to go back to her hotel, but we promised to all meet up one last time the next day, our final in the city.

As soon as Marcia and I were back in our hotel room, I sent a desperate e-mail to Susie: "I am dying here. It never ends. November 1st is suddenly a long ways off." But aside from our phone call, Susie and I didn't talk while I was in Toronto. She had all but checked out of the Jake world. She wouldn't respond to my pleading e-mail until long after I was home.

Marcia turned on the TV. She caught an advertisement for an upcoming clip on the news about the film festival, and the announcer mentioned that Jake would be shown. With exhaustion setting in, I stood up and announced I was going to take a shower, unless she wanted to take one first.

Marcia looked offended. "You're not going to wait around to see Jake?"

Wait around to see Jake?

Oh, for fuck's sake. As if I hadn't just spent my *entire fucking vacation* bending my schedule around this guy. I couldn't even *take a shower* without someone insisting he take priority?

I whirled around to face Marcia. The first word came out cold: "No." Her eyes widened, and I continued, "Sometimes it just gets to the point where I can *hardly stand to look at his face.*"

There was a devastating silence in the room as I awkwardly stepped around her and into the bathroom. Marcia was still conspicuously quiet as she tapped away at her computer when I emerged from the shower. Taking a deep breath, I apologized and explained that I was having a hard time dealing with the constant Jake talk and that I was disappointed we hadn't done much with the film festival itself. Marcia said she understood and then called me over to look at some new pictures that had gone up while we were out for the day. I thought I might cry.

The following morning, as we packed up, Marcia asked me, "What would make this worth it to you?" And when I told her I didn't want to talk about it, she tried another way: "Did you expect more from him?"

I couldn't bring myself to talk about it with her. I was hanging on by a thread as it was. I was desperate to go home and detox. I was past saving anyway, though I did feel bad for the first time that weekend for the way I'd acted around her. She'd been so nice, from letting me eat her breakfast to acquiescing every time I'd pushed for a change in plans. Even now, she was trying to understand, help me work through it. But she'd caught me at the end of a long journey. I hadn't been a good Prophecy Girl for her, and I felt a tinge of regret for that.

I hadn't expected much of anything from Jake, but I'm sure she'd been expecting better from me.

Nicely as I could, I told her I was all right, just tired, and asked if she was ready to go meet Cindy.

Our threesome met for the final time over lunch, and then it was time to say good-bye. Cindy was beside herself. "I just don't want to go back," she moaned. "I'd been looking forward to this for so long." She waxed a little about Jake's unknown whereabouts and then, after a lingering farewell, Cindy got into her taxi and left us. Marcia and I headed to the airport for a departure that was decidedly more strained than our arrival.

But I felt freer the minute I boarded the plane.

Two more months now. Just two more months.

A Conversation (Assign to It Whatever Meaning You'd Like)

"How was Toronto? Did you see anyone famous?" asked A Co-Worker.

"Oh, I saw so many people! I saw Brad Pitt, Angelina Jolie, Eric Bana, Jodie Foster, Jake Gyllenhaal …"

"Wait, Jake?"

"Jake Gyllenhaal."

"Yeah, what's he been in?"

"*Brokeback Mountain.*"

"I never saw that."

"*Donnie Darko*? *Jarhead*? He's been in a lot of movies that no one has ever heard of. Oh, and *The Day After Tomorrow.*"

Pause.

"Um, who's he dating?"

"Reese Witherspoon."

"Oh!" Recognition at last. "Yeah! I saw them in some magazine."

Five Conveniently Timed
Ending-Signaling Things

I was sifting through the gazillion shots of Jake from last weekend on IHJ and I was overwhelmed by [one] particular picture. Because peeking above the shoe, what is THAT?! It appears to be none other than the flirtatious edge of a sock (!!). I might swoon.

I was so struck by the beauty of Jake's barely-visible ankle that I decided to write a haiku about my feelings:

> *Your socks, exquisite.*
> *I ache to see their full size.*
> *Brown, or trick of light?*

My God, I should have gone into poetry. I think we should all write haikus about Jake now. In fact, I'm going to write another one.

> *Jake, why are you sad?*
> *You look like you will vomit.*
> *Don't ruin your tie.*

—"Sock Watch: A Poetic Vision."
Jake Watch, September 13, 2007

I never wanted to do Jake Watch more than I did after I got home from Toronto.

Insane! I know!

It seems much more likely that I would want to fill these last pages with angsty reflection on feeling unappreciated and that sort of crap. But no. That was not my state of mind.

The strange thing about deciding to stop at the start of November was that Jake Watch would have ended then anyway. The blog went through a natural dying process that conveniently fell within the timetable I had laid out months earlier. In its last two months, unresolved issues came to a close, long-held misconceptions were corrected, and for a brief time, the fun of it all was back, as pure as it had been a year and a half earlier.

That's what I came home to: the beginning of an inevitable end.

Toronto had been very intense while it was happening, but it gave me a sense of purpose unlike any I'd known during my earlier days as a blogger.

I knew I was walking away soon.

I knew that Jake, by virtue of his lack of participation, had surprisingly little influence on his own online image.

I knew that when Jake Watch was gone, that image would be bequeathed, in its entirety, to whoever happened to outlast us.

I had seen in Toronto what I would be leaving behind. Being around those other fans, knowing they were going to be holding the torch when I was gone, lit a fire in me to go out on top. Jake Watch was unique; there was nothing like it on the internet. I didn't want to leave it as a shell of its former self. I wanted it to be just as good on the last day as it had been on the first day. I wanted what Susie and I had done to be remembered long after we were gone.

Before I took my final bow, I wanted to rewrite the standards for everyone.

I wanted to show every Jake fan out there just how you did this shit.

Of course, none of my grandiose plans up until this point had panned out, so there's no logical reason why they should start now.

Ending-Signaling Thing Number One: Boo's Inbox Runs Dry

First on the agenda when I got home was dealing with the aftermath of what had been revealed in Vanessa's interview, namely that Boo was no longer with Jake. Was he dead? Did Jake give him away? What did any of it *mean*? (Way to be vague in answering your interview questions, Gyllenhaal.) All we could say for sure was that he was no longer with Jake.

Boo got a MySpace makeover. I added Jake's quote ("I don't have my puggle ...") to the main page and then rechristened the profile by tacking an "In Memory of" to the front of Boo's name.

Legions of horrified dog lovers responded by sending me their condolences.

Exasperated, I posted a notice clarifying that I didn't know what had happened to Boo, but he wasn't with Jake anymore, and I was commemorating that fact, and not necessarily his death. And then the strangest thing happened ...

People stopped writing Boo.

Boo hadn't replied to anyone since the Uncle Jack Nasty days, but his silence had been painfully ineffective in reducing the number of messages in his inbox. As soon as the "In Memory of" sunk in, though ... nothing. It was eerie. As much as I liked to complain about the people who wrote to him (and oh did I like to complain), it was disconcerting when they stopped. I had started his profile when I had started with Jake Watch. There had never been a time when I'd been responsible for one but not the other.

It wasn't that I missed the messages—little did he know that getting rid of that dog was probably the nicest thing Jake could have done for me—but Jake Watch felt different without them. It drove home the point that things were changing ...

The MySpace changes didn't stop with Boo. While I was no closer to an answer as to why the Jake in '08 profile had been deleted, Jake's lack of knowledge strongly suggested that no one in his camp had been offended or asked that it be removed. That alone was enough to compel me to recreate it. Version 2.0, bolder and better than the original, made its debut less than a week after I returned home.[1]

With that, my full focus returned to the blog and the ever-present issue of privacy.

Many, many pages ago, I mentioned that my stance on privacy protection was headed toward a "draconian end." Well, we're approaching that end now. Stephen's dire words ("Jake can't do *anything*!") had been ringing in my ears for close to a year, and with each passing month, I became a little more severe. Even before I'd gone to Toronto, I'd taken

---

1   www.myspace.com/gyllenhaalforpresident. The original profile was at www. myspace.com/jakein08, but in the month it took me to decide to recreate it, someone else swept in and claimed that URL.

to not mentioning Jake's whereabouts when he showed up in paparazzi photos. Cities, times, dates, anything that might narrow down when or where a set of photos was taken, I tried to avoid. If I did publish any of those details, I made sure they were inaccurate.

After Toronto my restrictions tightened. I strongly favored pictures of Jake by himself, and sometimes even cropped shots so his companions weren't visible. Instead of deleting only the most invasive comments about his private life, I deleted all of them. I ignored any set of photos I arbitrarily deemed to be "too intrusive" and, likewise, avoided any pictures in which Jake looked angry at the person behind the camera. I didn't tell anyone that I was doing this, and sometimes when Susie popped in for an unexpected post, she would publish things that hadn't made it past my strict guidelines. But that was rare. And secretive as I was in my devious plot to whitewash all personal info from Jake Watch, I was almost always the only person who noticed when there was a breach in policy.

Every day that passed, my convictions seemed to be confirmed in the careful way Jake and Reese kept their relationship under wraps, even as *Rendition*'s impending release required they make frequent public appearances together. I knew, I just *knew*, they were making some sort of statement about privacy by keeping quiet. The only way to show my respect for their decision, in my mind, was to continue as I had in censoring Jake Watch.

It was one of the things that propelled me through to the end, the certainty that I was doing the *right thing*, that it was my responsibility to use my role in the fan community to set a good example.

I knew people simply went elsewhere when we didn't provide the information they wanted. But I felt smug in my confidence that no one was getting anything from *me*.

Ending-Signaling Thing Number Two: The Right to Post Copyright-Infringed Interview Content Leads to a Transatlantic Meltdown

Then again, with all of my bowdlerizing and whatnot, it was even more difficult than usual to scrounge up things to write about.

Susie and I rarely went looking for news; from the earliest days, we relied heavily on our readers to send us tips. But as the months wore on and we lost more and more dedicated news scouts to apathy or other Jake sites, we were left to pilfer our information from other fansites. By the time Jake Watch headed toward the finish line, we were *always* the last place to find news. Even if we were fortunate enough to receive information quickly, it still took time to put our distinctive Jake Watch–brand spin on things. No one learned anything first on Jake Watch.

People did sometimes post tips in the comments section, though, and that is where I found a message in September alerting everyone to the fact that Jake would be on the cover of the October issue of *Interview Magazine.*

Parasite that I was, I immediately started checking other sites and, sure enough, found specifics elsewhere. In fact, the specifics were coming from Cindy. She already had parts of the interview and had helpfully posted them on her blog as an "exclusive." Cindy was in England, and *Interview Magazine* is an American publication. The issue must have been extremely new if Cindy was the only person with any information, so I concluded that someone on this side of the Atlantic, a person with early access to such publications, must have been feeding her the interview.

Oh, Jesus, I thought. Because I knew where this was headed. Me. In my car. Looking for that goddamned magazine. At least the mystery of how Cindy came across her information was solved relatively quickly. She wrote that a reader named "Dbay" had sent the snippets to her. Dbay … Dbay … why did that name sound so familiar to me? I couldn't put my finger on it, but I had a feeling I should be really pissed off that Dbay had given this "exclusive" to Cindy and not me …

It was a Friday afternoon, and I might have had plans. But no longer. Dbay be damned, I was going to find that magazine. I was tired of Jake Watch, the one-time darling of the fan world, stuck in its perpetual last place.

Two hours later, as I drove home empty-handed, I started composing a really guilt-inducing post in my head. Something about how I'd run all over town trying to find this magazine, and everyone should feel sorry for me. And I wanted to throw something in there about Dbay's clear snub of the Jake Watch community and how we should all take it personally. If only I could figure out who the hell Dbay was.

I was expecting scanned images of the article to be available by the time I got back to my computer. But there weren't, meaning I wasn't the only person having difficulty finding the magazine. Cindy, however, was back with more excerpts, courtesy of the mysterious Dbay. Cindy had also, in the interim, bought a copy on eBay and had one of her readers call a

U.S. Barnes and Noble to confirm that the magazine would be on shelves by the end of the week. Oh, fabulous. I felt so much better about wasting my afternoon running around town after hearing that. Why didn't *I* just call Barnes and Noble? Because apparently I'm an idiot and have to find out when magazines hit American stores from somebody in England.

Dbay … Dbay … That name was still bothering me. And I was hungry. So I put a hot dog in the microwave and about halfway through the twenty-five-second cook cycle, I yelled to my empty apartment, *"Fucking Doris!"*

Doris! How could I have forgotten *Doris*? Doris, from Chapter 3. Doris, who worked in a library (that's how she got the magazine first!) and wrote me rambling and occasionally incoherent e-mails dissecting Jake in great detail. Doris, who insisted there was no reason to reply to her e-mails and always ignored everything I said if I did happen to reply. Doris, who didn't have internet access at home and once drove to her workplace *in the middle of an ice storm* to check on Jake news. Doris, who chastised me for using the term "grandpa sweater" in a post because she felt that older readers (i.e., Doris) might find it offensive. Doris, who wrote Susie after my first trip to New York and labeled me a "real" stalker, speculating that Jake had purposefully ignored me due to my deplorable behavior.

Wait a minute. Doris, who thought *I* was a stalker, was now giving her top-secret information to Cindy? *Cindy?!* As it turned out, my actual indignity was, like, *way* stronger than the hazy notion of it I'd been carrying around all afternoon.

I could do nothing but sit back and watch disconsolately as Cindy continued to update throughout the day. I envisioned Doris bent over a computer, busily typing up the entire interview and sending it along while Cindy's traffic numbers soared. Well, I had better things to do than sit around and watch that scary scenario play out, so after update number three went up and it became obvious that there weren't going to be any scans anytime soon (I was pretty sure Doris didn't have a scanner), I wrote Susie a quick e-mail, filling her in, and then occupied my time with things other than Jake for the duration of the day. Like eating my hot dog.

It was with no small amount of surprise that I saw that a post had been put up on Jake Watch when I finally got back online that evening. Susie, whom I had not heard from in days, made a rare blogging appearance, posting an entry that was titled "Fuck That Shit" and started off: "Oh, that's just perfect. Jake will be in *Interview Magazine* soon. Magical. Enjoy the following extracts I have exclusively pulled out of my ass and have not stolen from another site. Good day!" Following that were the excerpts cut and pasted directly from Cindy's site.[2]

Susie did that type of thing on occasion. She possessed an unparalleled ability to storm in and whip up a controversy. I honestly don't know what Jake fans do for fun nowadays; back then we relied on Susie to mix things up when times got slow. God love her, she was always leaving me half-amused, half-horrified.

But for Cindy and the people who read Cindy's blog, the reaction to Susie's post was decidedly on the side of horrified. Over in England, Cindy downed an entire bottle of wine and cried the night away while writing me (me?!) repeatedly and amassing sympathy from her readers.

We were condemned. We lost (even more) readers. Angry fans flocked to other sites to talk about how horrible we were. How disrespectful we were. How "maybe there shouldn't be a Jake Watch" (to quote a comment left on our site).

"I just made a post to crack you up and relieve some stress and it's like we've invaded Baghdad or something," Susie e-mailed after we surveyed the damage.

When things settled down (by which point Cindy and I had ceased all communication), a longtime Jake Watch reader e-mailed me to say she had a subscription to *Interview Magazine*, and her copy of the October issue had come early in the mail. She would give us the interview. The entire interview. And her scanner was broken, so she was going to stay up as late as she needed to that night to type up the article for us. She was a longtime commenter, though I didn't know much about her, and her selfless desire to help us out left me speechless.

"Increasingly it's becoming less fun to be a Jake fan, online anyway," she wrote to me. "Maybe I'm making more out of it than I should but there has always been a certain creepiness to Jake's online fandom and it keeps getting creepier … I love JW because it's not obsessive … [and] because you respect Jake's privacy, and are funny and smart and not at all creepy!"

Susie and I estimated that about 75 percent of the people who read our blog never left a comment. And of those who did leave us feedback, we only got to know a few of them personally. It was despairingly easy to forget that there was a whole audience out there, the majority of the audience even, who weren't represented by the antics of those who made the most noise. This reader was one of those we didn't know very well, and the possibility

---

2   http://jakegyllenhaalwatch.blogspot.com/2007/09/fuck-that-shit.html.

that there were others who silently shared her point of view was heartening. I couldn't stop thanking her for what she'd done for us.

The lesson we learned, then, was that sometimes you can antagonize harmless bloggers and still wind up being the first on the internet to post an interview with Jake Gyllenhaal (and if I just confessed to copyright infringement, I apologize and rest assured the interview was later removed). Several people who had recently found us to be awful forgot their anger when offered a chance to read *our* exclusive.

But the whole ordeal highlighted something important: the acquisition of that interview was the story. The controversy, the discussions, the switching of allegiances—far more emotional energy was expended on obtaining the interview than on the actual content of it.

Which begs the question: was there a way to ensure that the content itself lived up to our standards of entertainment?

Well, I'll tell you ...

Ending-Signaling Thing Number Three: I Accidentally Lead Some French People to Believe That Jake Is Releasing an Album of Civil War Songs

The anonymously-penned introductory paragraph describes Jake as "6 feet tall" and "bigger in life than he appears onscreen." (I can relate to this because when I see Jake onscreen, I always envision him as no taller than 5'11".)
—*"Interview* Interview!"
Jake Watch, September 28, 2007

The *Interview* interview was odd. The interviewer was none other than *Zodiac* director David Fincher, with whom Jake covered a myriad of topics, such as Jake's possible exposure to radioactivity when he was younger. And there was a bit where they talked about the Civil War.[3]

The article was accompanied by several bizarre photographs of Jake doing things like rowing a boat, fly fishing, and chopping wood. Lightly mocking the photographic spread, I wrote a post about Jake giving up acting to become a lumberjack. He showed up the next day in some

---

3   *Interview Magazine*, October 2007.

paparazzi pictures, so I wrote another post, this one about how he was giving up his life as a lumberjack to become an actor again. Then a picture showed up online that had been taken for the magazine but hadn't made it into the publication: Jake holding a guitar. By this point I was beating a thematic dead horse but, out of ideas, I wrote a post stating that Jake was giving up acting to become a musician, and I dragged the Civil War discussion into it purely out of desperation:

> *Oh my God, it's Jake, unposed, and caught in the extremely natural act of strumming a guitar at sundown in the mountains. It's like an ad for people to visit East Tennessee ... with Jake ...*
>
> *The picture accompanies an interview in which Jake divulges that he is hard at work on his first album. In keeping with the patriotic resolve that inspired his bid for the White House, his CD will feature several covers of acoustic hits from the Civil War era. Listen ... I can hear the soft, lilting chords of "Battle Hymn of the Republic" from here ...*
>
> —"Emergency Post on Account of Us Being Right,"
> Jake Watch, September 29, 2007

By Jake Watch standards, it was a pretty stereotypical entry. But apparently it was a little too believable.

Within hours, my post, in its entirety, showed up in the popular gossip community Oh No They Didn't (ONTD) under the heading, "That's Right Ladies, He Sings, Too." By the time I learned what had happened and checked it out for myself, the story had over sixty replies, mostly from people debating the plausibility of what I'd proposed:

"This is BS."

"BULLLLLLLLLLLLL."

"He used to be in a band, so I don't see why he wouldn't go at it again. Damn I would be front row at that concert!"

"Fake. Civil War inspired songs? Come on. Even Jake's not that boring."

"I would so download it"

"No, Jake, don't. (I'd buy it though.)"

"Jake Watch is the funniest fansite in the world and if you read like 2 posts there you'd realize this is NOT real news."

"Please Jake please. I beg you do nooootttttttt make an album PLEASE. I am so tired of that whole scene."

And, my personal favorite, from an actual former classmate: "He *was* in a band in high school and sang in all our school musicals too. He's quite talented."

The post only lasted about twenty-four hours on ONTD before it was removed. But ONTD was such a well-used source for general celebrity gossip that by the time the Civil War story was taken down, it had already made its way to several *other* gossip sites. Our readers, falling over themselves in hysterics, combed the internet and found all sorts of headlines, like "Holy Cow! Jake Gyllenhaal Set to Release an Album!" and "Jake Gyllenhaal Hard at Work on His Own Album?"

I gleefully told a friend of mine that I had started an internet rumor, and after I explained, she said, "But that isn't even a good rumor."

Which was true. Jake Gyllenhaal quitting acting to release an album of acoustic Civil War songs was not a good rumor. It was a *terrible* rumor. Which is why I felt it was so imperative that I do everything in my power to perpetuate it.

I named his album (*Jake Sings the Civil War: An Acoustic Collection*). I drafted an album cover using the picture of him with the guitar (complete with a Civil War battle scene superimposed behind him). And I made up a fake playlist with fake guest musicians ("Battle Hymn of the Republic"— guest vocalist MIMS [glory, glory, hallelujah, muthafucka!]).[4]

Even Susie was risen from her indifference. "I bow down to you. Remember that time I did a really shitty cut and paste of my name on Jake's arm during Tattoogate and some people on IMDb thought it was real? But this is better!!!"

The Civil War album got enough coverage that if any of us had bothered to check, we probably would have found it on the newsfeed on Jake's official site.

Seemingly unrelated to all of this was Susie's and my elaborate theory about Jake *actually* quitting acting. It was about this time that he destroyed any notion that we knew what we were talking about, because just prior to our Civil War fun, he signed on to do a film called *Brothers*, costarring Tobey Maguire. (He would, in fact, spend the following two years it took me to write this book doing nothing but signing on to new movies, proving we could not possibly have been further off the mark.)

The day I put up my second post about the Civil War album, it was revealed that Natalie Portman had also been cast in *Brothers*. Because the

---

4   http://jakegyllenhaalwatch.blogspot.com/2007/10/jake-watch-exclusive-more-info-on.html.

gossip world was really only big enough for one Jake-related story at a time, pretty much everyone ran with the casting news that day rather than my oddly believable album cover.

But a French gossip blog aimed at gay men took the bait. The blogger went so far as to say he had doubted the news about Jake's impending musical debut until he saw the album cover, and then he posted the cover as an "exclusive." Oh, the laughs we got from that guy ... Good times. (Never mind that somehow the most fun part of blogging had now become laughing at other bloggers.)

Most of the articles disappeared after a few days, taken down once the authors realized the story was a joke. Emphasis on the word "most."

Definitely not all.

Amazingly enough, as I write this, there are *still* a few Civil War album headlines out there.

By then it was October, and the release date for *Rendition* was rapidly approaching. As with *Zodiac*, a slew of interviews came to light. There was even a rumor about a TV appearance in Britain with a guy named Jonathan Ross.

"Jake Watch is offering an 'I'm Stalking Jake!' button FREE OF CHARGE to anyone who asks Jake about his new album and/or his Presidential campaign," I wrote on Jake Watch, mock addressing anyone who might interview Jake.[5] Back in April I had written New Line Cinema to ask if I could aid them in any way in officially promoting the release of *Rendition*. They never got back to me. I wasn't expecting any of the interviewers to get back to me either, but I thought this approach was a cheaper alternative to mailing the buttons ahead of time.

The true miracle of the nonexistent Civil War album was that it gave Jake Watch one last worthless cause to rally behind. An anonymous commenter suggested that we write to Jonathan Ross to tell him about the free button offer, and from there a campaign was launched to contact as many talk show hosts as possible. Even Susie wrote a couple of e-mails, and she came out of semipermanent retirement to live blog Jake's appearance on Jonathan Ross's Friday night show, which gave Jake Watch a sizable traffic boost from those outside of England who couldn't see the show but wanted to get in on the excitement. It was like old times that night.

---

5   http://jakegyllenhaalwatch.blogspot.com/2007/10/christian-bale-has-more-fans-than-jake.html.

Huzzah! Jake has arrived in London; city of cities and questionable Olympic infrastructure spenditure. And thank god he did arrive as it's kind of essential to tonight's post. Nice to see him still using public transport as opposed to propelling himself across the Atlantic on the gusts of his own ego and a flock of underprivileged children as I hear Brangelina like to do.

—"Friday Night with Jonathan Ross
with Guest Star Jake Gyllenhaal
As Live-Blogged By britpopbaby,"
Jake Watch, October 13, 2007

"What a sense of satisfaction," Susie wrote me when she finished blogging.

The satisfaction, though, came solely from our renewed sense of community. It did not come from any success in our pleas for attention. Jonathan Ross did not earn an "I'm Stalking Jake!" button. Nor did anyone else. Not David Letterman, not Ellen DeGeneres, not Jon Stewart …

Speaking of Jon Stewart …

Ending-Signaling Thing Number Four: Those Wacky Gyllenhaal Men Continue to Act Predictably Even in Unpredictable Circumstances

Three days after Jonathan Ross, Danielle of The Sarsgaard Soiree and her friend Nicole were waiting for Jake outside of *The Daily Show* studio. They caught him as he walked into the building (grabbing autographs and pictures) and then again when he came back out (grabbing more autographs and pictures). Back in Memphis, I got a breathless phone call.

"Oh my God!" Danielle could hardly talk for laughing so hard. "You should have been here!"

Danielle and Nicole had had a relatively uneventful encounter as Jake walked into the building. But they were standing on the wrong side of the doorway when he came back out after his interview. His bodyguard, seeing the two of them standing there, had ushered them over to where Jake was signing autographs for some other fans. And then Jake, taking Nicole's pen and signing away, seemed to notice that Nicole had stuck around through the filming and said, "You're a good fan."

"He actually said, 'You're a good fan'?!" I gasped.

"Yes! We have video of it! We taped the whole thing!" Danielle laughed. I could hear Nicole giggling with her in the background.

"You *have* to send that to me," I said, in utter shock. Jake Gyllenhaal? Called someone "a good fan"? That was … no. That could not have happened. Jake Gyllenhaal did not do things like go around calling people "good fans."

I called my mother.

"Becky, I just do not believe that he said that," she said.

"Well, I didn't, either, but they have it on video!" I insisted.

"Wait until you watch the video," she said.

I did watch the video. I heard him say "good fan." And I posted the video on Jake Watch before live blogging his appearance on *The Daily Show*.[6]

And then the next day Danielle wrote me to say that after repeated viewings, she and Nicole had come to the sinking conclusion that Jake had not said "good fan."

He had said, while signing Nicole's magazine (*Interview Magazine*, no less), "Good pen."

I watched the video again, and no question: "Good pen."

And the world made sense again.

Only a few weeks from the end, I opened my e-mail inbox and almost deleted what I thought was a spam message. It had come from an unfamiliar sender, but the subject line, "Ramona's Gift," gave me pause. Instead of deleting it, I opened it.

"Dear Becky," it started. And then there was a long paragraph, followed by the unlikely signature, "Sincerely, Stephen Gyllenhaal."

That definitely fell under the category of unexpected.

I went back to the top and started at the beginning.

Cantara, it appeared, had made good on her promise to send Stephen the picture Susie had taken of Ramona's plaque at the Chester Zoo, and this was Stephen assuring me that he would show the photo to Maggie and Peter. He also apologized for what had happened the night of the poetry reading: "I can't remember what I said exactly, but I know that I

---

6   http://jakegyllenhaalwatch.blogspot.com/2007/10/remember-that-time-that-jake-hosted.html.

can sometimes be thoughtless and a little distracted … I guess we're all learning all the time."

"Well, I'll be a son of a bitch," I told my computer screen. After all this time. He was *still* talking about learning!

I was sure Cantara had put him up to it, equally sure he wasn't lying when he said he didn't remember what he said, but I was flattered either of them had taken the time to do this for me, to recognize that something had gone wrong that night and to acknowledge it was worthy of an apology. That *I* was worthy of an apology.

"I got one too!" Susie wrote the next day, after I shared the news. "My e-mail said exactly the same."

Oh. Well. Maybe I wasn't quite so special then if Susie, who had not even been there that night, had gotten the same words. Whatever. It was still nice of him to write us.

"I think he must have sent it to you first and then Cantara must've told him to send it to me too because at the top it had a little explanation. I feel bad now because our ownership of that damn red panda expires next month," she wrote.

Susie wasn't sure if we should write him back, and Cantara asked explicitly that I not, but, oh ho! Too late. I already had. As if I would have let an opportunity slip by now that the lines of communication were open! In a lengthy e-mail, I explained the blog to him, emphasized our respect for his family, apologized for my own immaturity the night of the reading, and stressed that I would not share the contents of his e-mail with our readers without his permission but that it would mean so much to the community to hear what he had to say. I hit send and I waited and I waited and …

… yeah, he never wrote me back.

Ending-Signaling Thing Number Five: My Morally Righteous Stand against Privacy Invasion Is Left to Burn on a Pile of Piggyback Rides and Photo Ops to Sell a Doomed Movie

Not having any desire to see *Rendition* (again) on opening weekend, I used those days to draft my farewell letter to the Jake Watch community.[7]

---

7   Meaning that yes, of the two Jake movies that were released during the lifetime of Jake Watch, I saw neither of them on opening weekend. Susie didn't either.

I didn't list a date. The plan was to post the letter one week in advance, just to give our readers some warning, and then continue posting as usual through the final seven days. No countdowns, no celebrations. The last post would be a comprehensive listing of our best work, and that would be it. The end.

I wrote the post a few days in advance and found the process to be surprisingly emotional. I couldn't help but feel like I was letting everyone down, selfishly taking something away from them. Despite my vast and numerous complaints, I was going to miss it. It took me a couple of days to figure out how I wanted to say good-bye.

I started off simply. "Hmmmm," I wrote. "Have you ever wondered what life would be like with no Jake Watch? Well, we have ..."

I had just finished editing the final draft, a day or two before it would go up, when the first photos started trickling in.

Rendition's opening weekend came and went, and the box office numbers didn't look good. Jake, along with Reese, was in Italy at the time, at the Rome Film Festival (actually, so was Cindy). And though there had been the usual rumors about Jeese because of their public appearances for the movie—was it official? unofficial? would they show up to anything as a couple?—I ignored them. As I always did. They were the same rumors and discussions that had accompanied every film festival, every premiere, every public appearance so far.

I heard about the pictures before I saw them. It's strange because there was a lag; the photographs were taken over opening weekend, but it wasn't until the following week that they showed up online. And so wrapped up was I in my personal turmoil, wondering who would be most upset to see the site go and how I would ever again justify taking three to four vacations every year, that even when people said to me, "PG, have you seen the pictures?" I didn't really understand.

And then I saw the pictures. At which point I did understand. For there. In Rome. Were Jake. And Reese. With ice cream cones. And piggyback rides. And her hand in his back pocket. And my entire worldview, the one that had been so painstakingly crafted around the four simple words of "Jake can't do *anything*!", the one that had guided me through an entire year of my blogging life, fell apart in an instant.

All those months they dodged questions, avoided being photographed, all those months *I* had been deleting comments, that time the publicist *crawled across the floor in the middle of an interview* ... all of that was apparently not part of some grand gesture regarding the intrusion of privacy, but instead was done because they were *holding out for opening weekend.*

And they hadn't used any of the roughly ten gazillion interviews they'd done, in every available medium, to reveal themselves, but had gone with the paparazzi.

The paparazzi. The Jake-can't-do-anything paparazzi.

All I could think was now? *Now!?* They couldn't have waited *one more week* so I could have slunk away with some dignity? Because right now, all that moral superiority of mine was looking pretty damned stupid.

I watched in disbelief as a few pictures turned into tens and then hundreds ...

"It's the principle of the thing!" I yelled to Kara over the phone. She had had the unfortunate luck to call about the time I scrolled down to a picture of Jake and Reese posing for tourists, which, having not long ago heard a story of Jake refusing to let a fan take his picture on the street, struck me as particularly offensive.

"It's going to look like I shut down Jake Watch because I was jealous or some shit when really I've been planning this for months!" I said. (I was right too. Lots of people, to this day, will tell you we quit because of Reese.) "And the whole reason I stuck it out this long is because I had some fucking idiotic idea that I was doing the right thing by not talking about his private life and being all anti-paparazzo or whatever. And *this* is the way they unveil their relationship? *This?!* I look like a *complete fucking dumbass* now because if he doesn't care, why the hell should I? I make *fun* of people who think he's something that he's not, but I'm no better than any of them!" (And I wasn't.) "You can't have it both ways! You can't tell me that they're ruining his life and then expect me to buy it when he turns around and pulls a stunt like this. I just ... I can't ... I can't believe that he actually *put on a show* for the paparazzi," I ground out.

"Do you really think he was putting on a show?" Kara asked when she could get a word in.

"Piggyback rides, Kara. Fucking *piggyback rides* in the middle of a public square in *Rome* during an international film festival *the very weekend* their film opened in the U.S. It's a publicity stunt."

"You have a point," she conceded.

"And hello?!" I added. "Way to steal the limelight from my impending announcement!"

Maybe it wouldn't have been so bad if they hadn't spent the entire week before denying that they were together. Or if the pictures hadn't been so cringe-inducingly staged. Or, you know, if I hadn't spent the past year of my life bending over backward to set an example and proselytizing about Respecting Celebrities' Private Lives only to learn *seven days before I was going to quit* that not even Jake Gyllenhaal was above publicity stunts.

There was a guy on another site who believed that Jake was gay, and the day the pictures came out, he was so distraught that he forced himself to stay away from his computer so he could grieve in peace. But a friend of his left comments on his mood and a fellow fan, on that same site, ridiculed him for taking it "personally." The guy's friend shot back, "To him this is personal." In some other life, like maybe back in Chapter 8, I would have forwarded that statement to Susie along with a derisive comment. But I was no longer in any position to be judging people for what they did and did not take personally.

After I rambled to Kara for several more minutes, she started getting frustrated with my one-track conversation. I snapped at her when she tried to change the subject, and then we argued until I realized I was talking to a dial tone. I'd been friends with Kara for years, and she'd never once hung up on me.

But she did over some dumb paparazzi pictures of two people we didn't know. We didn't talk again for two weeks.

I can't think of many occasions when I felt more idiotic than I did after talking to Kara. I felt stupid for taking Stephen's words at face value, stupid for being as upset as I was, stupid for holding some guy I didn't know to arbitrarily high standards, and especially stupid for taking it all so personally.

There was nothing personal about it. It had nothing to do with me.

I'd been counting down to that week for six months, but even if I hadn't been, I still would have walked away from Jake Watch exactly when I did. Not because of those pictures, but because of my reaction to them.

It was time to get away from all of this.

Closing Up Shop

Aside from a few snarky comments about the timing, Susie and I didn't talk much about what was going on with Jake in those final days. In the weeks and months since New York, we'd drifted apart. I didn't even blink when she forgot which day my farewell letter was supposed to go up and wrote me the night before to say she was planning a post. I asked her to hold off.

The letter went up as written and as planned, though with a short note at the top explaining that our decision had nothing to do with events earlier in the week. I had expected disappointment, but nothing could have prepared me for the thoughtful and heartfelt things that people wrote, and not just from the regulars. So many readers we thought we'd lost came forward to say that, though they may have stopped commenting, they had never stopped reading.

"My love of Jake Gyllenhaal has significantly waned, but my love of this blog has only grown."

"I am typing this as I sit in the lobby of a hotel in a place I never would have been, waiting to meet up with my best friend … whom I never would have known if not for Jake Watch. That's the kind of impact this blog has had on our lives …"

And in response to my apology for never securing them any interaction with Jake:

"You proved a Jake-free Jake could be a wonderful thing."

And:

"Hell, I still like looking at the boy—he's such a beauty—but I feel I've learned a lot about the star-making machinery surrounding him while following all of your escapades—things I wish I didn't know."

And on and on …

"I need this blog like the deserts need the rain, no one else can put the insanity of fandom into some much needed perspective like you girls can."

"I do not know which hurt worse, reading this, or seeing the pic of Jake and Reese holding hands … :*(I am going to cry now."

"I know it's not over yet—but I still have to say: WOW, it's been one *hell* of a ride …"

And proving we never did get over the tragedy that was the official website:

"How ironic that Jake Watch is the one to go while the crappiest official website ever lives on."

britpopbaby kept things in perspective: "In typical fashion, just as we do our pre-prepared dying swan act, he shows up and makes it all about him. Damn you, Gyllenhaal! Damn yooooooooooooou! He'll just never leave us be to have 'our moment'. That's what you get working with actors."

I went to Pittsburgh that weekend to visit my friend Melissa. It was my first trip in almost two years without a work- or Jake Watch–related agenda. I came home hungover and ready to move on. Susie had stepped in to do some last-minute posting while I was away. I had spent the days before I left pulling together our final post, so by the time I was back, the two of us had nothing left to do except finish out the week and walk away.

And then with just two days to go, Susie sent me an e-mail:

"I'm kinda scared of throwing this out there but, dare we hold out a bit longer?"

It was unequivocally the worst thing she could have possibly said to me at that point. I had a twin reaction to the one I'd had five days earlier: Now? *Now* she wanted to keep going!?

When I go back and read Jake Watch now, it's easy for me to forget just how bitter the two of us were at the end. Through the final days, Prophecy Girl was cheerful as ever. She said things like, "And so tonight marks the third and final live blogging experience in the *Rendition* Publicity Blitz, referred to in some circles as 'Jake Week.' We don't refer to it as such in our circle because on Jake Watch, every week is Jake Week."

But when I go back and read the e-mails Susie and I sent to each other, I sometimes find insight into PG's inspiration. And it's not nearly so happy: "I'm going to work in a dig against the phrase 'Jake Week' in *The Daily Show* post because for some reason, seeing that phrase is starting to annoy the shit out of me."

Even more telling is that Susie didn't respond to that. When she wrote me back the next day, her topic was Nicole's "good fan" video (before we were informed of the mistranslation). "Bite me," she wrote, after two lines of expletives. And then hours later, when I responded, I ignored her completely to complain about something else.

We weren't talking to each other anymore; we were just bitching. What had started as a serendipitous and wonderfully productive partnership had been reduced to two or three lines a couple of times a day, revealing nothing except we were too tired to even pretend to listen to each other. We had had some great, happy times in our last two months, and some of my favorite posts ever came in that era. But by October 30, the day Susie asked me to keep going, there was no part of me that wanted to continue.

I didn't want to fight with her, so as calmly as I could, I asked what she wanted to do yet. And God. She had a whole list.

I thought then about how I had been the one to choose our end date and how I had pushed her to let the blog continue months after she wanted to stop. Having been the one to create Jake Watch, it must have been hard for her to let me set the agenda and keep going after she wanted out. It was hard for me, as I read her e-mail, to think about stepping away and letting her complete her list on her own. And yet I knew I would have to. I couldn't do it anymore, and I owed it to both of us to acknowledge that. I had set my stopping point and worked toward it, and now it was her turn to figure out how she wanted to end it for herself.

On November 1, the day we had planned to shut down, Susie put up a Sock Watch, which she anticipated as being the first in a series of all of our regular features. But after she posted it, she changed her mind. "I now feel at peace in a strange way," she wrote to me. That was it. All she'd needed. Simple as that, we were both okay.

So on November 2, 2007, just one day after our originally planned ending date, our final post went up, published under the name "Jake" so neither britpopbaby nor Prophecy Girl would have the last word.[8]

After exactly nineteen months and 675 posts, Jake Watch had shut down for good.

---

8 http://jakegyllenhaalwatch.blogspot.com/2007/11/last-post.html.

Becky: "It's up. We're done. Holy shit."

Susie: "You know what, I bet a load of fucking golden pictures show up now with fucking socks and blatant stalkers and everything!"

It's All About *Learning*, A.K.A. The Obligatory Epilogue-Like Chapter

"You don't know how much this place is missed!! Please come back!!"
—comment left on Jake Watch,
April 7, 2008

So it was over.

Kind of.

I spent my first few weeks of freedom much as I'd spent my last few weeks of service: gorging on Heath Ledger movies. "Getting back to my roots," I called it, thinking back to the more innocent days of hitting up the theater for *A Knight's Tale*. I kept it simple; I stayed away from the internet and stuck to watching his movies. I told people Heath got me through the last months of Jake Watch. I wasn't exaggerating, considering the way *Casanova* and *The Four Feathers* took up residence in my DVD player.

Jake Watch ended just as trailers and posters for *The Dark Knight* began leaking, and I, along with a group of JW veterans (and half of the rest of the world), got swept up in the excitement. My friend Erin asked if I had any future stalking missions planned, and together we decided to go to *The Dark Knight* premiere the following July. It would be nothing like a Jake Watch trip. No pressure, no obligations, just a vacation in L.A. that happened to include screaming along with other fans at a red carpet event. Maybe we'd get Heath's autograph …

"It would be so great if you went to *The Dark Knight* premiere and got a picture of Heath's back! Who knows, maybe he'll bring his mom and she'll give you the evil eye," a former reader joked when I told her of my plans. I laughed.

A month later, he was gone.

He died on my twenty-sixth birthday. All I wanted out of that day was to drink a beer on my lunch break. It was a Tuesday, it was my birthday, I wanted a beer at noon. My parents came to take me to lunch, but then somehow the whole office was going with us, and then my brother locked his keys in his car, and lunch was late ... I didn't get my beer.

I came back to work and a former reader had sent me nine pictures of Heath as a birthday gift. Nine pictures that I brought up individually, looked at carefully, and then gushed over horribly in the e-mail I sent back to her. I wrote the e-mail, switched tabs, hit refresh, and saw the headline. There couldn't have been more than two seconds between "send" and "I just saw the NYC 5 PM news—Heath Ledger was found dead in his downtown, NY apartment today..."

And I *knew* it was true. I knew it because of "5 PM news" and "found dead" and that cold rush you feel when you've learned something terrible ... but all I could think about was the e-mail I'd just sent. I could not fathom how I could have been writing that stupid girly e-mail when he was dead. *Dead.* He was already gone, and I was simpering about how hot he looked in orange.

Cantara was the first to call, and I'll never forget the emotion in her voice ... or in Megan's as she cried along with me when she called a few minutes later ... or in Kara's as I broke the news later that night. She hadn't heard and was just calling to wish me a happy birthday. I don't like thinking about that day, or the ones that immediately followed. They were awful.

Heath's death marked the start of a rough 2008, which also saw the dissolution of the Gyllenhaal parents' thirty-year marriage and the death of Mark Ruffalo's brother. The year felt too long to me. I spent so much of it being sad.

It's a terrible ending to this story.

Which is why I can't leave it like this.

Back in fifth grade, I watched The Beatles movie *Help!* on TV one night, and I liked it so much that I made a board game in its honor. My brother and I took turns playing as each of the four Beatles, pictures of their heads glued onto pennies, in the race around the board to get to Ringo's ring. (It sounds better in concept than it was in execution.) I liked making board games; in fact, I spent almost as much time in my youth constructing them as I did playing them. So when Susie came to me shortly before the end of Jake Watch and suggested we make a board game called "Jakes and Ladders," as a play on the game Snakes and Ladders, I was all for it.

It was truly a harbinger of Jake Watch's impending demise that I couldn't finish the game. Susie didn't have any ideas past the title, and I wasted several evenings after work trying to come up with a viable game concept. I got nowhere. I'd never in my life started a game and not finished it. But whatever spark of inspiration I needed to make Jakes and Ladders work, it just wasn't in me. It was one of only two major Jake-related projects that Susie and I laid out and saw past the discussion phase but then never finished.

The other project was a book. *This* book. The Jake Watch book.

We had the idea independently and almost simultaneously, though it was a couple of months before we started talking to each other about it. I started jotting down notes in February of 2007 on the days I wasn't editing *The Day After Tomorrow Never Dies*. By April, I had about twenty pages. That was when Susie first mentioned the idea, and the two of us swapped notes. Her thoughts were all still in her head, and what I'd put to paper so far wasn't of much help: "Every time in the past two months when I've gotten outrageously upset in any way, I've written diatribes to myself," I wrote. "So I've got that and some Boo letters. And a truncated version of the NYC story that isn't remotely humorous."

Not the most auspicious of starts.

We put the idea aside after that, though we brought it up to each other frequently. When we set the end date for Jake Watch, we talked about writing it when the blog was done. We'd have more time then. We'd have more perspective too. Right up to the end, we planned to write it together. I even referenced it in my farewell letter. I mentioned that one of the reasons we were quitting was "directly related to Jake and Jake Watch."

"Our biggest undertaking ever," I called it, though I didn't say what it was. We were going to set aside the time that we had previously devoted to the blog and use it to write. It would be a fitting end. Two wannabe writers capping off their partnership by writing a real book.

But when the blog ended, the time between our e-mails to each other lengthened, and when we did write, we didn't talk about the book. Soon we stopped writing altogether.

We never got started down the path of doing this as a joint project. We'd gone nonstop for a year and a half, and when it was over, we didn't particularly want to talk about it. It was hard to find the enthusiasm to write about any of this. Ours was not a story of glorious achievement. It was one of multiple borderline-pathetic failures.

Then again, when had failure ever stood in the way of Jake Watch?

So now we're going to get very meta-textual.

I didn't have a plan for the book I started writing alone, three weeks before Heath died. I just started writing.

And then ... everything stopped.

It took me a long time to pick myself up after that, though looking back, I was upset about more than just Heath's death. Jake Watch had been hard. I didn't feel good coming out of it. For all my logical philosophizing about being okay if it didn't "go anywhere," that had been easier to accept while I was still doing it. When it was over, when all the crises and dramas and projects were gone, there was nothing to distract my focus from the sum of what had happened. And what had happened was that it really *hadn't* gone anywhere. I was still at the same job, still clueless about the direction of my life ...

Worse yet, there were all these feelings of inadequacy. I thought I'd done some great things with the blog, but I also remembered the times when I'd worked and worked only to have Susie casually dismiss it all ... There was Stephen who, time and again, didn't deem me worth remembering ... There was Jake, and Jake's management, even the guy who ran Jake's website, all of whom had systematically ignored me ... There was Cantara, who always valued Susie's opinion more than my own ... There was the seemingly endless list of flops, failures, disappointments ...

It was difficult to deal with, and difficult not to dwell on it. I'd never before had the time to sit back and think it all over, but now ... now I had more time than I knew what to do with. Clinging to what was familiar, I had thought that going to *The Dark Knight* premiere would be a fun and carefree way to put some of it behind me. I remember telling people that twenty-five had been a hard year for me and hearing in return, "Twenty-six will be better!" But the day I turned twenty-six, the last of what made sense fell apart ...

Heath's death wasn't just the end of the happiness that had come from *Brokeback Mountain*; it was the real world claiming me back again. It was inescapable. I just kept thinking that if only I hadn't gotten so wrapped up in that movie, I would be handling this better. I wouldn't be hurting so much right now. I wouldn't feel so awful every time I thought of Jake, because Jake was a real person, and he had lost his friend, and ups and downs aside he had been a big part of my life for a long time, and it hurt terribly to think about what he must be going through ...

I kept writing. By May, I had about thirty-five thousand words.[1] But book writing is not blogging, and stuck in a blogger's mentality of quick posts and quicker feedback, I decided I might be more successful if I had someone look over what I'd written. Should I keep going? Was it worth the effort? My final Jake Watch–related judgment error occurred at the exact moment that I decided to seek someone else's opinion to validate what I was doing. Because what did I do? I turned to the only person I knew in the publishing world: Cantara.

I know, I know. You're probably sitting there shaking your head at me. It's fine. I deserve it.

My relationship with Cantara had peaked and troughed in the year and a half since I'd met her, but she'd kept in touch, and the two of us wrote regularly. Through a series of events too long and boring to get into here, Cantara and her husband, Michael, edited my draft and agreed to help me find a publisher. If they were unsuccessful, they would publish it themselves, provided I edit it down to thirty thousand words.

Well, that's that! I thought. *Success at last!* Who knew it was so easy to write a book? And wouldn't you know … my good pal Stephen Gyllenhaal just happened to be finishing a novel at exactly this same time. Cantara was trying to break him into the literary scene in a big way, so instead of publishing his book herself, as she had with *Claptrap*, she set the goal of finding him a larger publisher. For a short time that summer, Cantara was working to find publishers for both Stephen and me at the same time. At last, my work was on par with the literary prowess of the great Stephen Gyllenhaal …

But you know what? Writing a book isn't that easy. Finding a publisher isn't that easy. Working with Cantara certainly wasn't that easy. There were false starts and delays and changes that I didn't approve, and for the second time in as many years, Cantara found herself on the receiving end of a lengthy e-mail from me about my expectations and how they hadn't been met and …

blah …

blah …

blah.

Why was I still doing this? Why was it two years later and I was still in the same place? It was September 2008, and it might as well have been October 2006.

---

1   As a point of reference, the book you just slogged through is about 108,000 words.

And when Marcia read something on Cantara's website about my undertaking (which Cantara and Michael had—to my surprise—renamed *JakeWatch!* [*sic*] *A Fan's Memoir*), she contacted me for the first time in months to ask what I was doing. Over the course of several highly uncomfortable e-mails, I realized that she thought I had set her up. And I think she thought I had participated in Jake Watch as a social experiment, solely to write about later, and that I had targeted her specifically as a good case study. Everything I wrote to her came out wrong. Faced with the seemingly simple task of convincing her that my goal in writing a book had nothing to do with ruining her life, I failed at even that.

This didn't seem to be going very well.

So I quit writing for a while.

———————————

By November 2008, Jake Watch felt very far away. It had been a year since we quit, and that portion of my life seemed like something from the distant past. The few times I'd gone back and skimmed through the blog, it felt foreign. Like I was reading someone else's work.

But that month, Susie e-mailed me out of the blue. "Hey, remember me? britpopbaby?" she asked, as if she were writing to me after decades and not months. "I decided to check JW after not even looking at it for like a year. I laughed at bits and remembered how much we fucking ruled at what we did … In other news, I'm mortified about how 'normal' I've become—JW was some crazy shit but in an odd way I miss it."

It was also around that time that I got an e-mail from Alice, whom I'd spoken to only a few times since Toronto. She'd found an old mention of my book on Cantara's website and had read a sample chapter we'd circulated months earlier. Interest in that chapter had been humiliatingly low, and of the few former readers who read it, the feedback I got was uniformly along the lines of, "I don't want to hurt your feelings, but …"

But Alice had actually liked it. She'd liked it so much that she wanted to read more. Like Susie, she'd been thinking about Jake Watch lately, and she told me:

"There was an extended period during my JW time that I thought you were perfect. Now at 50 years old I'm not delusional, of course I know that people cannot be perfect, but during JW you were perfect to me, you could do no wrong. I'm not making this up, this is how I thought of you. I guess that sounds weird, I dunno, I never said that or had something like that said to me, but I just thought I'd let you know. Unrealistic expectations from perfect strangers?"

Aside from being an incredibly flattering and humbling sentiment, I thought that was a rather pristine description of what we had all gone through with Jake. And it got me thinking …

What the hell was wrong with me? I wanted to write a book. So why had I not? Why was I getting so wrapped up in other people's reactions? Why was I seeking validation from people who had never validated me before? Why was I acting like I'd been wronged in some way?

Alice's e-mail made me reconsider the way the rest of the world had perceived me while I was writing the blog. I was so quick to focus on the ways in which I thought I had fallen short. That, in turn, meant that my motivation when I first tried to write this was all wrong. I was writing it because I thought I'd failed with the blog. I wanted a "success" to justify all my hard work, but I was simultaneously terrified that I was repeating my past mistakes. That the book itself would be yet another failure.

But sometimes the value of a thing isn't in the end result. Sometimes it's in the doing of it.

As I wrote back and forth with Alice and Susie both, I was left wondering why I had gotten so wrapped up in the negatives. I mean, my God, it wasn't like anything legitimately bad had happened to me. It was Jake Watch. It was kind of awesome. I did tons of cool things that I never would have done otherwise. I hadn't "failed" at all. What I'd done was grow up. That vaguely empty feeling I'd been attributing to a lack of acceptance on others' part was really a lack of acceptance on my part. Jake Watch was over, and I could either let it incapacitate me or I could get the hell over it, and myself, and use what I'd learned to move forward.

If I was going to write a book, I had to write it for the same reason I had written Jake Watch: because I wanted to. I didn't need any other reason. In fact, it wouldn't work if there *was* any other reason.

Jake Watch was never a blog about why. It was a blog about *why not*. If I wanted to write the damned book, I should just write the damned book. Because for God's sake, why not?

So in 2009, with Susie's blessing, I wrote the damned book.

In the meantime, so did Cantara. Damn her. (Just kidding, 'cause whatever.)

She announced midyear that she was going to be writing her own memoir about the Gyllenhaals. In testing the interest in what she was doing, she e-mailed the first few chapters to a group of friends and associates, and I was among them. In one installment, she told her side of the Babygate controversy and offered the following intriguing insight into how she played us (after describing how she found the picture of Jake and his dad on Jake Watch):

> I emailed [Susie] back, telling her in so many words that the Gyllenhaals were familiar with what was being said about them on the internet. Of course they all took the high road, ignoring the sites that attempted to pry into their private affairs and pander to the crudest opinions. But they also appreciated responsible, respectful sites like JakeWatch [*sic*] and their friendly rival, IHeartJake [*sic*], where fans were obviously more interested in Jake and Maggie's careers rather than their personal lives.
>
> Reader, I confess to a minor deception. No such appreciation from the Gyllenhaals existed. In fact, to hear it from Stephen, he and the whole family regarded any reference to them at all on the internet as an intrusion and an insult.

And wouldn't it have been nice to know *that* before I went traipsing off to New York. Had I only known I wasn't an ally, but "an intrusion and an insult."

Ah, well. It's not like this revelation came as a shock or anything. I tried to act affronted the first time I read it, but my heart just wasn't in it. And maybe that was the best thing to come out of Jake Watch for me: to be able to read such things and not take them personally. At the very least, this skill came in handy when 2010 rolled around. I thought I'd been ignored a lot during my years as a blogger, but man. I didn't know the meaning of the word until I tried to get this baby published ...

But that's another story.

In a weird, symmetrical twist, as I finish this book, Jake's filming yet another movie with Anne Hathaway. They're in Pittsburgh, and Jake is living in (of all places) Melissa's neighborhood, Melissa who entertained me my last weekend of Jake Watch. She and her friends see him all the time. All that effort I put into catching up with him, and they run into him going about their daily lives.

I still keep in touch with a few Jake Watch readers, but I've lost touch with most. Some I'd forgotten about until I started digging around in my inbox for quotes. Early on, I ran across this e-mail from a fan who had a film festival experience similar to my own:

"[Another fan] kept squeezing my arm, repeating: 'You're gonna see Jake, aren't you excited?' And God I was TERRIFIED. I remember thinking to myself: what kind of fucking MESS have I gotten myself into?"

Yeah …

That, too, could be classified as a rather pristine description of what we all went through.

There was a lot of truth in those simple words that Stephen said to me at the poetry reading. It really *is* all about learning. And a good lesson to learn is that you should never stalk Jake without bringing backup in the form of a sane person.

But of all the other lessons I learned, the most important is that no matter what else has changed … goddammit *I will never get over the fact that* Brokeback Mountain *didn't win Best Picture.*

I mean, for Christ's sake! That's just the dumbest thing I've ever heard in my entire life. Like *Crash* ever drove masses of people to internet hysteria.

Tell you what, you find me evidence of *that,* and I'll gladly reward you with one nice, clean white pair of Jake Gyllenhaal's socks.

Acknowledgments

I would like to thank my brain for not developing dementia after reliving all of this ten billion times during the editing process … No, only kidding! It takes a village to birth a book. Or something like that. I have many people to give thanks to:

To Susie. Thank you. For everything. From going through this experience with me to encouraging me to write this. And for creating Jake Watch!

To Mom and Dad, for supporting me and listening to me through the entire writing process, which wound up taking so much longer and being so much harder than I ever anticipated. Nothing I could say here could ever convey how much I appreciate your help.

To John/Jops/Gee, for never letting me take myself too seriously, and for insisting on the Fourth of July, between Bud Lights, that people would want to read this.

To Melissa, for being my first editor and my last. Next time I do this, I hope to have the means to pay you for your brilliant and expert advice. And thanks for letting Jake move into your neighborhood and for sending me that Bigfoot-quality picture of him that finally gave me a reason to be Prophecy Girl again.

To Kara, for withstanding four years of hysterical phone calls. Miraculously, you'll still travel with me after New York (again, I'm sorry!); you are an amazing friend.

To Greta and Crystal, for making my first trip to Los Angeles one of my favorite vacations ever, and for tolerating me during the second one.

To Megan, for getting me into running (stress relief!) and for listening to me ramble … and ramble … and ramble over countless miles. I thank you, too, for always acting as if there was no question I could write this.

To Kathryn, for the phone calls and for reading my blogs and for leaving me comments on JW! If I ever stalk David Boreanaz, I'm forcing you to come with me.

To Cantara, for the good times (and, all right, the bad) and for asking me about my progress and making me believe I could finish this. I thank you and Michael both for your support.

To Suzanne and Aunt Joan, for reading this and treating it like it was a story worth telling when neither of you knew what you were getting into when I sent it to you.

To Jess and Malin, for the most supportive e-mails I've ever gotten. To Jane and Leslie, for your continued cheerleading and friendship. And to Sam and Chris, for doing the impossible and reading *every blog I've ever written*; from *The Day After Tomorrow Never Dies* (and before) till now, you guys have been there for me.

To the readers of Jake Watch, for taking the time to read what we wrote for you. *Thank you.*

And lastly, to Jake, for the inspiration, the entertainment, and the reality check. I wish you luck in all that you do … starting with getting rid of all the Fake Yous that now populate Twitter.

About the Author

Becky Heineke is unbearably talented. There is nothing she can't do (except all of the things you just read about in this book, and then some other things). She has so many blogs she can't keep up with them all, but the only ones anyone reads are the ones about Jake Gyllenhaal.

A native of Memphis, Tennessee, Becky is a graduate of Rhodes College, where she earned a degree in biology. Since graduating, she has gone to art school, lived and worked in Cork, Ireland, and learned the importance of saving for retirement while working in a financial office.

She lost her job to the recession, so she's really glad you bought this book (the royalty will buy her about two packages of ramen noodles). Becky still writes under the name Prophecy Girl at her very exciting website: www.imstalkingjake.com.